Bloom's Modern Critical Views

Bloom's Modern Critical Views

Bloom's Modern Critical Views

DEREK WALCOTT

Edited and with an introduction by
Harold Bloom
Sterling Professor of the Humanities
Yale University

CHELSEA HOUSE
P U B L I S H E R S
A Haights Cross Communications Company
Philadelphia

Library of Congress Cataloging-in-Publication Data

Derek Walcott / edited and with an introduction by Harold Bloom.
    p. cm. -- (Bloom's modern critical views)
Includes bibliographical references and index.
  ISBN: 0-7910-7395-5
 1. Walcott, Derek--Criticism and interpretation. 2. West
Indies--In literature. I. Bloom, Harold. II. Series.
  PR9272.9.W3 Z65 2002
  811'.54--dc21
                                            2002151622

Chelsea House Publishers
1974 Sproul Road, Suite 400
Broomall, PA 19008-0914

http://www.chelseahouse.com

Contributing Editor: Jesse Zuba

Cover designed by Terry Mallon

Cover photo © Reuters NewMedia Inc./CORBIS

Layout by EJB Publishing Services

Contents

Editor's Note

My Introduction centers upon Derek Walcott's recent long poem, *Tiepolo's Hound*, which I read as a parable of Walcott's problematic relation to poetic tradition.

The Irish poet, Seamus Heaney, renders a gracious tribute to Walcott's volume, *The Star-Apple Kingdom* (1979), particularly commending the long poem, "The Schooner Flight," while Calvin Bedient assays a somewhat lower place to *The Fortunate Travellers* (1981).

Helen Vendler, in the essay reprinted here with which I am most in agreement, shows how vulnerable Walcott is to the influence of stronger precursors: W. B. Yeats, Hart Crane, Dylan Thomas, Pound, Eliot, and Auden. Joseph Brodsky however praises Walcott's poetry as "Adamic," and insists he is neither a traditionalist nor a modernist.

In a very generous overview, Peter Balakian finds in Walcott an eminence akin to such poets as Yeats, Rilke, and Neruda, after which Rita Dove praises Walcott's "wise artistry."

Stewart Brown usefully examines Walcott's apprentice verse, and emerges unbothered by Walcott's eclecticism in absorbing such contemporaries as Robert Lowell and Brodsky, even in much later work.

We move to Walcott's plays with David Mikics, who in a very adroit essay, exploits the Magical Realism he feels allies Walcott to the great Cuban novelist, Alejo Carpentier.

Omeros, Walcott's epic, is lauded by Gregson Davis for *not* being shadowed by Homer, after which Paula Burnett returns us to Walcott's dramas, which she sees as being comparable to the best of Brecht.

In an excellent essay, Jahan Ramazani considers *Omeros* as the exemplar of an authentic "postcolonial poetics of affliction," while Paul Breslin centers upon *Another Life*, a poetic autobiography which he judges to be a narrative experiment of considerable power.

In this volume's final essay, Wes Davis attempts to contextualize Walcott in the nuances of West Indian History.

Introduction

After reading each of Derek Walcott's books as they have appeared, I remain uncertain as to the question of his aesthetic eminence, though few seem to share my inability to render any verdict, even for myself. Walcott is an excellent narrator, and is blessed with many verbal gifts. My own bafflement ensues from a concern with poetic voice that centers my own love for reading and appreciating poetry. Has Derek Walcott developed a voice altogether his own, the mark of a major poet, or does one hear in him the composite voice of post-Yeatsian poetry in English?

I want to see if my recent reading of Walcott's long poem, *Tiepolo's Hound*, will resolve my doubts. The strategy of *Tiepolo's Hound* turns upon a brilliant doubling of Walcott and the West Indian Impressionist painter Camille Pissarro, born in 1830, exactly a century before Walcott. In Pissarro, a Sephardic Jew and so a fellow exile and outsider, Walcott discovers an aesthetic quest he regards as being profoundly akin to his own.

The poem's final section, XXVI, opens with a poignant identity forged between Pissarro and Walcott:

He enters the window frame. His gaze is yours.

Primed canvas, steaming mirror, this white page
where a drawing emerges. His portrait sighs

from a white fog. Pissarro in old age,
as we stand doubled in each other's eyes.

To endure affliction with no affection gone
seems to have been the settlement in those eyes,

whose lenses catch a glinting winter sun
on mansards and the rigid smoke of chimneys.

This is eloquent and memorable, but do I hear Walcott's voice or an adaptation of the nuanced cadences of Wallace Stevens? Does it matter whose voice it is, when the expression has this much aesthetic dignity? I uneasily recall the poetry of Archibald Macleish, whose eclectic assimilation of Eliot, Pound and others was so wittily satirized by Edmund Wilson in his *The Omelet of A. Macleish*. Here are the closing lines of *Tiepolo's Hound*, which seem to me quite beautiful, but again I hear Wallace Stevens's "hum of thoughts evaded in the mind":

Let this page catch the last light on Becune Point,
lengthen the arched shadows of Charlotte Amalie,

to a prayer's curling smoke, and brass anoint
the branched menorah of a frangipani,

as the lights in the shacks bud orange across the Morne,
and are pillared in the black harbour. Stars fly close

as sparks, and the houses catch with bulb and lampion
to the Virgin, Veronese's and Tiepolo's.

Soon, against the smoky hillsides of Santa Cruz,
dusk will ignite the wicks of the immortelle,

parrots will clatter from the trees with raucous news
of the coming night, and the first star will settle.

Then all the sorrows that lay heavily on us,
the repeated failures, the botched trepidations

will pass like the lights on bridges at village corners
where shadows crouch under pierced constellations

whose name they have never learnt, as the sickle glow
rises over bamboos that repeat the round

of the chartered stars, the Archer, aiming his bow,
the Bear, and the studded collar of Tiepolo's hound.

I cannot deny the distinction of this verse, but the pervasive tonalities of Stevens's kind of impressionism trouble my ear. Walcott, the leading Anglophone poet of the West Indies, is a cultural figure of real importance, and deserves his fame. If I do not find him to be a strong poet, unlike John Ashbery or Seamus Heaney, Geoffrey Hill or James Merrill, Jay Wright or Anne Carson, is that because I set too high a value upon the agonistic element in poetry? My uneasiness may reflect primarily upon myself, and not upon Derek Walcott.

SEAMUS HEANEY

The Murmur of Malvern

A poet appeases his original needs by learning to make works that seem to be all his own work—Yeats at the stage of *The Wind Among the Reeds*. Then begins a bothersome and exhilarating second need, to go beyond himself and take on the otherness of the world in works that remain his own yet offer rights-of-way to everybody else. This was the kind of understanding and composure Yeats had won by the time he published *The Wild Swans at Coole*, and it is the same kind of authority which Derek Walcott displays in *The Star-Apple Kingdom*.*

'The Schooner Flight', the long poem at the start of the book, is epoch-making. All that Walcott knew in his bones and plied in his thought before this moves like a swell of energy under verse which sails, well rigged and richly cargoed, into the needy future. I imagine he has done for the Caribbean what Synge did for Ireland, found a language woven out of dialect and literature, neither folksy nor condescending, a singular idiom evolved out of one man's inherited divisions and obsessions, an idiom which allows an older life to exult in itself and yet at the same time keeps the cool of 'the new'. A few years ago, in the turbulent and beautiful essay which prefaced his collection of plays, *Dream on Monkey Mountain*, Walcott wrote out of and about the hunger for a proper form, an instrument to bleed off the

From *The Government of the Tongue*. © 1989 by Seamus Heaney.

accumulated humours of his peculiar colonial ague. He has now found that instrument and wields it with rare confidence:

> You ever look up from some lonely beach
> and see a far schooner? Well, when I write
> this poem, each phrase go be soaked in salt;
> I go draw and knot every line as tight
> as ropes in this rigging; in simple speech
> my common language go be the wind,
> my pages the sails of the schooner *Flight*.

The speaker fixes his language in terms that recall Walcott's description of an ideal troupe of actors, 'sinewy, tuned, elated', and the language works for him as a well-disciplined troupe works for the dramatist. It is not for subjective lyric effects but for what James Wright has called 'the poetry of a grown man', one grown to that definitive stage which Yeats called 'the finished man among his enemies'.

For those awakening to the nightmare of history, revenge—Walcott had conceded—can be a kind of vision, yet he himself is not vengeful. Nor is he simply a patient singer of the tears of things. His intelligence is fierce but it is literary. He assumes that art is a power and to be visited by it is to be endangered, but he also knows that works of art endanger nobody else, that they are benign. From the beginning he has never simplified or sold short. Africa and England are in him. The humanist voices of his education and the voices from his home ground keep insisting on their full claims, pulling him in two different directions. He always had the capacity to write with the elegance of a Larkin and make himself a ventriloquist's doll to the English tradition which he inherited, though that of course would have been an attenuation of his gifts, for he also has the capacity to write with the murky voluptuousness of a Neruda and make himself a romantic tongue, indigenous and awash in the prophetic. He did neither, but made a theme of the choice and the impossibility of choosing. And now he has embodied the theme in the person of Shabine, the poor mulatto sailor of the *Flight*, a kind of democratic West Indian Ulysses, his mind full of wind and poetry and women. Indeed, when Walcott lets the sea-breeze freshen in his imagination, the result is a poetry as spacious and heart-lifting as the sea-weather at the opening of Joyce's *Ulysses*, a poetry that comes from no easy evocation of mood but from stored sensations of the actual:

In idle August, while the sea soft,
and leaves of brown islands stick to the rim
of this Caribbean, I blow out the light
by the dreamless face of Maria Concepcion
to ship as a seaman on the schooner *Flight*.
Out in the yard turning gray in the dawn,
I stood like a stone and nothing else move
but the cold sea rippling like galvanize
and the nail holes of stars in the sky roof,
till a wind start to interfere with the trees.

It is a sign of Walcott's mastery that his fidelity to West Indian speech now leads him not away from but right into the genius of English. When he wrote these opening lines, how conscious was he of another morning departure, another allegorical early-riser? The murmur of Malvern is under that writing, for surely it returns to an origin in *Piers Plowman*:

In summer season, when soft was the sun,
I rigged myself up in a long robe, rough like a sheep's,
With skirts hanging like a hermit's, unholy of works,
Went wide in this world, wonders to hear.
But on a May morning, on Malvern Hills,
A marvel befell me—magic it seemed.
I was weary of wandering and went for a rest
Under a broad bank, by a brook's side;
And as I lay lolling, looking at the water,
I slid into a sleep ...

The whole passage could stand as an epigraph to Walcott's book in so far as it is at once speech and melody, amorous of the landscape, matter-of-fact but capable of modulation to the visionary. Walcott's glamorous, voluble Caribbean harbours recall Langland's field full of folk. Love and anger inspire both writers, and both manage—in Eliot's phrase—to fuse the most ancient and most civilized mentality. The best poems in *The Star-Apple Kingdom* are dream visions; the high moments are hallucinatory, cathartic, redemptive even. Here, for example, is a passage from 'Koenig of the River', where Koenig appears on his shallop like some Dantesque shade arisen out of the imperial dream, being forced to relive it in order to comprehend it:

Around the bend the river poured its silver
like some remorseful mine, giving and giving
everything green and white: white sky, white
water, and the dull green like a drumbeat
of the slow-sliding forest, the green heat;
then, on some sandbar, a mirage ahead:
fabric of muslin sails, spider-web rigging,
a schooner, foundered on black river mud,
was rising slowly up from the riverbed,
and a top-hatted native reading an inverted
newspaper.
              'Where's our Queen?' Koenig shouted.
'Where's our Kaiser?'
                        The nigger disappeared.
Koenig felt that he himself was being read
like the newspaper or a hundred-year-old novel.

There is a magnificence and pride about this art—specifically the art, not
specially the politics—that rebukes that old British notion of 'Commonwealth literature': Walcott possesses English more deeply and sonorously
than most of the English themselves. I can think of nobody now writing with
more imperious linguistic gifts. And in spite of the sheen off those lines, I
suspect he is not so much interested in the 'finish' of his work as in its drive.
He has written lyrics of memorable grace—'In a Green Night' and 'Coral'
come to mind as two different kinds of excellence—and his deliberately
designed early sonnet sequence 'Tales of the Islands' guaranteed the
possibility of these latest monologues and narratives. His work for the stage
has paid into his address to the poetry until the latter now moves itself and
us in a thoroughly dramatic way. 'The Star-Apple Kingdom', for example, is
a discursive and meditative poem, a dive into the cultural and political matter
of post-colonial Jamaica, yet the pitch of the writing could hardly be
described as either meditative or discursive. Again, there is a dream-heavy
thing at work, as if the years of analysis and commitment to thinking justly
had resolved themselves for the poet into a sound half-way between sobbing
and sighing. The poem does not have the pure windfall grace of 'The
Schooner Flight'—in places it sags into 'writing'—but its pitch and boldness
make a lovely orchestration of the music of ocean and the music of history:

What was the Caribbean? A green pond mantling
behind the Great House columns of Whitehall,

behind the Greek façades of Washington,
with bloated frogs squatting on lily pads
like islands, islands that coupled sadly as turtles
engendering islets, as the turtle of Cuba
mounting Jamaica engendered the Caymans, as, behind
the hammerhead turtle of Haiti-San Domingo
trailed the little turtles from Tortuga to Tobago;
he followed the bobbing trek of the turtles
leaving America for the open Atlantic,
felt his own flesh loaded like the pregnant beaches
with their moon-guarded eggs—they yearned for
Africa ...

Walcott's poetry has passed the stage of self-questioning, self-exposure, self-healing, to become a common resource. He is no propagandist. What he would propagate is magnanimity and courage and I am sure that he would agree with Hopkins's affirmation that feeling, and in particular love, is the great power and spring of verse. This book is awash with love of people and places and language: love as knowledge, love as longing, love as consummation, at one time the Sermon on the Mount, at another *Antony and Cleopatra*:

He lies like a copper palm
tree at three in the afternoon
by a hot sea
and a river, in Egypt, Tobago.

Her salt marsh dries in the heat
where he foundered
without armour.
He exchanged an empire for her beads of sweat,

the uproar of arenas,
the changing surf
of senators, for
this ceiling over silent sand—

this grizzled bear, whose fur,
moulting, is silvered—
for this quick fox with her
sweet stench.

('Egypt, Tobago')

There is something risky about such large appropriations, but they are legitimate because Walcott's Caribbean and Cleopatra's Nile have the same sweltering awareness of the cynicism and brutality of political adventures. He is not going beyond the field of his own imagery; he is appropriating Shakespeare, not expropriating him—the unkindest post-colonial cut of all.

Conscious-maker that he is, Derek Walcott is certainly aware that when the whirligig of time brings in such revenges, they turn out to be more ironies than revenges. His sense of options and traditions is highly developed and his deliberate progress as a writer has not ended. Much that he inherited as inchoate communal plight has been voiced, especially in the dramatic modes of this volume, yet I am not sure that he won't return inwards to the self, to refine the rhetoric. 'Forest of Europe', the poem dedicated to Joseph Brodsky, is aimed at the centre of Walcott's themes—language, exile, art— and is written with the surge of ambition that marks him as a major voice. But I feel that the wilful intelligence has got too much of the upper hand in the poem, that the thrill of addressing a heroic comrade in the art has forced the note. I rejoice in everything the poem says—'what's poetry, if it is worth its salt / but a phrase men can pass from hand to mouth?'—yet the poem is not securely in possession of its tone. Which could never be said of Shabine, who deals with the big themes in his own nonchalant way:

> I met History once, but he ain't recognize me,
> a parchment Creole, with warts
> like an old sea bottle, crawling like a crab
> through the holes of shadow cast by the net
> of a grille balcony; cream linen, cream hat.
> I confront him and shout, 'Sir, is Shabine!
> They say I'se your grandson. You remember Grandma,
> your black cook, at all?' The bitch hawk and spat.
> A spit like that worth any number of words.
> But that's all them bastards have left us: words.

NOTE

* *The Star-Apple Kingdom*, Farrar, Straus & Giroux, 1979.

CALVIN BEDIENT

Derek Walcott, Contemporary

Something like genius, like a convicting and convincing necessity, woke in "The Schooner *Flight*," the long lead poem in Derek Walcott's last volume, *The Star-Apple Kingdom* (1979). And the rest of the book did not much let one down. *The Fortunate Traveller*, by contrast, shows more gift than genius. Walcott's characteristic strength remains a combination of facility and passion but the proportions are not quite right. I miss in the new book a near approach to the "necessary and unalterable"—the qualities Proust located in "the beauty of landscapes or of great works of art," things more genuine than ourselves. The assured diction and tone, the limber eloquence, the varied metrical craft, the auditory imagination perhaps second in consummate concentration only to Geoffrey Hill's (if also now and then to Seamus Heaney's), the visual imagination clear as air and almost as surprisingly detailed as space, the cultural sensitivity acute as anyone's, plus the usual sheaf of personal griefs—these continue to engross. But the volume makes one long to find the facility forgotten, surpassed in some awful absorption. (This nearly happens, to be sure, in "Wales" and perhaps does in "Jean Rhys.")

Here Walcott is a rolling stone, not a landscape of the mind. He suffers the twentieth-century dislocation. He lacks authority. He whiffles; his uprootedness is sometimes indulged. He seems to write, now and again, on

From *Parnassus: Poetry in Review* 9, no. 2 (Fall/Winter, 1981). © 1982 by the Poetry in Review Foundation.

whim, nostalgic for a home in poetry but finding none—not even (in a beautiful phrase from *Sea Grapes*, his volume of 1976) "the river's startled flowing."

Restless incertitude is conspicuous—as are starts away from it—in the first five poems, all on America. Here Walcott roams the East Coast as if looking for an America to call home. (Born in St. Lucia and imprinted as a Trinidadian, he has taught recently at Harvard and Columbia.) Now, Walcott is welcome to America; she could use a poet who would see her; she is tired of those lovers who keep her up all night talking about themselves. But his gifts of observation, his mimicry of some of our poets, and his home-need do not turn the trick. Except in the South he's too eager to please and be pleased. His citizenship is would-be, griefless and untried.

Besides, his mimicry of Robert Lowell and Elizabeth Bishop is soft. "Upstate" copies the latter's offhand unfoldment: "A knife blade of cold air keeps prying / The bus window open.... The door to the john / keeps banging. There're a few of us: a stale-drunk or stoned woman in torn jeans," and so on. But the poem devolves from the precarious Bishop model and misses her sort of sliding, infinitely gentle cohesion. It slithers, rather, to "I am falling in love with America":

> I will knock at the widowed door
> of one of these villages
> where she will admit me like a broad meadow,
> like a blue space between mountains,
> and holding her arms at the broken elbows
> brush the dank hair from a forehead
> as warm as bread or as a homecoming.

As Allen Grossman notes in *Against Our Vanishing*, Bishop's "management of perception" in the absence of decisions about "how we know" and "what there is" "excites admiration at the point where it expresses the consequences for sentiment of the relentless focus which she everywhere practices." In "Upstate" the descriptive discipline relents, giving way to the "rush" of a romantic homecoming.

For all five poems, grouped under the section title "North," the ideal reader would be the kind of "consumer" described by Theodor W. Adorno in his *Introduction to the Sociology of Music*: one for whom "the unfoldment of a composition does not matter," for whom "the structure of hearing is atomistic: the type lies in wait for specific elements, for supposedly beautiful melodies, for grandiose moments." How else read "Old New England," with its shudderingly perfect bits:

> and railway lines are arrowing to the far
> mountainwide absence of the Iroquois.

Why complain that Walcott is not in fact a New England poet, that the "our" in "The crest of our conviction grows as loud / as the spring oaks" or "our sons home from the East" is ersatz when most American poets would sell their convictionless souls to be able to write like this? Still the poem is excessively written in proportion to what it has to say—is virtuosic merely. It reads like a smooth dream of phrases that not even Vietnam ("our sons home from the East") can wake up. In a way that is its point, but the poet's hunger to absorb New England, and Robert Lowell, places him curiously inside the dream, insulated there, enjoying it.

If Walcott is free for this maundering it's because he's in the strictest sense Contemporary. Back in his great poem "The Schooner *Flight*" he sailed, so it seemed, by the last breath of Romantic quest, one grown refreshingly tropical. He proved one of those poets (the great example is Shakespeare) whose country has emerged out of the shell of the blind elements as a thing preternaturally comely and kind, a blood-warm goddess. She was the Maria Concepcion who

> ... was all my thought
> watching the sea heaving up and down
> as the port side of dories, schooners, and yachts
> was painted afresh by the strokes of the sun
> signing her name with every reflection;
> I knew when dark-haired evening put on
> her bright silk at sunset, and, folding the sea,
> sidled under the sheet with her starry laugh,
> that there'd be no rest, there'd be no forgetting.

Through his persona Shabine, both fabulous and human, and the wakeful naiveté of unabashed yearning—"The bowsprit, the arrow, the longing, the lunging heart— / The flight to a target whose aim we'll never know"—the poet pushed passion to its utmost cathartic emergence and expression. That was yesterday. Today, his heart as perplexed as it is full, he's back in the modern world, where "the mania / of history veils even the clearest air, / The sickly sweet taste of ash, of something burning."

This is no pose. It is felt as debility, not nobility. Walcott's mind says it may be over, the human adventure. He's Contemporary in that he doesn't know what to do with his humanness, regret or refine it (it's too late to rejoice in it). Neither does he know how to use it for his own or others' good. Contemporary in that for him everything is tentative, in transit. Contemporary, too, in his disconnection. True, he's far from free, despite wishing, of his Caribbean origins, his "white" and "black" racial inheritances, the stateliness of *their* English and the dandelion tea of *their* dialect, friendship and family, the poetry of sea grapes, sea almonds, and the indigo sea.... Still he's unsure of who he is, an unfinished man.

Although a few have managed to make tentativeness and transitiveness a cause—William Carlos Williams for instance, early on—for others the Contemporary is a diffuse, deadening fate, life without a fuse. It was so for Lowell, it is so for Ashbery. How like Lowell is Walcott when writing of his two divorces, particularly (in "Store Bay") the second:

> I still lug my house on my back—
> a mottled, brown shoulder bag
> like a turtle's—
> to the shadow of a rock,
> quivering from sunstroke
> and my second divorce.

Defensively the last line comes as if an afterthought and modestly, for nowadays what's more banal than personal crisis? It highlights "the house on my back" as the poignant emblem of two generations. (Walcott was born in 1930, a few years before the peripatetic Bishop published *North and South*, titular parent to the geographical divisions of *The Fortunate Traveller*.) The sense of a lonely laboring, of shock, of scarifying repetition, the homelessness, the transiency build to a wish for utter disconnection:

> I unplug the hotel lamp and lie in bed,
> my head full of black surf.
> I envy the octopus with ink for blood,
> his dangling, disconnected wires
> adrift, unmarried.

Lug and unplug: the whole plot in an ugly rhyme. "On fading sand," he has earlier said, "I pass / a mackerel that leapt from its element, / trying to be different— / its eye a golden ring, / married to nothing." Evidently the effort to be a poet, to transform immediate into reflective emotion, golden, unmarried, contributed to the divorce, a divorce not complete enough since blood not ink flows in the poet's veins. The Contemporary poet knows too well the brief route back from every dream:

> To the thud of reggaes
> from a concrete gazebo,
> a yellow glass-bottom launch,
> trailing weed from its jaws,
> sharks in from the coral gardens
> for the next shoal of picnickers.

"Change me, my sign," Walcott asks in the poem about his first divorce, "The Hotel Normandie Pool," "to someone I can bear."

The "High Moderns," to quote Grossman again, could still aspire to "central and gigantic utterance." Pound, Eliot, Stevens, and even Yeats had themes they thought crucial and beneficial to many, timely, essential. In the main they thought they had something more "important" to write about than their divorces or breakdowns—or they boldly took from these the pulse of their civilization. For them the poet was not the private man in the public eye but impersonal man disclosing the verbs and nouns of being. Their advocacy of impersonality was not modesty but a passion to haul in their verbal nets all reality; it was a passion to heal.

With the Contemporaries the trick is rather to extricate from the confusion and disconnections of their always provisional lives a socially valid part of themselves, someone they can accept and like. How try for the total picture when the paint is still wet on their faces, burning their eyes? For them history has become maniacal and just to have the assurance of an "I" in the great deliquescence of the "We" is task enough, or so it seems.

The Contemporary is the weakening of the will to form, as despair of an overall purpose is communicated from life to the poem. Vigorous evolution becomes obsolete when the launch is already returning (you knew it would) trailing weed from its inoperable jaws. Here is a serious dilemma. We want art to be truthful but not to drain our energy. Form is its means of quickening us. What for the Contemporary is left of structural refinements of hearing, formal ambush, architectonic mystery and economy?

The soul, as Whitehead said, consists of discovery, and discovery must remain the principle, or faith, governing art. There's no totally satisfactory alternative, in art, to a religious concentration: to a divination that coincides with the labor of design. "The Store Bay" discovers the self-punishing desire for disconnection. The end is not given entire in the beginning but is a depth that the opening line, like a plumb-string, enters cold. Too much of the longer "Hotel Normandie Pool" is strung out along the surface. The poet himself talks on and then a towel-draped Ovid at poolside talks on, exile consoling exile.

Yet politics, too, is a way of quickening form and if Walcott in his post-colonial loneliness, his need to invent an identity, illustrates the Contemporary (without performing it in mock-fever, like John Ashbery or W. S. Graham), he has the advantage of a troubled patrimony, one that, when it riles him, rouses his idle deracinated abilities. His wandering and memory of Dachau and the passport of his perfect English may make him "international—Delmore Schwartz's label for T. S. Eliot (who however ventured beyond internationalism to divinity, as a would-be isolate and ascetic)—but he remains bound in a way to the Caribbean, in a marriage all blows and departures. And in his politics he finds the privileged, pivotal point of the Contemporary, gaining purpose from, precisely, tentativeness and disconnection, turning in accusation against their source. (What a relief as the satirist, renouncing helplessness and assuming mastery, puts Power at the mercy of his pen.)

What ails the West Indies is (it seems) the Contemporary blight itself, a want of confidence and self-release. On these former colonies the various groups of people either wrangle or keep to themselves. Or so V. S. Naipaul found when, revisiting the islands in 1960, after years of expatriation, he made this summary:

> For seven months I had been travelling through territories which, unimportant except to themselves, and faced with every sort of problem, were exhausting their energies in petty power squabbles and the maintaining of the petty prejudices of petty societies. I had seen how deep in nearly every West Indian, high and low, were the prejudices of race; how often these prejudices were rooted in self-contempt; and how much important action they prompted. Everyone spoke of nation and nationalism but no one was willing to surrender the privileges or even the separateness of his group.

Naipaul himself, as here in *The Middle Passage* (1962) and in his remorseless novel *Guerrillas* (1976), has been deliberately the sort of writer the West Indian—insecure and resisting satire—needs, one who will "tell him who he is and where he stands." And Walcott, starting from scratch and anger, has singlehandedly created a mature West Indian branch of English poetry.*

Toward this end he has had to hand not only his beautiful formal English but what Naipaul calls the "lively and inventive Trinidad dialect," which he yet uses sparingly. It can be no small privilege and excitement to "represent" in "English" poetry the language of calypso and by way of identifying the collectivity that authenticates him as a poet with a people. Shabine's radiantly aggressive idiolect, at once racy and majestic, models what it means to be a self-made individual. In his new poem "The Spoiler's Return" Walcott lashes the Trinidadians in something closer, perhaps, to their own tongue (while avoiding the barbarousness endemic in dialect literature). Satire delights in this idiom with its jazzy resistance to the genteel:

> The shark, racing the shadow of the shark
> across clear coral rocks, does make them dark—
> that is my premonition of the scene
> of what passing over this Caribbean.
> Is crab climbing crab-back, in a crab-quarrel,
> and going round and round in the same barrel,
> is sharks with shirt-jacs, sharks with well-pressed fins,
> ripping we small fry off with razor grins;
> nothing ain't change but color and attire,
> so back me up, Old Brigade of Satire,
> back me up, Martial, Juvenal, and Pope
> (to hang theirself I giving plenty rope)....

And later: "All you go bawl out, 'Spoils, things ain't so bad,' / This ain't the Dark Age, is just Trinidad, / is human nature, Spoiler, after all, / it ain't big genocide, is just bohboh."

Light and glittering, perhaps two out of every three couplets cut. Certainly the form, with its flourishes, means to intimidate and the couplets with their slip-nooses of rhyme would bag evil. But the social grief is enormous: "... all Power has / made the sky shit and vermin of the stars" neglects to laugh. Spoiler "feel to bawl / 'area of darkness' with V. S. Nightfall" and finally he quits: he goes back to Hell ("One thing with Hell, at least it organize / in soaring circles ..."). Satire may imply an imperious unforgiveness that itself seems to affirm rational man. But who's listening? The rude rousing revenge sours. The poem disturbs satire with pathos. In an unkindest cut that cuts both ways, it shuts up in despair.

"The Spoiler's Return" is a razzle-dazzle but, after its kind, it rambles. "The Liberator" shows more securely what political purpose can do for poetic form. Here satire succeeds to irony in a justice almost bleedingly deep. The poem risks a sympathetic inwardness with the will-rot of Antillean cultures as well as protests against it. In a Venezuelean jungle the guerrilla followers of a certain Sonora "bawl for their mudder and their children haunt them. / They dream of mattresses, even those in prison." "We was going so good," sums up Sonora. "But then, they get tired." If he can say no more neither can Walcott, who's in the sticky position of sounding detached and English, untested: it's Sonora who suffered, who was there. No wonder Walcott lets the sweated dialect take over:

> In a blue bar at the crossroads, before you turn
> into Valencia or Grande, Castilian bequests,
> in back of that bar, cool and dark as prison,
> where a sunbeam dances through brown rum-bottles
> like a firefly through a thicket of cocoa,
> like an army torch looking for a guerrilla,
> the guerrilla with the gouged Spanish face named
> Sonora again climbs the track through wild bananas,
> sweat glued to his face like a hot cloth
> under the barber's hand. The jungle is steam.
> He would like to plunge his hands in those clouds
> on the next range. From Grande to Valencia
> the blue-green plain below breaks through the leaves.
> 'Adios, then,' said Estenzia. He went downhill.
> And the army find him. The world keep the same....

Reasserting itself at the end, where the opening lines are repeated with a difference, the standard English is tantamount to the majestic clouds on the next range, into which the likes of Sonora will never plunge their hands. But meanwhile English words have talked and a man different from the poet and his readers has emerged and become more important than the correct words. (His words are in the context the correct ones.) If he sounds clownish when he says, "A fly, big like a bee, dance on my rifle barrel / like he knew who was holding it already dead," he speaks with a representative liveliness that has its own dignity and his mimetic enfranchisement is not unrelated to a possible political one—one that "a loss of heredity," as the last line of the poem somewhat fecklessly notes, "needs to create."

Hovering within the poem is the old complaint of the best laid plans of mice and men. The flesh is weak, heroism hard, we know that. But the poem gently exceeds a specific cultural malaise without diminishing it. Walcott may lack the ideologue's assurance of where to fix the blame, but here nothing is forgotten or excused or absolved.

The long title poem, ambitiously scaled to an international betrayal of the poor, is less happy, if in its tone and procedure wonderfully hush-hush:

> We are roaches,
> riddling the state cabinets, entering the dark holes
> of power, carapaced in topcoats,
> scuttling around columns, signalling for taxis,
> with frantic antennae, to other huddles with roaches;
> we infect with optimism, and when
> the cabinets crack, we are the first
> to scuttle, radiating separately
> back to Geneva, Bonn, Washington, London.

Queerly the speaker knows his own evil to a "t"—he even privately rehearses "the ecstasies of starvation," mimicking his victims. Who, exactly, does he represent? And why emphasize "white" evil as in "The heart of darkness is not Africa. / The heart of darkness is the core of fire / in the white center of the holocaust... / the tinkling nickel instrument on the white altar," as if Conrad had been wrong to locate it in everyone? Improbably the speaker foresees at the end his own nemesis: "through thin stalks, / the smoking stubble, stalks / grasshopper: third horseman, / the leather-helmed locust" and this also seems too convenient. A brilliantly scary Third World political cartoon of The Man, the poem perhaps errs in endowing the speaker—that beetle-like criminal—with the poet's own blazing conscience: a poetic economy that falsifies.

"The Season of Phantasmal Peace," which follows it, is its sentimental obverse, a fable of "all the nations of birds" lifting together "the huge net of the shadows of this earth / in multitudinous dialects" and flying it at a seasonless height invisible to those "wingless ones / below them who shared dark holes in windows and in houses." In this precious fantasy men can't see the net of shadows except as light "at evening on the side of a hill in yellow October," and, to add to the confusion, the "season" of this "seasonless" Love "lasted one moment ... / but, for such as our earth is now, it lasted long." These conundrums are idle. The poem is effectively counter-political, distracting the reader from actual conditions. (Anyway this earthling would like the shadows, at least those "of long pines down trackless slopes," left where they belong.)

Even in political poetry the muse must be with you, your wits about you. But suppose Walcott were always to get it right, still you would want him on call for other things. If his exile's loose-endedness is a problem, heterogeneity is with him a grace, almost a way. (Even among the four political poems just examined the range of tone is unusual.) His powers long to travel and his sensibility enlarges everything to its widest limits.

At the level of style alone Walcott offers God's plenty. In addition to the aphoristic pentameter of the Spoiler, all tang, you find in *The Fortunate Traveller* morally exhausted hexameters:

> Under the blue sky of winter in Virginia
> the brick chimneys flute white smoke through skeletal lindens,
> as a spaniel churns up a pyre of blood-rusted leaves;
> there is no memorial here to their Treblinka—
> as a van delivers from the ovens loaves
> as warm as flesh, its brakes jaggedly screech
> like the square wheel of a swastika....

You find trimeters packed with word-painting and word-music:

> The edge-erasing mist
> through which the sun was splayed
> in radials has grayed
> the harbor's amethyst....

And maybe a dozen other manners. If so much versatility produces misgivings (it suggests a talent of easy virtue), the happier view is that Walcott is the sort of poet, very rare, in whom the accumulated resources of a tradition break on the present like a brilliant surf.

When you think of the volume as a whole you may miss purpose like a "tightened bow" but feel ready to scrap with anyone who wanted to take from you, say, "Early Pompeian," "Hurucan," "Wales," or "Jean Rhys," various though their subjects and treatments are and though only the last two are free of faults. One would miss in the first the delicate appreciation of the deepening and quickening of womanhood, the monstrous size of the father's grief over the stillbirth, and the demonic metaphors that, hurtingly inspired, wrest for their tenors the last affective truths. Or from "Hurucan" numerous descriptions of the furious storm, which proves "havoc, reminder, ancestor, / and, when morning enters, pale / as an insurance broker, god."

What have these poems, the first slowly traversing grief, the other all reportorial frenzy, a race to keep up with the hurricane, in common with the tidy, dignified "Wales," except a seizing craft and a demonic intensity of metaphor? "Wales" is peaceful and exciting, as classic art has always been. Patient, impersonal, remote, it reads like an inspired aside in some divine annal of the earth. The muse of history herself might be bemused by this concentrated yet casual evocation of a landscape saturated in past times:

> Those white flecks cropping the ridges of Snowdon
> will thicken their fleece and come wintering down
> through the gap between alliterative hills,
> through the caesura that let in the Legions,
> past the dark disfigured mouths of the chapels,
> till a white silence comes to green-throated Wales.

How assured each syllable is, validated by a usage that feels both old and young as the hills. (Among other felicities it is right that the short flinty *i* should not relent till the "white silence comes to green-throated Wales.") The authority of the writing seems uncanny, since Walcott can only have visited the country. It is with a ferreting genius that this Caribbean deprived of history goes after its insignia in other lands. In Wales he can feel even in the bones of the conqueror's language, which happens also to be his, a deep resistance to modernity:

> A plump raven, Plantagenet, unfurls its heraldic
> caw over walls that held the cult of the horse.
> In blackened cottages with their stony hatred
> of industrial fires, a language is shared
> like bread to the mouth, white flocks to dark byres.

All three poems reflect, however differently, an imminent or actual "loss of heredity." (The rumor of this runs wild throughout the volume.) Jean Rhys has the same intelligence. A child when the nineteenth century was "beginning to groan sideways from the ax stroke!" she developed, like Sonora, a need to create, or so Walcott imagines in his beautiful poem on her Dominican childhood, where photographs mottled "like the left hand of some spinster aunt" place her among "bone-collared gentlemen / with spiked mustaches / and their wives embayed in the wickerwork / armchairs." In the "furnace of boredom after church" (for the photographs are quickened into cinematic biography) "A maiden aunt canoes through lilies of clouds / in a

Carib hammock, to a hymn's metronome" while the child "sees the hills dip and straighten with each lurch." She will become, this girl whose senses are sharpened by "the cement grindstone of the afternoon," a writer about women whose every waking moment—in Paris, in London—seems a lurch. (Often they are left in one.) But back before the mania of history, when "grace was common as malaria," this fierce writer foresaw, from a lion-footed couch, her own hard salvation, such as it was: her calling as a writer.

> ... the gas lanterns' hiss on the veranda
> drew the aunts out like moths
> doomed to be pressed in a book, to fall
> into the brown oblivion of an album,
> embroiderers of silence
> for whom the arches of the Thames,
> Parliament's needles,
> and the petit-point reflections of London Bridge
> fade on the hammock cushions from the sun,
> where one night
> a child stares at the windless candle flame
> from the corner of a lion-footed couch
> at the erect white light,
> her right hand married to *Jane Eyre*,
> foreseeing that her own white wedding dress
> will be white paper.

One notices the sureness and seductive power of the detail and, increasingly, of the pacing. Admirable too is the unforced biographical allusion (Rhys was to know a very different London from the souvenir scenes fading on the cushions and to write the story of the first Mrs. Rochester, mad and Creole, in *Wide Sargasso Sea*). And the contrast between the "brown oblivion" of the spinster aunts and the white-paper wedding dress is poignantly complex (since writing is both sexual and abstinent, the page an eternal union and virginal). Besides dowering Rhys's parched sensibility with his own lush and delicate range of impressions, with this poem, so different from the others, Walcott at once fixes and graces her, and implicitly himself, with the myth of what Graham Greene called the "fatal moment." Here the accidents and irrelations of a Sunday afternoon transcend themselves, becoming the provocation of a marriage and a destiny. The gentle, Proustian movement of the poem, the syntax branching and branching as if desiring never to break with the moment, first conceals then delivers the inexorable. Even the solecism of the recurring "at" (in "at the erect white light") is suitably riveting. The structure is not ambitious but (in both senses) holds. As writing, we are given to understand, holds every writer—in a curiously alert fascination and a marriage with the muse that is too like celibacy to be altogether happy: at best a privileged loneliness.

"Jean Rhys" is contemporary in the sense most poetry is—it is written as if from a tragically privileged position within time, not an inhumanly privileged one outside it. Beyond that it's Contemporary in the peculiar sense intended in this review: it faces on time not as what coheres but as what disperses, not as what can be mastered but as what must be endured. This, too, is old. What is new is the nakedness with which it is suffered.

NOTE

* Andrew Salkey's anthology, *Breaklight* (1971), like his own long poem *Jamaica* (1973), seems designed to make the Caribbeans feel good, indeed a little righteous, about being Caribbean, and heady with their future ("Culture come when you buck up / on you'self"). Walcott, with his comparatively international intellect, his assimilation of English poetry, and his peculiarly strong sense of Contemporary loneliness, stands apart. He "participates in the celebration of a West Indian consciousness that has evolved from an unlikely history and from an insular separateness," as Lloyd W. Brown puts it in *West Indian Poetry*, but "his much greater emphasis on the persistence of individual separation tempers his perception of a communal or regional identity." So does his analysis "of the ... tensions ... between the moral and emotional promise of a communally perceived ideal and the human failings which blunt that promise."

HELEN VENDLER

Poet of Two Worlds

Derek Walcott is a poet, now over fifty, whose voice was for a long time a derivative one. His subject was not derivative; it was the black colonial predicament (Walcott comes from St. Lucia). But there was an often unhappy disjunction between his explosive subject, as yet relatively new in English poetry, and his harmonious pentameters, his lyrical allusions, his stately rhymes, his Yeatsian meditations. I first met his work in an anthology that had reprinted his "Ruins of a Great House," a poem now several decades old:

> A smell of dead limes quickens in the nose
> The leprosy of Empire.
>   'Farewell, green fields,
>   'Farewell, ye happy groves!'

*   *   *

> I climbed a wall with the grill ironwork
> Of exiled craftsmen protecting that great house
> From guilt, perhaps, but not from the worm's rent
> Nor from the padded cavalry of the mouse.

From *The New York Review of Books* 29, no. 3 (4 Mar. 1982). © 1982 by NYREV, Inc.

And when a wind shook in the limes I heard
What Kipling heard, the death of a great empire, the abuse
Of ignorance by bible and by sword.

A green lawn, broken by low walls of stone
Dipped to the rivulet, and pacing, I thought next
Of men like Hawkins, Walter Raleigh, Drake,
Ancestral murderers and poets.

It was clear that Walcott had been reading Yeats—the "Meditations in Time of Civil War," "On a House Shaken by the Land Agitation," and so on. Walcott's place did not seem to me then, and does not seem now, a poem, but rather an essay in pentameters. The emotional attitudes of Walcott's early verse were authentic, but shallowly and melodramatically phrased. Walcott borrowed theatrically, for instance, from Yeats's *Supernatural Songs* to express a genuine dilemma.

How choose
Between this Africa and the English tongue I love?
Betray them both, or give back what they give?
How can I face such slaughter and be cool?
How can I turn from Africa and live?

It is always dangerous for a young poet's future when he begins, as Walcott did, with a subject. Language may become, then, nothing but the ornament to his message, the rhetoric for his sermon. Walcott did not escape this ornamental view of language (and his uncertainty as to his own genre caused him to spend twenty years writing for the theater, forming a theater company, and directing plays, the most direct and urgent form of literary communication).

But there were other aspects, not anthologized, to Walcott's early verse. One was the presence of island patois—unsteady, not well managed, but boldly there, confronting the Yeatsian poise:

Man, I suck me tooth when I hear
How dem croptime fiddlers lie,
And de wailing, kiss-me-arse flutes
That bring water to me eye!

But the ever-present baleful influence of Yeats suddenly overshadows the patois speaker, and the song ends on an unlikely "literary" note:

.... Flesh upon flesh was the tune
Since the first cloud raise up to disclose
The breast of the naked moon.

Somewhat later, a shrewd social observation made itself felt in Walcott's work, as in this sketch of blacks who had returned to the native islands after having been in the United States; Walcott sees

... The bowed heads of lean, compliant men
Back from the States in their funeral serge,
Black, rusty Homburgs and limp waiters' ties
With honey accents and lard-coloured eyes.

Hart Crane, Dylan Thomas, Pound, Eliot, and Auden followed Yeats in Walcott's ventriloquism. It seemed that his learnedness might be the death of him, especially since he so prized it; one of the epigraphs in his book-length autobiographical poem *Another Life* (1973) runs, "It is never the sheep that inspire a Giotto with the love of painting; but, rather his first sight of the paintings of such a man as Cimabue" (Malraux). The sentiment appealed to Walcott precisely because he was afraid of drowning in his topic—"Too many penitential histories passing / for poems," he remarks wryly. And he knew that not politics, and not opinions, but an inner dynamic, holds an artwork together:

I can no more move you from your true alignment,
mother, than we can move objects in paintings.

Walcott's agenda gradually shaped itself. He would not give up the paternal island patois; he would not give up patois to write only in formal English. He would not give up his topic—his geographical place, his historical time, and his mixed blood; neither would he give up aesthetic balance, "the rightness of placed things." He was in all things "a divided child," loyal to both "the stuffed dark nightingale of Keats" and the "virginal unpainted world" of the islands; he was divided again between writing poetry and writing plays, divided yet again between writing plays and directing them. From St. Lucia he went to Trinidad, from Trinidad to the United States, becoming not only the colonial but also the exile and, in his returns to the West Indies, the prodigal son. Walcott has written of "the inevitable problem of all island artists: the choice of home or exile, self-realization or spiritual betrayal of one's country. Travelling widens this breach."

And yet Walcott's new book is called, not entirely ironically, *The Fortunate Traveller*. The degree to which Walcott is able to realize a poem still varies. He is still, even as a fully developed writer, peculiarly at the mercy of influence, this time the influence of Robert Lowell, as in the poem "Old New England":

> A white church spire whistles into space
> like a swordfish, a rocket pierces heaven
> as the thawed springs in icy chevrons race
> down hillsides and Old Glories flail
> the crosses of green farm boys back from 'Nam.

This represents Walcott's new apprenticeship to the American vernacular, as he lyrically describes it:

> I must put the cold small pebbles from the spring
> upon my tongue to write her language
> to talk like birch or aspen confidently.

But no one can take on a new idiom overnight, and Walcott's pentameters stubbornly retain their British cadences. It is American words, and not yet American rhythms, that find their way unevenly into these new poems. They ruin some lines and enliven others. Since the only point of using colloquialisms is to have them sound colloquial, Walcott loses momentum when his Americanisms ring ill on the ear. Here is a monologue by a person planning a movie, impatient of the suggestion that there be any lyric interludes in it, such as shots of the sea:

> The plot
> ... has to get the hero off somewhere
> else 'cause there's no kick in contemplation
> of silvery light ....

The person who would, say "'cause there's no kick in" something or other would not say "contemplation of silvery light"—the voice goes false whether you read backward or forward. There is more of this mismanagement of tone in this satiric portrait; it closes,

> Things must get rough (in the movie)
> pretty damn fast, or else you lose them, pally.

The "pally" for "pal" is a painful lapse, and one feels no better about it when one sees that it is there to rhyme with "alley" five lines earlier. No rhyme is worth destroying the illusion of plausible voice.

This sort of uncertainty in diction is disconcerting in Walcott, since he has many virtues: he is always thinking, he does not write sterile exercises in verse, he is working out a genuine spiritual history from his first volume to his current one, he keeps enlarging his range of style and the reaches of his subject. And when he errs, he often errs in a humanly admirable direction, the direction of literal truth. The trouble is, literal truth is often the enemy of poetic truth. Take his description of climbing up a hill in "Greece":

> Beyond the choric gestures of the olive,
> gnarled as sea almonds, over boulders dry
> as the calcareous molars of a Cyclops,
> past the municipal frothing of a cave,
> I climbed....

Anyone who has seen Greece will recognize the literal truth of the wind-bent olive trees, the dry gray rocks, and the sea issuing in spray out of hill-caves. Walcott's native sea almonds are there to establish the foreignness of the climber, as he thinks back to another point of reference; the Cyclops is there to establish the climber as a reader (a point necessary later in the poem). The periodic sentence ("Beyond this, over that, past the next thing, I climbed") is there to enact syntactically the long ascent. Why, then, does the passage fail? It is at this point that one enters the disputed field of decorum, surprise, and necessity—where the axioms are that a word or a form should seem necessary when it occurs and yet should "surprise by a fine excess."

Objects can always seem overmeticulous. And yet, does it fall satisfactorily on the ear to have "olive" in the singular and "sea almonds" in the plural? Isn't the line-break after the word "dry" an awkward interpolation into the phrase "dry as molars"? Are the molars of a Cyclops any more or less calcareous than other molars? And where, for that matter, is the rest of the Cyclops? And why are his discarded molars lying around the landscape? And why should an innocent cave seem to be frothing at the mouth like the proverbial madman (since nothing is subsequently made of the "maniacal" cave)?

In short, there is no psychic coherence as these details are assembled. Though each is made carefully to resemble a literal portion of the landscape, taken all together they do not resemble a soul in act. About poetry the same argument must be made that Ruskin never wearied of making about

Turner—that it was the mind of Turner, powerfully charging every pictorial detail with its own psychological freight, that made the data of the painting (whether realistic or impressionistic) converge into a single complex whole.

When Walcott has a single poem of concentration to govern his images, the poem manages its parts better. In "Hurucan" he summons and evokes the god of hurricanes, who stands allegorically for the force of the colonial oppressed:

> We doubt that you were ever slain
> by the steel Castillian lances.

In some parts of the poem, the old ugly overpreciseness remains ("flesh the gamboge of lightning, / and the epicanthic, almond-shaped eye / of the whirling cyclops"), but when the rhythm breaks loose, the images follow like a flood:

> ... Florida now flares to your flashbulb
> and the map of Texas rattles,
> and we lie awake in the dark
> by the dripping stelae of candles,
> our heads gigantified on the walls,
> and think of you, still running
> with tendons feathered with lightning,
> water worrier, whom the chained trees
> strain to follow,
> havoc, reminder, ancestor....

This is one of Walcott's poems of the South; *The Fortunate Traveller* is divided into portions called North, South, North, and the division is a symbolic one, putting the two terms into a continual dialectic rather than a sullen opposition. The patois poems in this new volume still seem to me unconvincing:

> So back me up, Old Brigade of Satire,
> back me up, Martial, Juvenal, and Pope
> (to hang theirself I giving plenty rope),
> join Spoiler' chorus, sing the song with me
> Lord Rochester, who praised the nimble flea.

The experiment is worth trying (and Walcott has used patois in every phase of his play-writing, too), but, once again, however much it reflects the truth of Walcott's own divided mind and inheritance, it has not yet found a conclusive and satisfying aesthetic relation to his "high" diction, as the passage I have just quoted suggests. A macaronic aesthetic, using two or more languages at once, has never yet been sustained in poetry at any length. There are Hispano-American poets now writing in a mixture of Spanish and English, where neither language gains mastery; once again, such work may accurately reflect their linguistic predicament, but the mixed diction has yet to validate itself as a literary resource with aesthetic power. These macaronic strategies at least break up the expected; and anyone can understand Walcott's impulse to wreck his stately and ceremonious rhythms. Often writers must follow a new impulse as a clue to an elusive style, and consolidate the old before they can find the new.

When Walcott's lines fall effortlessly and well, as in a remarkable poem of exile called "The Hotel Normandie Pool," he seems the master of both social topic and personal memory. At the pool Walcott has a vision of a fellow-exile, Ovid, banished to a Black Sea port, forced, while writing his *Tristia* (poems talismanic for Mandelstam and Heaney as for Walcott) to leave behind the pastoral of Rome for the harsher music of another climate:

> Among clod–fires, wolfskins, starving herds,
> Tibullus' flute faded, sweetest of shepherds
> Through shaggy pines the beaks of needling birds
> pricked me at Tomis to learn their tribal tongue
> so, since desire is stronger than is disease,
> my pen's beak parted till we chirped one song
> in the unequal shade of equal trees.

This seems to me Walcott at this most natural, worldly, and accomplished. The Latinity enters the ear without affectation, the mirror image of a beaked pen and the beaks of birds rivets the stanza together, and no labored effects of unnatural diction mar the lines. Ovid sums up the predicament of the educated colonial poet writing in the language of Empire:

> "... Romans"—he smiled—"will mock your slavish rhyme,
> the slaves your love of Roman structures."

Walcott's steady ironies and his cultivated detachment in the midst of a personal plight make him an observer to be reckoned with: he will remain for this century one of its most candid narrators of the complicated and even desperate destiny of the man of great sensibility and talent born in a small colonial outpost, educated far beyond the standard of his countrymen, and pitched—by sensibility, talent, and education—into an isolation that deepens with every word he writes (regardless of the multitude by whom he is read). This is in part the story of many writers—it could be said to be the story of Beckett. But in Walcott's case the story is deepened by the added element of mixed blood, an unconcealable and inescapable social identity. This has driven Walcott to the theater, and to his tidal efforts against solitude. But these efforts recede, and the writer finds himself where he was: alone, with the brief moment of community and coherence dissipated by time and the dispersal of companions.

The wars between races and nations now seem permanent to Walcott as personal isolation is permanent; but just as a momentary incandescence of joint effort is possible, so, in a time of wars, there can be a merciful respite of quiet, a "season of phantasmal peace." It is, one could say, the lyric season when a hush falls on the epic conflict, and a chorus can be heard in the polyphony of song. And though one may quicken to the Walcott of observant sharpness, brusque speaking, and social passion, voiced in patois, it is lyric Walcott who silences commentary. The best poem in this new collection is the poem Walcott placed last, "The Season of Phantasmal Peace." It is too long to quote whole, but it must be quoted in part. It begins at twilight as migrating birds lift up the shadows of the earth and, as they fly past uttering their various sounds, cause a "passage of phantasmal light," and by their singing, unify the various dialects of the earth:

> Then all the nations of birds lifted together
> the huge net of the shadows of this earth
> in multitudinous dialects, twittering tongues,
> stitching and crossing it.

Into the birds' song there comes "an immense, soundless, and high concern / for the fields and cities where the birds belong." This is one of the oldest topics of poetry—the singers of the earth concerned for mute and earthbound fellow men. The birds here feel, in the painfully beautiful close of the poem, "something brighter than pity" for the rest of us,

> for the wingless ones
> below them who shared dark holes
> in windows and in houses,

and the birds begin their work of brief, but tangible, charity:

> And higher they lifted the net with soundless voices
> above all change, betrays of falling suns,
> and this season lasted one moment, like the pause
> between dusk and darkness, between fury and peace,
> but, for such as our earth is now, it lasted long.

The poem says nothing explicit about Empire and the oppression of colonies, about dialects of white English and island English, about the power to rise above the immediate that is conferred on a poet by his allegiance to song, about the social identification that a black poet especially feels for those who share dark holes in houses, or about the betrayals and desertions entailed in a life lived between black and white, empire and outpost, island and mainland. But the poem is the transcendent clarification of all that darkness; and it holds the darkness back for its own instant of phantasmal peace. It is unashamed in its debt to Shakespeare, Keats, and the Bible; but it has assimilated them all into its own fabric.

Walcott, the best diagnostician of his own case, has said that "the urge towards the metropolitan language was the same as political deference to its centre, but the danger lay in confusing, even imitating the problems of the metropolitan by pretensions to its power, its styles, its art, its ideas, and its concept of what we are." The balancing of influences makes the writer "the mulatto of style," as Walcott once put it, attempting to avoid the pitfalls everywhere around him:

> Most of your literature loitered in the pathos of sociology, self-pitying and patronised.... And [black writers'] poems remained laments, their novels propaganda tracts, as if one general apology on behalf of the past would supplant imagination, would spare them the necessity of great art.

It is typical of Walcott to use the severe word "necessity," not about social protest but about art; the essay from which I have been quoting, "What the Twilight Says" (from *Dream on Monkey Mountain and Other Plays*), ought to be more widely known, both as a meditation on aesthetics and as a short autobiography of powerful and exhausting emotion, the background to all the poems.

JOSEPH BRODSKY

The Sound of the Tide*

Because civilizations are finite, in the life of each of them comes a moment
when centers cease to hold. What keeps them at such times from
disintegration is not legions but languages. Such was the case with Rome,
and before that, with Hellenic Greece. The job of holding at such times is
done by the men from the provinces, from the outskirts. Contrary to popular
belief, the outskirts are not where the world ends—they are precisely where
it unravels. That affects a language no less than an eye.

Derek Walcott was born on the island of Saint Lucia, in the parts
where "the sun, tired of empire, declines." As it does, however, it heats up a
far greater crucible of races and cultures than any melting pot north of the
equator. The realm this poet comes from is a real genetic Babel; English,
however, is its tongue. If at times Walcott writes in Creole patois, it's not to
flex his stylistic muscle or to enlarge his audience but as a homage to what he
spoke as a child—before he spiraled the tower.

Poets' real biographies are like those of birds, almost identical—their
real data are in the way they sound. A poet's biography is in his vowels and
sibilants, in his meters, rhymes, and metaphors. Attesting to the miracle of
existence, the body of one's work is always in a sense a gospel whose lines
convert their writer more radically than his public. With poets, the choice of
words is invariably more telling than the story line; that's why the best of

From *Less Than One*. © 1986 by Joseph Brodsky.

them dread the thought of their biographies being written. If Walcott's origins are to be learned, the pages of this selection are the best guide. Here's what one of his characters tells about himself, and what may well pass for the author's self-portrait:

> I'm just a red nigger who love the sea,
> I had a sound colonial education,
> I have Dutch, nigger, and English in me,
> and either I'm nobody, or I'm a nation.

This jaunty four-liner informs us about its writer as surely as does a song—saving you a look out the window—that there is a bird. The dialectal "love" tells us that he means it when he calls himself "a red nigger." "A sound colonial education" may very well stand for the University of the West Indies, from which Walcott graduated in 1953, although there is a lot more to this line, which we'll deal with later. To say the least, we hear in it both scorn for the very locution typical of the master race and the pride of the native in receiving that education. "Dutch" is here because by blood Walcott is indeed part Dutch and part English. Given the nature of the realm, though, one thinks not so much about blood as about languages. Instead of— or along with—"Dutch" there could have been French, Hindu, Creole patois, Swahili, Japanese, Spanish of some Latin American denomination, and so forth—anything that one heard in the cradle or in the streets. The main thing is, there was English.

The way this third line arrives at "English in me" is remarkable in its subtlety. After "I have Dutch," Walcott throws in "nigger," sending the whole line into a jazzy downward spin, so that when it swings up to "and English in me" we get a sense of terrific pride, indeed of grandeur, enhanced by this syncopatic jolt between "English" and "in me." And it's from this height of "having English," to which his voice climbs with the reluctance of humility and yet with certitude of rhythm, that the poet unleashes his oratorial power in "either I'm nobody, or I'm a nation." The dignity and astonishing vocal power of this statement are in direct proportion to both the realm in whose name he speaks and the oceanic infinity that surrounds it. When you hear such a voice, you know; the world unravels. This is what the author means when he says that he "love the sea."

For the almost forty years that Walcott has been at it, at this loving the sea, critics on both its sides have dubbed him "a West Indian poet" or "a black poet from the Caribbean." These definitions are as myopic and misleading as it would be to call the Saviour a Galilean. This comparison is appropriate if only because every reductive tendency stems from the same terror of the infinite; and when it comes to an appetite for the infinite, poetry often bests creeds. The mental as well as spiritual cowardice, obvious in these attempts to render this man a regional writer, can be further explained by the unwillingness of the critical profession to admit that the great poet of the English language is a black man. It can also be attributed to completely busted helixes or bacon-lined retinae. Still, its most benevolent explanation is, of course, a poor knowledge of geography.

For the West Indies is a huge archipelago, about five times as big as the Greek one. If poetry is to be defined by the subject matter alone, Mr. Walcott would have ended up with material five times superior to that of the bard who wrote in the Ionian dialect and who, too, loved the sea. Indeed, if there is a poet Walcott seems to have a lot in common with, it's nobody English but rather the author of the *Iliad* and the *Odyssey*, or else the author of *On the Nature of Things*. For Walcott's descriptive powers are truly epic; what saves his lines from the corresponding tedium, though, is the shortage of the realm's actual history and the quality of his ear for the English language, whose sensibility in itself is a history.

Quite apart from the matter of his own unique gifts, Walcott's lines are so resonant and stereoscopic precisely because this "history" is eventful enough: because language itself is an epic device. Everything this poet touches mushrooms with reverberations and perspectives, like magnetic waves whose acoustics are psychological, whose implications are echo-like. Of course, in that realm of his, in the West Indies, there is plenty to touch— the natural kingdom alone provides a great deal of fresh material. But here's an example of how this poet deals with the most *de rigueur* of all poetic subjects—with the moon—which he makes speak for itself:

> Slowly my body grows a single sound,
> slowly I become
> a bell,
> an oval, disembodied vowel,
> I grow, an owl,
> an aureole, white fire.
> (from "Metamorphoses, I / Moon")

And here's how he himself speaks *about* this most unpalpable poetic subject— or rather, here's what makes him speak about it:

a moon ballooned up from the Wireless Station. O
mirror, where a generation yearned
for whiteness, for candour, unreturned.

(from *Another Life*)

The psychological alliteration that almost forces the reader to see both of the
Moon's *o*'s suggests not only the recurrent nature of this sight but also the
repetitive character of looking at it. A human phenomenon, the latter is of a
greater significance to this poet, and his description of those who do the
looking and of their reasons for it astonishes the reader with its truly
astronomical equation of black ovals to the white one. One senses here that
the Moon's two *o*'s have mutated via the two *l*'s in "ballooned" into the two
r's of "O mirror," which, true to their consonant virtue, stand for "resisting
reflection"; that the blame is being put neither on nature nor on people but
on language and time. It's the redundance of these two, and not the author's
choice, that is responsible for this equation of black and white—which takes
better care of the racial polarization this poet was born to than all his critics
with their professed impartiality are capable of.

To put it simply, instead of reductive racial self-assertion, which no
doubt would have endeared him to both his foes and his champions, Walcott
identifies himself with that "disembodied vowel" of the language which both
parts of his equation share. The wisdom of this choice is, again, not so much
his own as the wisdom of his language—better still, the wisdom of its letter:
of black on white. He is simply a pen that is aware of its movement, and it is
this self-awareness that forces his lines into their graphic eloquence:

Virgin and ape, maid and malevolent Moor,
their immortal coupling still halves our world.
He is your sacrificial beast, bellowing, goaded,
a black bull snarled in ribbons of its blood.
And yet, whatever fury girded
on that saffron-sunset turban, moon-shaped sword
was not his racial, panther-black revenge
pulsing her chamber with raw musk, its sweat,
but horror of the moon's change,
of the corruption of an absolute,
like a white fruit
pulped ripe by fondling but doubly sweet.

(from "Goats and Monkeys")

This is what "sound colonial education" amounts to; this is what having "English in me" is all about. With equal right, Walcott could have claimed having in him Greek, Latin, Italian, German, Spanish, Russian, French: because of Homer, Lucretius, Ovid, Dante, Rilke, Machado, Lorca, Neruda, Akhmatova, Mandelstam, Pasternak, Baudelaire, Valéry, Apollinaire. These are not influences—they are the cells of his bloodstream, no less so than Shakespeare or Edward Thomas are, for poetry is the essence of world culture. And if world culture feels more palpable among urine-stunted trees through which "a mud path wriggles like a snake in flight," hail to the mud path.

And so Walcott's lyric hero does. Sole guardian of the civilization grown hollow in the center, he stands on this mud path watching how "the fish plops, making rings / that marry the wide harbour" with "clouds curled like burnt-out papers at their edges" above it, with "telephone wires singing from pole to pole / parodying perspective." In his keensightedness this poet resembles Joseph Banks, except that by setting his eyes on a plant "chained in its own dew" or on an object, he accomplishes something no naturalist is capable of—he animates them. To be sure, the realm needs it, not any less so than does the poet in order to survive there. In any case, the realm pays back, and hence lines like:

> Slowly the water rat takes up its reed pen
> and scribbles leisurely, the egret
> on the mud tablet stamps its hieroglyph ...

This is more than naming things in the garden—this is also a bit later. Walcott's poetry is Adamic in the sense that both he and his world have departed from Paradise—he, by tasting the fruit of knowledge; his world, by political history.

"Ah brave third world!" he exclaims elsewhere, and a lot more goes into this exclamation than simple anguish or exasperation. This is a comment of language upon a greater than purely local failure of nerves and imagination; a semantic reply to the meaningless and abundant reality, epic in its shabbiness. Abandoned, overgrown airstrips, dilapidated mansions of retired civil servants, shacks covered with corrugated iron, single-stack coastal vessels coughing like "relies out of Conrad," four-wheeled corpses escaped from their junkyard cemeteries and rattling their bones past condominium pyramids, helpless or corrupt politicos and young ignoramuses trigger-happy to replace them and babbling revolutionary garbage, "sharks with well-pressed fins / ripping we small fry off with razor grins"; a realm where "you bust your brain before you find a book," where if you turn on the radio, you may hear the captain of a white cruise boat insisting that a hurricane-stricken island reopen its duty-free shop no matter what, where "the poor still poor, whatever arse they catch," where one sums up the deal the realm got by saying "we was in chains, but chains made us unite, / now who have, good for them, and who blight, blight," and where "beyond them the firelit mangrove swamps, / ibises practicing for postage stamps."

Whether accepted or rejected, the colonial heritage remains a mesmerizing presence in the West Indies. Walcott seeks to break its spell neither by plunging "into incoherence of nostalgia" for a nonexistent past nor by eking himself a niche in the culture of departed masters (into which he wouldn't fit in the first place because of the scope of his talent). He acts out of the belief that language is greater than its masters or its servants, that poetry, being its supreme version, is therefore an instrument of self-betterment for both; i.e., that it is a way to gain an identity superior to the confines of class, race, or ego. This is just plain common sense; this is also the most sound program of social change there is. But then poetry is the most democratic art—it always starts from scratch. In a sense, a poet is indeed like a bird that chirps no matter what twig it alights on, hoping there is an audience, even if it's only the leaves.

About these "leaves"—lives—mute or sibilant, faded or immobile, about their impotence and surrender, Walcott knows enough to make you look sideways from the page containing:

> Sad is the felon's love for the scratched wall,
> beautiful the exhaustion of old towels,
> and the patience of dented saucepans
> seems mortally comic ...

And you resume the reading only to find:

> ... I know how profound is the folding of
>   a napkin
> by a woman whose hair will go white ...

For all its disheartening precision, this knowledge is free of modernistic despair (which often only disguises one's shaky sense of superiority) and is conveyed in tones as level as its source. What saves Walcott's lines from hysterical pitch is his belief that:

> ... time that makes us objects, multiplies
> our natural loneliness ...

which results in the following "heresy":

> ... Gods loneliness moves in His smallest
>   creatures.

No "leaf," neither up here nor in the tropics, would like to hear this sort of thing, and that's why they seldom clap to this bird's song. Even a greater stillness is bound to follow after:

> All of the epics are blown away with leaves,
> blown with careful calculations on brown paper,
> these were the only epics: the leaves ...

The absence of response has done in many a poet, and in so many ways, the net result of which is that infamous equilibrium—or tautology—between cause and effect: silence. What prevents Walcott from striking a more than appropriate, in his case, tragic pose is not his ambition but his humility, which binds him and these "leaves" into one tight book: "... yet who am I ... under the heels of the thousand / racing towards the exclamation of their single name, / Sauteurs! ..."

Walcott is neither a traditionalist nor a modernist. None of the available –isms and the subsequent –ists will do for him. He belongs to no "school": there are not so many of them in the Caribbean, save those of fish. One would feel tempted to call him a metaphysical realist, but then realism is metaphysical by definition, as well as the other way around. Besides, that would smack of prose. He can be naturalistic, expressionistic, surrealistic, imagistic, hermetic, confessional—you name it. He simply has absorbed, the way whales do plankton or a paintbrush the palette, all the stylistic idioms the North could offer; now he is on his own, and in a big way.

His metric and genre versatility is enviable. In general, however, he gravitates to a lyrical monologue and to a narrative. That, and the tendency to write in cycles, as well as his verse plays, again suggest an epic streak in this poet, and perhaps it's time to take him up on that. For almost forty years his throbbing and relentless lines kept arriving in the English language like tidal waves, coagulating into an archipelago of poems without which the map of modern literature would effectively match wallpaper. He gives us more than himself or "a world"; he gives us a sense of infinity embodied in the language as well as in the ocean which is always present in his poems: as their background or foreground, as their subject, or as their meter.

To put it differently, these poems represent a fusion of two versions of infinity: language and ocean. The common parent of these two elements is, it must be remembered, time. If the theory of evolution, especially that part of it that suggests we all came from the sea, holds any water, then both thematically and stylistically Derek Walcott's poetry is the case of the highest and most logical evolvement of the species. He was surely lucky to be born at this outskirt, at this crossroads of English and the Atlantic where both arrive in waves only to recoil. The same pattern of motion—ashore, and back to the horizon—is sustained in Walcott's lines, thoughts, life.

Open this book and see "... the grey, iron harbour / open on a sea-gull's rusty hinge," hear how "... the sky's window rattles / at gears raked into reverse," be warned that "At the end of the sentence, rain will begin. / At the rain's edge, a sail ..." This is the West Indies, this is that realm which once, in its innocence of history, mistook the lantern of a caravel for a light at the end of a tunnel and paid for that dearly—it was a light at the tunnel's entrance. This sort of thing happens often, to archipelagoes as well as to individuals; in this sense, every man is an island. If, nevertheless, we must register this experience as West Indian and call this realm the West Indies, let's do so, but let's also clarify that we have in mind the place discovered by Columbus, colonized by the British, and immortalized by Walcott. We may add, too, that giving a place a status of lyrical reality is a more imaginative as well as a more generous act than discovering or exploiting something that was created already.

NOTE

* This piece originally appeared as the introduction to *Poems of the Caribbean* by Derek Walcott (Limited Editions Club, 1983).

PETER BALAKIAN

The Poetry of Derek Walcott

It may seem audacious for a young poet to liken his situation to that of St. John on Patmos receiving revelation, yet Derek Walcott's early poem "As John to Patmos" is an *ars poetica* and a written vow. This early (the poem was written when the poet was in his twenties) he expresses *his* sacred sense of vocation and *his* moral and aesthetic commitment to his native realm—his island, St. Lucia, and the entire Caribbean archipelago: "So I shall voyage no more from home; / may I speak here. / This island is heaven." After evoking the island's almost mystical landscape, he consecrates his need "To praise love-long, the living and the brown dead." While the early poems included in *Collected Poems* are more modest in their intentions and less complex in their metaphorical richness than what will follow, there is still a remarkable maturity and confidence in them. (It is astonishing to realize that "Prelude" was written by a poet in his teens.) These poems allow us to see the young poet developing the idiom and grappling with the problems that will come to define his life's work and his distinctive sensibility.

Derek Walcott's *Collected Poems: 1948–1984* is a large selected poems of over 500 pages and includes work from all of his books, beginning with *In a Green Night: Poems 1948–1960*, which was first published in England by Jonathan Cape in 1962. Because 1948 marks the public beginning of Walcott's career (his first book, *25 Poems*, was published in that year), this

From *Poetry* 148, no. 3 (June 1986). © 1986 by The Modern Poetry Association.

new collection enables the reader to gain a sense of this major poet's growth and evolution. And, because all of his books prior to *Sea Grapes* (1976) are out of print, *Collected Poems* makes available the entirety of Walcott's book-length poem, *Another Life* (1973), and many other important poems from the first half of his career.

The poems from his early books, *In a Green Light, Selected Poems* (1964), and *The Castaway and Other Poems* (1965) reveal his mystic sense of place and a lush imagination which is always poised against a high eloquence. In an extraordinary early poem, "Origins," he is already able to create a language that can contain one of his major concerns—the creation myth of his native place. His ability to discover the sources of a hitherto unnamed place puts him in the company of the lyrical epic poets of the Western hemisphere, especially Whitman and Neruda. Walcott's Adamic ability to embody rhythmically and metaphorically the natural history of his world and transform it into culture-making language is what Emerson called Naming in the highest poetic fashion. "Origins" is a prologue to poems like "The Sea Is History," "Schooner *Flight*," "The Star-Apple Kingdom," "Sainte Lucie," and his book-length epic, *Another Life*. In "Origins," as in these later poems, Walcott is able to find in the cosmogonic conditions of his landscape a protean identity as a man and an epic consciousness for his culture. The warm Caribbean waters become an amniotic bath for this poet whose memory encompasses, at once, phylogeny and ontogeny. "In my warm, malarial bush-bath, / The wet leaves leeched to my flesh. An infant Moses, / I dreamed of dying, I saw / Paradise as columns of lilies and wheat-headed angels." Out of the Proustian remembrances of his childhood and his deeper racial memory comes a force of imagination in a surging rhythm that defines what he refers to as "the mind, among sea-wrack, see[ing] its mythopoetic coast":

> O clear, brown tongue of the sun-warmed, sun-wooded Troumassee
> of laundresses and old leaves, and wind that buried their old
> songs in archives of bamboo and wild plantain, their white sails
> bleached and beaten on dry stone, the handkerchiefs of adieux
> and ba-bye! O sea, leaving your villages of cracked mud....

The selections from *In a Green Night* (1962) show us Walcott's various formal virtuosities. His rhyming quatrains of iambic tetrameter in poems like "Pocomania" and "In a Green Night," or his sonnet sequence, "Tales of the Islands," reveal his ability to mine traditional forms of English poetry without ever compromising his passionate energy or his language's inner music. One senses that the vestiges of form are in the deeper structures of so many of Walcott's later freer poems. For example, the inner cohesion of the lyrical epic, *Another Life*, is in part created by the delicate balance between Walcott's eruptive imagination and the harnessing control of his tradition-bound intellect.

Other poems from the 1962 collection, such as "A Far Cry from Africa," "Ruins of a Great House," "Two Poems on the Passing of an Empire," show Walcott beginning to wrestle with the complex identity that will unfold in his later books—his irreconcilable and pluralistic cultural situation as a transplanted African in a colonial English society. Perhaps he sums up his life's dilemma when he cries out at the close of "A Far Cry from Africa":

> I who am poisoned with the blood of both,
> Where shall I turn, divided to the vein?
> I who have cursed
> The drunken officer of British rule, how choose
> Between this Africa and the English tongue I love?
> Betray them both, or give back what they give?
> How can I face such slaughter and be cool?
> How can I turn from Africa and live?

For his ability to embrace his Black West Indian identity and to accept, with the ingenuity of an artist, the language of his inherited culture accounts for much of the genius and richness of his idiom. Using the English tongue he loves does not preclude his moral outrage at the crimes that the Empire has committed against his people. He hears in the mansion of English culture a death-rattle in each room. In "Ruins of a Great House" he sees clearly "Hawkins, Walter Raleigh, Drake, / [as] Ancestral murderers and poets," and confesses that his "eyes burned from the ashen prose of Donne." Knowing his love affair with English literature, one senses the complexity of Walcott's mind.

For the most part the poems from *The Gulf* (1970) are more personal than the earlier work and bear the imprint of some of Lowell's tone and mood in *Life Studies* and *For the Union Dead*. Travelling between the West Indies and the States, Walcott has acquired a new sense of North–South tension. With his juvenalian eye, he observes another empire in the midst of its internal conflicts and violence. In the title poem, a flight over Texas provokes his vision of America as "detached, divided states, whose slaughter / darkens each summer now, as one by one, / the smoke of bursting ghettos clouds the glass." In "Elegy," written on the night of Robert Kennedy's assassination, Walcott's sober view of America ends with his recasting of that famous American couple of Grant Wood's "American Gothic": they stand "like Calvin's saints, waspish, pragmatic, poor, / gripping the devil's pitchfork / stare[ing] rigidly towards the immortal wheat."

In *The Gulf* and *The Castaway and Other Poems* (1965), Walcott's luxuriant images and tropes have become so rooted in his nature—in his pathological relationship to the world—that sight and insight, sensory perception and metaphorical meaning merge. In "The Flock," a stunning poem that opens *The Castaway*, his reflection on the imagination and the creative process begins with an image of birds migrating south: "The grip of winter tightening, its thinned / volleys of blue-wing teal and mallard fly / from the longbows of reeds bent by the wind, / arrows of yearning for our different sky." Before the poem is over the birds have become part of the imagination's topography without ever losing their naturalistic authenticity—natural fact and metaphor remain one.

Another Life (1972), written between 1965 and 1972, is an extraordinary leap forward in the evolution of Walcott's work. He has, in this poem of four books and twenty-three sections, "sung," in the epic meaning of the word, a life's story into a mythic journey. Beginning the poem in the middle of his life's journey, he exclaims near the end of the poem, "a man lives half of life / the second half is memory." And the memory in this poem is that of a collective mind and an intimately personal one. The texture, color, tone of the poet's childhood on St. Lucia and his rites of initiation into manhood and art are matched by a language so rich and sensuous that one feels in it that rare balance between the personal life and the fully metaphorical meaning of that life. Consequently, the poem is balanced between its narrative elements—the people, places, and events that have shaped the poet's life (his mother's house, the local townsfolk who become his heroes, his soul-mate the drunken painter Gregorias, his discovery of his history, his metaphorical marriage)—and the lyrical transfigurations of those elements. The poem is at once a paen to the culture of his island and the history of the Caribbean and a dramatization of the morphology of the poet's mind. In his double Culture and his divided self, he sees the music of language, the basis of metaphor, and the moral meaning of poetry. For all of the immensely cultured intellect in this poem (I cannot think of a poet who uses the history of Western painting as brilliantly as he does here), there is never anything effete or rarified in the Stevensian sense. He has managed to do what a modern epic poet must do: encompass history, myth, culture, and the personal life with the realm of aesthetic vision. Some of these passages illustrate what I mean.

His sacramental sense of culture, landscape, and history:

> At every first communion, the moon
> would lend her lace to a barefooted town
> christened, married, and buried in borrowed white,
> in fretwork borders of carpenter's Gothic,
> in mansard bonnets, pleated jalousies,
> when, with her laces laid aside,
> she was a servant, her sign
> a dry park of disconsolate palms, like brooms,
> planted by the seventh Edward, Prince of Wales ....

In his love celebration, the blood of nature becomes the blood of sacrament:

> And a vein opened in the earth,
> its drops congealing into plum,
> sorrel, and berry,
> the year bleeding again, Noel, Noel,
> blood for the bloodless birth,
> blood deepening the poinsettia's Roman blades
> after the Festival of the Innocents.

The Historical burden of his people:

> The bones of our Hebraic faith were scattered
> over such a desert, burnt and brackened gorse,
> their war was over, it had not been
> the formal tapestry bled white by decorum,
> it had infected language,
> *gloria Dei* and the glory of
> the Jacobean Bible were the same. The shoes
> of cherubs piled in pyramids
> outside the Aryan ovens.

The exuberant drunkenness of the young poet and his painter friend:

> while the black, black-sweatered, horn-soled fisherman drank
> their l'absinthe in sand back yards standing up,
> on the clear beer of sunrise,

on cheap, tannic Canaries muscatel,
on glue, on linseed oil, on kerosene,
as Van Gogh's shadow rippling cornfield,
on Cezanne's boots grinding the stones of Aix
to shales of slate, ochre, and Vigie blue,
on Gauguin's hand shaking the gin-coloured dew
from the umbrella yams,
garrulous, all day, sun-struck ....

Sea Grapes (1976) is in certain obvious ways a quieter and more austere book. After the outpouring of the long poem, it is as if Walcott were forced to retreat in order to examine the troubles of his present life. Poems like "Sea Grapes," "Fist," "Winding Up," and "Love After Love" deal with the tensions between the passionate life of love and poetry and his responsibilities to his domestic life and his solitary self. Nevertheless, the one long poem, "Sainte Lucie," shows us that he is never too far from his tribal self. This five-part poem, which is a kind of psalm to his island, is a mixture of French Creole and even a Creole song, touches of a vernacular speech, and Walcott's inimitable eloquence. In a way the poem looks forward to the continuing epic impulse that defines *The Star-Apple Kingdom* (1979).

Coming to *The Star-Apple Kingdom* after the poems that have preceded it, one becomes aware not only of Walcott's genius but of his stature as a major poet. His ability to renew himself, to revitalize his imagination, to rediscover the myth of his life and his culture, places him among the greatest poets of our century—Yeats, Neruda, Rilke, Williams, Elytis, for example—poets who write out of their obsessions without repeating themselves. Two of his most powerful poems, "The Schooner *Flight*" and "The Star-Apple Kingdom," reveal Walcott's seemingly inexhaustible resources. In "The Schooner *Flight*," he unites beautifully a vernacular tradition with his high eloquence so that the reader believes that his persona, Shabine, is both a common man and a speaker of poetry. Shabine, who is trying to escape the woes of his life by fleeing his island as a castaway, is able to sustain a tone that is both autobiographical and mythic. "I'm just a red nigger who love the sea, / I had a sound colonial education, / I have Dutch, nigger, and English in me, / and either I'm nobody, or I'm a nation." He becomes a kind of underwater Isaiah whose vision encompasses his people's history. He sees what it was to be a "colonial nigger," and as the rhythms of the sea provoke Shabine's inner eye ("I had no nation but the imagination"), he relives the Middle Passage, sees the corruption of the imperialist businessman and ministers, and as an angry prophet cries out: "I shall scatter your lives like a handful of sand, / I who have no weapon but poetry and / the lances of palms and the sea's shining shield!"

The language of the title poem, which is set in Jamaica, is able to hold in tension the pastoral munificence of the colonial world and its morally rotten underpinnings:

> Strange, that the rancour of hatred hid in that dream
> of slow rivers and lily-like parasols, in snaps
> of fine old colonial families, curled at the edge
> not from age or from fire or the chemicals, no, not at all,
> but because, off at its edges, innocently excluded
> stood the groom, the cattle boy, the housemaid, the gardeners,
> the tenants, the good Negroes down in the village,
> their mouths in the locked jaw of a silent scream.

As he recounts the history of the Caribbean, he sees the islands as beads on the rosary—and through this ingenious sacramental conceit he leads us back into history (the Conquistadors, "the empires of tobacco, sugar, and bananas," "the footbath of dictators, Trujillo, Machado," "the alphabet soup of CIA, PNP, OPEC"). But, as so often happens in Walcott's poems, the journey into the darkness of history enables him to validate his identity as a West Indian Black man so that he can "sleep the sleep that wipes out history" and envision, once again, another version of Genesis—what becomes for him almost an imaginative ritual allowing him to reclaim his people's strength. He imagines his "history-orphaned islands" from Cuba to Tobago as turtles coupling, and finds the history of his race in one black woman who sees "the creak of light" that divided the world between "rich and poor," "North and South," "black and white," "between two Americas," as she hears the transcendent silence of the beginning in the "white, silent roar / of the old water wheel in the star-apple kingdom."

Since the ten poems in *The Star-Apple Kingdom* (only eight are reprinted here) comprise a sustained book-length poem, it would seem hard to surpass such an effort in a short period of time. However, *The Fortunate Traveler* (1981) is again a surge forward—another poetic renewal. The book shows Walcott's various selves: an exiled poet writing with ambivalent passion about the North, the Augustan satirist writing in a comic vernacular in "The Spoiler's Return," and the elegist enlarging his familiar theme of exile into a modern vision. In one of the magnificent poems of the collection, "North and South," the poet confesses his identity as a "colonial upstart at the end of an empire, / a single, circling, homeless satellite." He becomes a modern exiled poet with a global vision of what empire means as he hears "its gutteral death rattle in the shoal / of the legions' withdrawing roar, from the raj, / from the Reich, and see[s] the full moon again / like a white flag rising over Fort Charlotte." Like Ellison's Invisible Man or Wright's Bigger Thomas, Walcott finds himself a deracinated Black man wandering through the snowy surreal white streets of the urban North (Manhattan). He is enervated by how far he is from the "salt freshness" of his "raw" culture, and tired of the decadence of America and Europe with its "literature ... an old couch stuffed with fleas." As the poem shifts to a winter Virginia landscape (amplifying the double meaning of North and South), the poet identifies himself as a slave, and as he imagines that a blue-eyed, red-haired aunt of his might be part Jewish, he makes a pact with all the oppressed peoples of the world and would rather have "the privilege / to be yet another of the races they fear and hate / instead of one of the haters and the afraid."

He extends this human empathy even further in the title poem. His self-effacing and poignant use of the famous refrain of St. Paul in Corinthians, "*and have not charity*," is the poem's hymning refrain; it serves as a benediction and an admonition. The poem is borne out of the poet's painful sense of the fissure between the need for a religious ethos and the absence of any moral order in our time. With his savage wit he recasts history so that "After Dachau" supplants "Anno Domini." As he contemplates the 10,000,000 people starving on the earth and the 765,000 skeletons in Somalia, that horseman of the apocalypse—famine—"the leather-helmed locust" stalks his imagination. The beast that Yeats saw "slouching toward Bethlehem" is now among us as Walcott looks at the twentieth century to see "The heart of darkness is the core of fire / in the white center of the holocaust." The poem reminds us of the meaning of *caritas* and the fact that all reform must begin in the human heart. For all the moral advocacy in this poem, Walcott never strays from the richness of his metaphor or collapses his poetic eloquence for the sake of a message. This is the kind of political poem that only a master can write.

The *Collected Poems* concludes with a selection of thirty poems from his most recent book, *Midsummer* (1984). The collection is comprised of fifty-four short lyric poems, which in their diary-like tone give the sense of a poet charting his preoccupations during the course of a year. Since the collection is a kind of book-length poem, I wish the entire book had been republished. In a certain sense, this is Walcott's most American book (although its personal tone is always ballasted by his sumptuous imagination). Here, he appears more at home in his exile, a cosmopolitan poet absorbing the pulse of many cultures; he exclaims "this is the lot of all wanderers, this is their fate, / that the more they wander, the more the world grows wide." He becomes the poet as ethnographer and we see him in the pensiones, hotels, motels, and inns of Rome, New York, Warwickshire, Boston, and even having a nightmarish vision of nuclear winter in Chicago. He has also found a more personal idiom for writing about one of his passions—painting.

His lyrical ruminations on Watteau, Gaughin, Van Gogh, and Chardin show us how Walcott's rich imagination continues to be informed by texture, tone, gradation of color, hard and soft lines, and shifting perspectives—and how much the art of Gregorias's friend is a love-affair with the world. In concluding, it is fitting to mention Walcott's love poems. For they are as full-bodied, erotic, compassionate, personal and mythic at once, as any love poems written in English in this century. "Bleeker Street, Summer," "Goats and Monkeys," the epithalamion in *Another Life*, "Egypt, Tobago," "Europa," and the astounding poem about his still-born daughter, "Early Pompeian," are poems that embody another dimension of *caritas*.

It is difficult to think of a poet in our century who—without ever betraying his native sources—has so organically assimilated the evolution of English literature from the Renaissance to the present, who has absorbed the Classical and Judeo-Christian past, and who has mined the history of Western painting as Walcott has. Throughout his entire body of work he has managed to hold in balance his passionate moral concerns with the ideal of art. By his fifty-fifth year Derek Walcott has made his culture, history, and sociology into a myth for our age and into an epic song that has already taken its place in the history of Western literature.

RITA DOVE

"Either I'm Nobody, or I'm a Nation"

1. Why a Collected? Why this essay?

Acelebrated poet reaches a point in his career where there needs to be a
retrospective consideration of the work. Several choices can be made. A
Selected Poems demands rigorous excerpting from previous books. A *New and
Selected Poems* is a way of assuring the public that one is not yet an institution.
A *Collected Poems* is like tossing in one's lot with the gods.

Derek Walcott's massive *Collected Poems 1948–1984* has an edge of
defiance, as if to say, "Dismiss me if you can." But who would want to dismiss
him? Walcott's poems stand out from the wash of contemporary American
poetry (so much of it so *mild*, like half-whispered, devious apologies) because
they are so boldly eloquent. The writing is some of the most exquisite in the
English language, resembling the Caribbean in its many voices—sometimes
crisp, sometimes tough, sometimes sweetly lyrical, or clear and treacherous
as water in a stream. The syntax is often elaborate, frustrating yet seductive
in the way it both reveals and obscures. When a Walcott poem fails, the
writing is rarely at fault.

A true Renaissance man, Walcott has consistently resisted being
cubbyholed. He has rejected neither his Caribbean heritage nor his British
education. Although in recent years he divides his time between Trinidad and

From *Parnassus: Poetry in Review* 14, no. 1 (1987). © 1987 by Rita Dove.

Boston, for a while he lived exclusively in the West Indies as director of the Trinidad Theatre Workshop. Although St. Lucia, his birthplace, forms his primary subject matter, he has also written about Manhattan and Mandelstam. In the eyes of the public, however, his unique position as the first English-speaking Caribbean poet of international renown threatens to make him "... a man no more / but the fervour and intelligence / of a whole country" (*Another Life*). And so the girth of this *Collected Poems* is also a demand to consider the whole man—not just his skin or age or prosody or heart or mind.

2. Two Early Poems—Precocity's *Ars Poetica*

> "... the writers of my generation were natural assimilators. We knew the literature of Empires, Greek, Roman, British, through their essential classics; and both the patois of the street and the language of the classroom hid the elation of discovery. If there was nothing, there was everything to be made. With this prodigious ambition one began."
>
> —Derek Walcott,
> "What the Twilight Says: An Overture"

In the very first poem—titled, significantly, "Prelude"—the young poet looks down on his island from a distance and puts it into geographical and historical perspective:

> I, with legs crossed along the daylight, watch
> The variegated fists of clouds that gather over
> The uncouth features of this, my prone island.
>
> Meanwhile the steamers which divide horizons prove
> Us lost;
> Found only
> In tourist booklets, behind ardent binoculars;
> Found in the blue reflection of eyes
> That have known cities and think us here happy.

Although he enjoys a giant's viewpoint, the "variegated fists of clouds" constitute a larger, more threatening entity which has beaten the island into submission. The poet recognizes his place in a line of bullies.

He then vows not to make his life "public" "[u]ntil I have learnt to suffer / In accurate iambics." This statement of aesthetics is an act of survival as well: coming from a marginal culture, Walcott realizes how quickly colonial attitudes would label the personal confessions of a West Indian impulsive, lecherous, and non-intellectual. Any of the contradictions and ambivalent urgings common to all human beings would be invisible to such a prejudiced observer; the poet's only chance to be heard is to beat the masters at their own game. With the practiced duplicity of a guerrilla, he plans to

> Make a holiday of situations,
> Straighten my tie and fix important jaws,
> And note the living images
> Of flesh that saunter through the eye.
>
> Until from all I turn to think how,
> In the middle of the journey through my life,
> O how I came upon you, my
> reluctant leopard of the slow eyes.

Beneath the surface politeness, he is a cool customer whose detached observations register human beings as subjects—not merely objects but "living images of flesh," a double removal. Still, these images "saunter," and the casual iambics of the next lines, plus the tripping syllables of "In the middle of the journey through my life," are lulling. The incantatory "O" brings us up short, approximating the sudden intake of breath the poet makes when he stumbles upon that which changes his life.

Dante's *Divine Comedy* also begins in the middle of a life. Is Walcott suggesting that he is at the same point—at age twenty-eight a precocious notion—or is he saying that once "boyhood has gone over" the remaining years constitute a struggle to recapture that beatific state? ("Never such faith again, never such innocence!" he exclaims, twenty-five years later, in *Another Life*.) The image of the leopard, moreover, is "reluctant," like a shy lover or a Muse ..." I think "Prelude," finally, welcomes passion—both sensual and communal—while warning against the pampering of personality that can lead to self-indulgent writing. Above all, it is the poet's vow to admit paradox and conflict into his intellectual makeup.

"Origins," the fifth poem in the book, was originally published in *Selected Poems* (1964). It is like a quilt of West Indian history, introduced with an epigram from Aimé Césaire; the roll of surrealistic images imitates the roll of the surf and is reminiscent of Césaire's *Return to My Native Land*. To begin, the slate is wiped clean. Tradition, history, culture, and identity are erased:

> The flowering breaker detonates its surf.
> White bees hiss in the coral skull.
> Nameless I came among olives of algae,
> Foetus of plankton, I remember nothing.

Walcott's admiration for the Hart Crane of "Voyages" and "O Carib Isle" accounts for the acoustical flamboyance here. The "flowering breaker" bombards the shoreline through the use of explosive consonants and that masterful word "detonates," with its echoing vowels. The sonic boom of the first two lines gives way to the quieter chains of nouns. The neutral material (coral skull, algae) provides a fruitful bed for the bees, the "I" with neither identity nor history. On this ground, then, one can plant. Nothingness, for Walcott, does not imply negation but rather a *tabula rasa* from which one can start afresh.

Western civilization intervenes, and the poet struggles to unite conflicting traditions in himself. His first efforts at assimilation apply the Western myths to oral African traditions:

> Between the Greek and African pantheon,
> Lost animist, I rechristened trees:
> Caduceus of Hermes: the constrictor round the mangrove....

Sections III and VI are italicized homages to island patois, the linguistical result of assimilation. Here the debt to Césaire is evident in the undulating string of images laid out for our delectation—the "clear, brown tongue of the sun-warmed, sun-wooded Troumassee / of laundresses and old leaves"— images which, however, become more jarring, near-surrealistic in the juxtaposition of sensations, such as the "cracked cobalt" of the "starched, linen seas," a rising agitation that subsides with the exclamation "*Ah, mon enfance!*" Part VI most resembles the Césaire of *Cahier d'un Retour au Pays Natal* (*Notebook of the Return to My Native Land*) with its associative progression of images through history: "their alphabet of alkali and aloe ... their bitter olive" have scoured the "sweet, faded savour of rivers" until we find a "twin soul, spirit of river, spirit of sea." This, however, is a positive process, a multiplication of strengths rather than a division.

Walcott's concerns, reflected in these two early poems, have not changed substantially over the years. Even when he evokes violent emotions—fury, love, grief—the writing is controlled, trenchant. In the midst of the most relentless self-scrutiny is the panning, photographic eye, returning to us flailed beachhead, yellowing coconut, the "padded cavalry of the mouse."

The primary vigor of patois informs poems like "The Liberator," "Parang," "The Schooner *Flight*," and "Pocomania," where the cadences of dialect syncopate the iambic line and patois words are liberally sprinkled without obliterating sense. In "Sainte Lucie," in the middle of a bilingual cataloguing of indigenous fruit, he cries, "Come back to me, / my language"; later in the same poem appear the lyrics of a native Creole song he once heard on the back of an open truck; he provides an English translation in the next section.

Walcott is a poet of circling and deepening; even the framing dates for this volume—1948 to 1984—hint that everything comes full circle. A prodigy and a black, he saw his dilemma early; a poet, he knew that the iambic line, with its thumbholds of word and image, was his thread out of the labyrinth.

3. SANTA LUCIA: THE RAW MATERIAL

"If your daily life seems poor, do not blame it; blame yourself, tell yourself that you are not good enough to call forth its riches. For anyone who creates there is no poverty and no poor, indifferent place."

—Rilke, *Letters to a Young Poet*

I had to go away to college to discover that I was supposed to be ashamed of my hometown—for wasn't Akron, with its brick factories and sooty clapboard houses, deplorable? Didn't the smell of rubber make me sick? Wasn't it true that the only river had been forced underground? (The gorge remains, choked with dogwood, oak, hickory; in summer it wafts sickeningly with the floral bouquet of rotting garbage.)

Tourists love the Caribbean for its white beaches and opal seas, its glossy vegetation trailing across restaurant lattices. How delightful to snack on pomegranates, tucking a nameless exotic flower behind your ear! How could anyone regret all this!

Derek Walcott was born in Castries, St. Lucia, a small volcanic island between St. Vincent and Martinique. Then a part of Her Majesty's Empire,

St. Lucia "enjoyed" a British imprint—Christianity, white manor houses. But behind the Great House sprawled the squalor of the poor blacks. All that a writer from St. Lucia could offer, in lieu of Thomas Hardy's cool and lonely heath, were bleached shores and, puffing toward them, steamers which "prove us lost: / Found only / In tourist booklets, behind ardent binoculars."

To get a hint of the complexity of the West Indian identity crisis, first look at the map. Register the distances between islands—"little turtles from Tortuga to Tobago"—and imagine the small towns trying to imitate suburban America, the capital cities wishing they were Washington or at least Havana; imagine the tiny communities separated by distances we find insignificant but they experience as absolute. Then look at a history book: the waves of conquests from Spain, the Netherlands, France, Great Britain; the African slave trade, the influx of cheap peasant labor from India and China. Imagine the Babel of languages, the frictions arising from different religions, eating habits, body gestures. Above all, imagine the northwestern hemisphere leaning its weight on the rest of the world, telling them that their ways are primitive, shameful, wrong, and must be changed.

Colonialism imposes on its subjects many indignities, but the most insidious one is a spiritual and cultural schizophrenia. (Walcott's dilemma is also biological, as one of his grandfathers was British. In the oft-quoted "A Far Cry from Africa" he asks: "I who am poisoned with the blood of both, / Where shall I turn, divided to the vein?"). Until Walcott realizes that assimilation means embracing every culture around one, his early lyrics are often stilted and hollow. The sonnets reprinted from *In a Green Night* (1962) are technically skilled but lifeless. This description of a Caribbean harbor could have been written by a tourist rather than by someone who grew up with the fishermen and listened to their stories:

> The fishermen rowing homeward in the dusk
> Do not consider the stillness through which they move,
> So I, since feelings drown, should no more ask
> For the safe twilight which your calm hands gave.
>
> ("The Harbour")

Yet he is learning; in an elevated manner reminiscent of Crane's shorter lyrics, Walcott applies his talents to the landscape and people, faithfully recording; by the time *Selected Poems* is published (1964), the improvement is startling. "Parang" not only re-creates the language of the people but succeeds in catching the ironical humor—*laughin' just to keep from cryin'*—any member of a suppressed group well better practice for survival. "Tales of the

Islands," a sequence of ten sonnets, compiles snatches of gossip, folkloric rituals—some devoutly believed, some performed for visiting anthropologists—saloon talk, and scenic views, resulting in a batch of mock-satirical "postcards."

In the struggle to prove Akron worthy of poetry, the lines of battle are at least clearly drawn. Walcott's task is complicated by that very postcard image of the West Indies. Every time he mentions the sea, we tend to sigh with envy. And so he gives us sea and shore and salt air in spades: blinding heat, stunned water, the smells of sweating humanity, the omnipresent galvanized roofs, the stars nailed into the sky, the rain like knives—he rams the scenery down our throats until we stop, being thrilled and start to listen.

4. History Lesson

"When there is no history there is no metaphor ..."
                                        —Michael S. Harper

"[T]here is too much nothing here."
                                        —Derek Walcott, "Air"

Derek Walcott claims time and again that the West Indies have no history, that without history a new race is rising from these tourist-ridden islands. He plays the devil's advocate by adopting the Official Version of Events; his bitter jibes at his countrymen for not making an impact on this record is his duplicitous way of attacking the foundations of Western civilization. Arguing negatively, he is permitted, through remorse and abuse, to lavish his attention on people, communities, and landscapes that aren't historically "important."

Michael Harper's history is a matrix of memory and responsibility. He rejects the Official Version, for it has no vision or morality. It is not, humanely speaking, truthful. I can imagine Walcott replying to Harper: "Without history, there is no memory." Or conversely: "Without memory, there is no history." The Middle Passage obliterated family ties, tribal connections, and the religious and communal rites that give sense to natural law. West Indian history is a how-to manual for the brutal destruction of whole races' systems for sustaining memory.

The amnesia of the people is reflected in the island vegetation whose rapid proliferation obliterates paths and manors alike. Human accomplishment disappears with time, sun, and rain. Uncontrolled growth is emblematic of the process of forgetting:

when the axe spoke, weeds ran up to the knee
like bastard children, hiding in their names,

whole generations died, unchristened,
growths hidden in green darkness, forests
of history thickening with amnesia ...

(*Another Life*)

Walcott's primary metaphor is the sea. The sea is History or, more precisely, a history book, her pages steadily turning, writing and erasing themselves. Sometimes the sea is a book of poems, left lying face down by an absent reader; more often, the sea is quintessential Nothingness. The islands take their lessons from the sea. As he points out in "The Sea Is History" (from *The Star-Apple Kingdom*), any event not recognized for its true essence does not exist. To the question "Where are your monuments, your battles, martyrs?" the West Indian replies: "Sirs, / in that grey vault. The sea. The sea / has locked them up." A list of humiliations follows—slave trade, imported peasant labor, conquerors and exploiters—to which the narrator blithely assigns biblical metaphors: the slave trade is Exodus, poverty is Lamentations, the sun setting is the New Testament. Only with the break-up of the British Empire does the clock start to tick:

then came the bullfrog bellowing for a vote,

fireflies with bright ideas
and bats like jetting ambassadors
and the mantis, like khaki police ...

"This," Walcott claims wryly, is the "rumour without any echo of History, really beginning." In other words, History begins with self-determination, no matter how corrupt the struggle to prevail, which, after all, is the last thing any empire that "sneers at all thoughts in the future tense" wishes. More suitable to the colonial game plan is the scenario of "Return to D'Ennery; Rain":

So azure and indifferent was this air,
So murmurous of oblivion the sea,
That any human action seemed a waste,
The place seemed born for being buried there.

5. PORTRAIT OF THE ARTIST AS A YOUNG MAN

> The dream
> of reason had produced its monster:
> a prodigy of the wrong age and colour.
> —Derek Walcott, *Another Life*

I first met Derek Walcott in the basement of the Performing Arts Building at my undergraduate university. He was in town to give a poetry reading that I would miss because of the dress rehearsal of my first play, a one-act incorporating pantomine, dream, and song into a forty-five-minute recounting of the last thirty years of Afro-American history. It was spring 1973, the year Walcott's phenomenal narrative poem, *Another Life*, was published. We shook hands and I croaked a hello; I had read *Dream on Monkey Mountain* the previous summer and couldn't believe that the author of that great play was standing outside the auditorium where my diluted imitation was struggling through missed cues and uncertain direction.

I did not read *Another Life* until much later. When I finally did, out of graduate school and on my way to Europe for the third or fourth time, I recognized its major themes as chords in my own life: loss of innocence, the search for a heritage; the schizophrenia of assimilation, the writer as exile to his homeland and to his own life.

Another Life's 4,000-plus lines are divided into four parts, which are then divided into twenty-three chapters. The narrative operates on many levels, often shifting times and perspectives in mid-line; it is a lyric *Bildungsroman*, Walcott's *Buddenbrooks* or *A la Recherche du Temps Perdu*. His usual rhetorical reticence disappears, and the telling is made more haunting by its elasticity; he cajoles, proclaims, rages, and whispers. There are straight descriptive passages, dramatic monologues, self-interviews, brief spurts of song. Walcott's experience as playwright and theater director finds a second life here, in poetry.

Part One, *The Divided Child*, recounts the first artistic stirrings. His ambition to become a great painter is undermined by the very literary metaphor that sets the opening scene:

> Verandahs, where the pages of the sea
> are a book left open by an absent master
> in the middle of another life—
> I begin here again ...

The absent master refers equally to the dead father, the drawing teacher Harold Simmons, God (who is either indifferent or dead), and the absence of racial memory. The image of the sea as a book occurs again and again, charting Walcott's deepening relationship to literature.

> And from a new book,
> bound in sea-green linen, whose lines
> matched the exhilaration which their reader,
> rowing the air around him now, conveyed,
> another life it seemed would start again ...

By Chapter 3, the narration is firmly in the hands of dramatic literature; the "town's characters, its cast of thousands" are presented in alphabetical order, from Ajax the "lion-coloured stallion" to Zandoli, rodent exterminator. "These dead, these derelicts," claims Walcott, "... were the stars of my mythology." He involves this cast in a mini-drama, but by Chapter 7, the narrator withdraws with an ironic commentary on his own creation:

> Provincialism loves the pseudo-epic,
> so if these heroes have been given a stature
> disproportionate to their cramped lives,
> remember I beheld them at knee-height ...

Is this sly disavowal prompted by embarrassment, or has Walcott anticipated our condescension? The ruse is Shakespearean, a clue that we will have to watch ourselves, a warning to avoid the easy judgment. Look at Julius Caesar, Macbeth, King Lear—what are heroes but plunderers, murderers, and vengeful, foolish men?

Part Two, "Homage to Gregorias," recalls Walcott's boyhood friend Dunstan St. Omer and their years together as apprentices of the artist Harry Simmons. Dunstan's name is changed to Gregorias because "it echoes the blest thunders of the surf ... / because it sounds explosive, / a black Greek's!"; it also suggests that St. Lucia, with its misted mountains and wilderness of ocean, has affinities to ancient Greece.

Soon realizing he does not have the gift for painting, the narrator envies "mad, divine Gregorias / imprisoned in his choice." But there is literature and the growing compulsion to articulate the dreams of his people who were "dazed, ignorant, / waiting to be named." Of Gregorias he says "He had his madness," then: "mine was our history." But where was this history to be found? Not in the school headmaster, "a lonely Englishman who loved parades, / sailing, and Conrad's prose," nor in the pupil's red-jacketed *History of the British Empire*. Not in the tapestry of Waterloo hanging in the house of one of his mother's sewing clients, not even in daydreams of Montparnasse in the twenties. (When I was ten I read an article in *Jet* about Dorothy Dandridge losing out to Elizabeth Taylor for the role of Cleopatra. Right then I knew that History didn't include me.) Taking a cue from Gregorias, the poet turns to his immediate environment for inspiration and sees "vowels curl from the tongue of the carpenter's plane." The two drink, talk through the night, criticize and praise each other's work, and make a vow:

> But drunkenly, or secretly, we swore,
> disciples of that astigmatic saint,
> that we would never leave the island
> until we had put down, in paint, in words,
> as palmists learn the network of a hand,
> all of its sunken, leaf-choked ravines,
> every neglected, self-pitying inlet
> muttering in brackish dialect, the ropes of mangroves
> from which old soldier crabs slipped
> surrendering to slush,
> each ochre track seeking some hilltop and
> losing itself in an unfinished phrase ...

The youthful fantasies accelerate, almost reveling in the squalor which they plan to extol—the endless sentence, so customary of Walcott, rolls through intricate couplings of landscape and language, finally slithering to a pause with the soldier crabs falling into slush ... those crabs being a foreshadowing of the disillusioned older poet who, looking back on those days, would exclaim: "Yet, Gregorias, lit, / we were the light of the world!"

That pun, with its cocky tenderness, erupts in Part Three into the purging, catalytic nature of fire. A conflagration devastates the town of Castries. Now the world of their youth is gone: "... with the fierce rush of a furnace door / suddenly opened, history was here." Castries' resurrection as "a cement phoenix" is paralleled by the poet's discovery of sex and the possibility of education abroad:

> Tea with the British Council Representative,
> tannin, calfskin, gilt, and thank you vellum much ...

I am hoisted on silvery chords upward,
eager for the dropped names like sugar cubes.
Eliot. Plop. Benjamin Britten. Clunk. Elgar. Slurp.
Mrs. Winters's cheeks gleaming. Polished cherries.
Lawns. Elegance. Remembering elms. England, then. When?
Down on her speckled forearm. More tea.
Thank you, my mind burrowing her soft scented crotch.
First intimations of immortality.
Other men's wives.

First love also sparks with the appearance of Anna, "gold and white ... light /
of another epoch." He makes her his lover and then, imitating literature,
idealizes her until she dissolves into all the literary Annas he has adored:
Anna Christie, Anna Karenina, Anna Akhmatova. Finally, inevitably, she
loses out to Art: "The hand she held already had betrayed / them by its
longing for describing her."

He leaves for study abroad, praying that nothing will change—a futile
wish, for though he returns many times, he carries the guilt of the prodigal
son. In Part Four, "The Estranging Sea," Walcott—"One life, one marriage
later"—encounters Gregorias and finds him

> unable to hold down a job, painting so badly
> that those who swore his genius vindicated
> everything once, now saw it as a promise never kept.
> Viciously, near tears, I wished him dead.

This self-punishing rage rapidly turns outward: news of the suicide of his
mentor, Harold Simmons, prompts a scathing denunciation of "the
syntactical apologists of the Third World," those ill-wishers who condemn
their promising artists before they have even begun. He envisions them
prodding Harry to his grave while exclaiming "from such a man / what would
you expect, / but a couple of paintings / and a dog's life?"

Finally it is the sea which opens the way to hope. If the sea is a book,
then the most natural action is to pick up that book and start to read; the next
step is to write the book oneself:

> for what else is there
> but books, books and the sea,
> verandahs and the pages of the sea,
> to write of the wind and the memory of wind-whipped hair
> in the sun, the colour of fire?

His fury spent, Walcott assesses his present position—"I was eighteen then, now I am forty-one"—and accepts what he has been and become. The next visit home he is able to see that it "is not bitter, it is harder / to be a prodigal than a stranger." He decides to visit neither Harry's grave nor Anna; instead, he asks forgiveness of the island for his desertion. Upon those who stayed so that he might leave—Anna, Gregorias, Simmons—he wishes rest. His only desire now is "to grow white-haired / as the wave, with a wrinkled / brown rock's face ... an old poet, / facing the wind."

6. CHILDHOOD'S AFTERMATH

> "It is summer-gone that I see, it is summer-gone."
> —Gwendolyn Brooks,
> "A Sunset of the City"

Another Life took seven years to write, years in which America exploded with student demonstrations and race riots. It is typical of Walcott's contrariness that he chose "to row, but backward"; to present an introspective exploration of his personal past at the very moment so many Afro-American writers were writing "for the people." Walcott insists that only through the particular fate can a universal one be posited; his response to the call for Black Pride is to contribute his version of a life, another life, in all its ambiguities.

Sea Grapes (1976) is the calm after the storm, a resignation borne of equal parts serenity and loss. These poems are *triste*—elegant, spare constructions, almost classical:

> Desolate lemons, hold
> tight, in your bowl of earth,
> the light to your bitter flesh ...
>
> ("Sunday Lemons")

If the green of the sea is the signature color of *Another Life*, *Sea Grapes*'s prevailing hue is gold—lemons, Valencia oranges, the goldsmith of Benares, "oaks yellowing October, / everything turning money." I am reminded of Yeats's "Sailing to Byzantium," where a similar yearning becomes the wish to escape the body into a form of "hammered gold and gold enameling." Gold, the color of fervor and denouement, of the fire and its embers.

Which is not to imply that Walcott has given up—on the contrary, there is a sweetness to this dignity that, rather than softening the effect of his rigorous attention to craft, makes these poems all the more troubling, their severe forms filled with mutable living tissue. The youthful paradise is gone; one cannot return home. Hence the Adam poems—Adam heartbroken by Eve's betrayal ("Adam's Song"), Adam's comprehension of labor and profit in "New World." Concomitant with the construction of a New World in these poems is the proliferation of bitter fruit—lemons, olives, limes, sour apples, green grapes.

The labor begins here, outside the walls. Where a lesser poet would fall silent or imitate earlier successes, Walcott rolls up his sleeves. His unique experience as unlikely prodigy, apprentice painter, literature student, poet, dramatist, and theater director; his cognizance of the bogus glories of "fame" and "world citizenship"—all this has prepared him for a new lesson: reconciliation with the irrevocable. As he says in "Dark August":

> ... I am learning slowly

> to love the dark days, the steaming hills,
> the air with gossiping mosquitoes,
> and to sip the medicine of bitterness...
> . . .

> I would have learnt to love black days like bright ones,
> the black rain, the white hills, when once
> I loved only my happiness and you.

7. THE STAR-APPLE KINGDOM

"Shabine sang to you from the depths of the sea."

The Star-Apple Kingdom is a lyrical celebration, an explosion of breathtaking imagery. The duality Walcott described in an essay titled "What the Twilight Says: An Overture" as "two lives: the interior life of poetry, the outward life of action and dialect" reaches a reconciliation in two major works: the title poem and "The Schooner *Flight*."

The volume opens with "The Schooner *Flight*," a rare persona poem. Shabine, whose name is "the patois for / any red nigger," leaves the "dreamless face" of his lover Maria Concepcion and boards the schooner

Flight. The names are not accidental: Shabine's ordeal is the allegory of Everyman, and his flight becomes a quest. Like Odysseus, he encounters terrors and defeats them; unlike Odysseus, he is running away rather than trying to return, although his ambitions are loftier:

> You ever look up from some lonely beach
> and see a far schooner? Well, when I write
> this poem, each phrase go be soaked in salt;
> I go draw and knot every line as tight
> as ropes in this rigging; in simple speech
> my common language go be the wind,
> my pages the sails of the schooner *Flight*,

The similarity between Shabine's aesthetic and Walcott's (a much earlier poem "Islands" states: "I seek ... to write / Verse crisp as sand, clear as sunlight, / Cold as the curled wave, ordinary / As a tumbler of island water ...") is intriguing; more important, however, are the differences between the two men: Shabine, never having left the islands, still belongs; the cab driver addresses him familiarly, and he suffers no agonizing sense of estrangement from the spirit of his community. Perhaps Shabine is the man Walcott might have become if he had stayed on St. Lucia; perhaps he is simply himself, one man in a nation of individuals. In any case, he embodies the universal in the particular. To those who would consider him exotic and look upon his culture with a vague nostalgia, Shabine is quick to call their bluff: "either I'm nobody," he says, "or I'm a nation."

Shabine has escaped a web of corruption and betrayal—now, on the high seas, he "had no nation ... but the imagination." A willing castaway, he is the privileged witness to miracles. God speaks through a harpooned grouper, and one dawn the ship enters the Middle Passage:

> where the horizon was one silver haze,
> the fog swirl and swell into sails, so close
> that I saw it was sails, my hair grip my skull,
> it was horrors, but it was beautiful.

The vision includes the ghosts of great admirals as well as slave ships, "our fathers below deck too deep ... to hear us shouting." Here is contemplation rendered palpable; Shabine is not as painfully self-conscious as Walcott and so is able to travel backward, over the troubled waters, to become whole. Later, during a life-threatening storm, what sustains him is the memory of those slave ships, superimposed on a church episode from childhood "when the whale-bell / sang service" and

> proud with despair, we sang how our race
> survive the sea's maw, our history, our peril,
> and now I was ready for whatever death will.

His last vision is of Maria Concepcion in the wake of the storm, marrying the sea and drifting away. "I wanted nothing after that day," Shabine states:

> I stop talking now. I work, then I read,
> cotching under a lantern hooked to the mast.
> I try to forget what happiness was,
> and when that don't work, I study the stars.

All the selections from *The Star-Apple Kingdom* are vintage Walcott: the hypnotic limbo of "Sabbaths, W.I.," the grimly brilliant "The Sea Is History." "Koenig of the River," a weirdly poignant negative of Shabine's journey, depicts Koenig, the last surviving crew member of a missionary group sent to inspect a camp in the swamp, as he succumbs to fever and delirium. But the real *tour de force* is the title poem, which Walcott rightly saves for last.

The protagonist of "The Star-Apple Kingdom" is more politically astute than Shabine, his introspection more bitter and cerebral. Hence his judgments are harsher, his visions more brutal, and revelation, when it comes, is more suspect. The poem begins with him perusing an old photo album; sepia snapshots from the Victorian era afford glimpses of "lily-like parasols" floating across a landscape dubbed "Herefords at Sunset in the Valley of the Wye." As dusk falls, he looks out over Kingston, imagining a silent scream from the oppressed—all those who were not included in the photographs—rising over the landscape. He falls asleep, finally, only to plunge into a nightmare procession of images from Caribbean history: the submerged cathedral of Port Royal, a "crab climbing the steeple"; Christianity contriving so that "the slave pardoned his whip." *La Revolucion* comes in the form of a woman, "a black umbrella blown inside out," who is simultaneously "raped wife, empty mother, Aztec virgin / transfixed by arrows from a thousand guitars." Refusing the bleakness of her vision, he cries out for

> ... a history without any memory,
> streets without statues,
> and a geography without myth.... no armies
> but those regiments of bananas, thick lances of canes ...

Still within the dream, he awakens to a vision of the partitioning of the West Indian republic: seven prime ministers who buy up the sea—

> one thousand miles of aquamarine with lace trimmings,
> one million yards of lime-coloured silk,
> one mile of violet, leagues of cerulean satin

and resell it at a profit to conglomerates. He then plunges into a deep sleep, one "that wipes out history." When he wakens—for real this time, his jaw still aching from the silent scream—he is able, finally, to cry out. The only person who hears him is an old woman scrubbing the steps of the cathedral; she hears his scream "as a dog hears, as all the underdogs / of the world hear." The acknowledged scream imposes on the world a silence lasting "for half an hour / in that single second—and though we cannot be sure if the old woman's cracked and wrinkled face conceals a smile, the poem assures us that the smile, if it exists, is "the same smile with which he now / cracked the day open and began his egg."

This is virtuoso writing: the roll of fierce images, dense with consonance, imitates the roar of the sea; the relentless dactylics of the last nine lines attain the grandeur of an Old Testament prophecy. Still, there is no resolution of conflicting energies; the outlook is nearly as bleak as at the outset. For though the anguished consciousness has found a kindred spirit, she is mute and ultimately inaccessible; the old woman is not about to join him for breakfast. Where does the torn soul go from here?

8. THE PRODIGY TURNS PRODIGAL

> I know the dark delight of being strange,
> The penalty of difference in the crowd,
> The loneliness of wisdom among fools ...
>   —Claude McKay, "My House"

The fate of any member of a minority who "makes it" is double-edged. As a model, he or she must be perfect; no slip-ups or "you've let us down." As a special case, he or she is envied, even reviled. Move away from the home court and you're accused of being "dicty"; return and you're a prodigal. Write about home and you blaspheme; choose other topics and you're a traitor.

In "The Spoiler's Return," a scathing portrayal of corruption, "the Spoiler" comes back to Laventille. He claims to have been to hell and back after leaving the West Indies with "no will / but my own conscience and rum-eaten wit." With Popian rancor he describes the Caribbean "scene": "Is crab climbing crab-back, in a crab-quarrel, / and going round and round in the same barrel ..."

(In August 1963, my parents dragged us to Washington, D.C. We stayed with relatives, great-aunts and uncles with scores of children and sub-children. The day before the March, Aunt Louise organized a crab bake: more terrifying than the claws scratching against the galvanized tub was the sight of them whole, boiled as bright a red as white people the second sunny day of summer, brilliant corpses we were supposed to dismantle and devour. Aunt Helen held no truck with my squeamishness; she pulled me over to the tub and pointed. "Look at that," she said, chuckling. "Niggers just like that—like crabs in a bucket, not a one get out 'cause the other pull him back."

I was impressed at the sight, and the curiously affectionate way she had used a word forbidden among the Negro bourgeoisie up North. The expression, I thought, she had made up herself. Now, more than twenty years later, I find it again, at the source.)

Everyone wants a prodigy to fail; it makes our mediocrity more bearable. Even before leaving for study abroad, Walcott felt the first twinges of the Prodigal Syndrome: envy from the outside, insecurity and guilt from within. It doesn't matter if the prodigal returns in shame or glory—the time away from "home" will always be suspect and interpreted as rejection. Frustration with this double bind can erupt into hate. "Laventille" depicts a funeral in a poor section of town; the narrator is impatient and grieved at the backwardness he witnesses:

> The black, fawning verger,
> his bow tie akimbo, grinning, the clown-gloved
> fashionable wear of those I deeply loved
> once, made me took on with hopelessness and rage
> at their new, apish habits, their excess
> and fear ...

Perhaps because he is confiding in a soulmate (the poem is dedicated to V. S. Naipaul, whose novels are grim studies of the squalor of the East Indian community in the Caribbean), Walcott allows hidden thoughts to burst through.

But that's not the end of the prodigy's tightrope act. There is the problem of being accepted on one's own terms in the larger world, where reactions can fluctuate from patronizing praise ("The best black writer since Ralph Ellison!") to outright disdain. Those "accurate iambics" are meant to legitimize Walcott's subject matter and to command respect both for his craft and his conclusions. The prosody can also help him contain his uneasiness with the dichotomy of mind and body—mind meaning English education and body referring to sensuality, connectedness. The traits of the body, however desirable, render one vulnerable. The attempt to dissociate mind from body is in Walcott's case complicated by the fact that Western civilization assigns the characteristics of the body—perceived as "feminine" and "inferior"—to the black race as well.

Walcott's struggle, internalized by his own mixed racial heritage, appears rather programmatically in the overquoted "I who have cursed / The drunken officer of British rule, how choose / Between this Africa and the English tongue I love?" When the body is denied, creative expression is diminished: "to be aware / of the divine union the soul detaches itself from created things," he states in "The Gulf"; later, in *Another Life*, he laments: "my sign was Janus, / I saw with twin heads, / and everything I say is contradicted." The wish for a separation of mind and body finds apt metaphors: mind becomes a "ripe brain rotting like a yellow nut"; an Indian trundles his wheelbarrow of "hacked, beheaded coconuts"; "the lopped head of the coconut rolls to gasp in the sand." Bodies on the subway ("A Village Life") are seen "each in its private hell, / each plumped, prime bulk still swinging by its arm / upon a hook." Marc Antony, stretched out next to a sleeping Cleopatra ("quick fox with her / sweet stench"), feels "dismembered, // his head / is in Egypt, his feet / in Rome, his groin a desert / trench with its dead soldier." In the last poem from *Midsummer*, wood lice become seraphim, "all heads, with, at each ear, a gauzy wing."

Even the "civilized" desire to relieve stress by a "vacation in the sun" can become an existential nightmare:

> We came here for the cure
> Of quiet in the whelk's centre ...
> To let a salt sun scour
> The brain as harsh as coral,
> To bathe like stones in wind,
> To be, like beast or natural object, pure.
>
> ("Crusoe's Island")

If you want to be "like beast or natural object, pure" you will also have to assume their negative qualities—to be a beast means to be less than human, less than reasonable; natural objects do not possess history, they do not have a sense of time—which, for man, is tantamount to oblivion.

The self-consciousness which comes from seeing yourself as unsuspecting others see you *and* knowing exactly what you're thinking at that moment becomes a technical innovation in Walcott's work, as he switches pronouns from "he" to "I" to "you" when discussing the self:

> for once, like them,
> you wanted no career
> but this sheer light, this clear,
> infinite, boring, paradisal sea,
> but hoped it would mean something to declare
> today, I am your poet, yours ...
>
>   ("Homecoming: Anse La Raye")

To change pronouns in mid-sentence not only shakes our complacency, our sense of knowing where we stand, but creates an intricate layering of remorse. Poem XI of *Midsummer* begins with the very traditional, almost clichéd, moment of self-confrontation in the mirror. What elevates a predictable moment to a dialectic is the matter-of-fact way Walcott calls this reflection his double, and then gives him a life independent of the real "other"—one of menial action, snipping hairs and shaving—while the other is condemned to remember "empty cupboards where her dresses / shone"— the small but "fatal" sadnesses born of introspection.

Walcott explores his reactions from all angles: from a distance, in "Prelude," as if watching a rare insect ("I go, of course, through all the isolated acts, / ... Straighten my tie and fix important jaws"), or from deep in the belly of the whale, as in "Mass Man," when he rages, half to himself and half to the laughing, dancing carnival celebrants:

> Upon your penitential morning,
> some skull must rub its memory with ashes,
> some mind must squat down howling in your dust,
> some hand crawl and recollect your rubbish,
> someone must write your poems.

9. NAMES ON THE SAND

Craftsman and castaway,
All heaven in his head ...

—Derek Walcott,
"Crusoe's Island"

A recurrent figure in Walcott's work is that of Robinson Crusoe, castaway: the man forced, as the sole survivor of a race, to become a God. The epigram to "Crusoe's Journal" invites us to see home as "a place I had lived in but was come out of." A repository of British education, this Crusoe returns to his island to find himself shipwrecked among familiar surroundings; he discovers that intellect can establish the distance helpful for accurate description, but only at the expense of emotion:

> the intellect appraises
> objects surely, even the bare necessities
> of style are turned to use,
> like those plain iron tools he salvages
> from shipwreck, hewing a prose
> as odorous as raw wood to the adze ...

The fate of being the West Indies' first internationally acclaimed poet bears with it the pressure of assuming the role of creator. As the first to "make it out," Walcott also has the dubious privilege of finding language that can "startle itself / with poetry's surprise / in a green world, one without metaphors...." The Adamic mission of naming is both an invigorating and a lonely enterprise, typically masculine in its separation of the human animal from the environment. Although he never quite escapes the alienation such a role provokes, Walcott, from his marginal perspective, is capable of seeing the irony in this:

> Being men, they could not live
> except they first presumed
> the right of every thing to be a noun.
> The African acquiesced,
> repeated, and changed them.

("Names")

Still, the star witness for the defense—the native West Indian who has stayed home, who has not experienced alienation—is mute. And so it is only one step farther to see Crusoe in any exile, from John writing *Revelations* on the isle of Patmos to a hungover poet suspended over Love Field in a Boeing 747.

In "Crusoe's Island," the privilege of naming swings rapidly around to the dark side:

> Craftsman and castaway,
> All heaven in his head,
> He watched his shadow pray
> Not for God's love but human love instead.

To become a god is to relinquish human ties, to lose the father and the Father. The freedom of being the sole spokesman is fraught with the burden of total failure with nothing to hang on to:

> I have lost sight of hell,
> Of heaven, of human *will*,
> My skill
> Is not enough,
> I am struck by this bell
> To the root.
> Crazed by a racking sun,
> I stand at my life's noon,
> On parched, delirious sand
> My shadow lengthens.

No matter how many times the prodigal returns home physically, he cannot obtain the purity of the stone or the crab. He cannot dissolve into the landscape that has yielded to the pressure of his observation. He cannot, in fact, touch the very people who are his legacy. At the poem's end he notices "Black little girls in pink / Organdy, crinolines" walking on the shore; in a brilliant recognition he dubs them "Friday's progeny, / The brood of Crusoe's slave." Thus Walcott becomes both Crusoe and Friday, "Crusoe's slave." The West Indian who loves those girls is a slave to the artist who stands outside their lives:

> And nothing I can learn
> From art or loneliness

Can bless them as the bell's
Transfiguring tongue can bless.

10. In the Air

> "I don't know the language
> Of this cool country
> And its pace is not mine."
> —Else Laskef-Schüler,
> "Homesick"

As Walcott's list of publications and achievements lengthens, so does the amount of time spent away from the islands. "We're in the air," a Texan remarks upon takeoff in "The Gulf." The rootlessness of the islander is augmented by the homelessness of the traveler. The idea of being the artist in the air begins to take precedence over the concept of Crusoe, firmly rooted—however lonely—on his island.

The Fortunate Traveller (1981) is generously represented in the *Collected Poems*. Although it is natural to favor one's most recent work, in this case I'm sorry the poet gave in to temptation, for many of these poems suffer from superficiality and a touch of the maudlin. Walcott is spending more and more time in the United States, and his adopted country has seduced him. He admits, in "Upstate," to failing in love with America (Kate Smith, move over!), and decides he must become a student again:

> I must put the cold small pebbles from the spring
> upon my tongue to learn her language,
> to talk like birch or aspen confidently.

But what a meek, eager-to-please student we have here! Wistfully he says, "Sometimes I feel sometimes / the Muse is leaving, the Muse is leaving America." And yet here comes the Muse by poem's end, arrayed in her traditional garb—virgin land smelling of just-baked bread.

Okay, one can't remain an angry young man forever—but I wish some of that indignant righteousness and impatience remained. The traveler seems weary, and several poems appear to have no *raison d'être* other than the fact that a writer should keep writing. Cruel? Perhaps, but it springs from disappointment; after *Another Life*, *Sea Grapes*, and *The Star-Apple Kingdom*,

I will not be satisfied with imitation Lowell. And though there are gems
("Map of the New World," or the vivid personae in "The Liberator" and
"The Spoiler's Return"), there are far more embarrassments, such as the
bland "Easter" and "Early Pompeian," where the attempt to describe a
stillbirth results in overwriting ("your sorrows were robing / you with the
readiness of woman") and festooned clichés ("the lamp that was struggling
with darkness was blown out / by the foul breeze off the amniotic sea").
Powerful oratory fizzles to rhetoric; I can only wince when, in "The Hotel
Normandie Pool," a raindrop "punctuates the startled paper" and Walcott
muses, as the pool surface wrinkles with rain, ". . . all reflection gets no
easier."

The title *The Fortunate Traveller* is meant to be ironic—perhaps more
than its author realized.

11. QUESTIONS OF TRAVEL

> CORPORAL: We cannot go back. History is in motion. The
> law is in motion. Forward, forward.
>
> SOURIS: Where? The world is a circle, Corporal. Remember
> that.
>   —Derek Walcott, *Dream on Monkey Mountain*

With *Midsummer*, a sequence of poems published in 1981, Walcott returns
to the West Indies for inspiration; or, more precisely, the West Indies return
to him. No matter where he finds himself—be it Rome, Argentina, or Van
Gogh's orchards—he carries his island inside. Emblematic of midsummer is
scorching heat that dries up vegetation and a glare that flattens perspectives.
"Midsummer's furnace casts everything in bronze"; similarly, each poem
paints itself and stiffens into elegy. One would think Walcott were bronzing
memories like baby shoes. The language is appropriately baroque, with
weariness and repetition built into the composition, and there is a sense of
just keep moving and everything will be all right.

But what is he running from that always pulls him back into its
gravitational field? Here and there, through the lush linguistic scenery, we're
given glimpses: "[t]he hills have no echoes" in poem VII and by XXI, "the
cloud waits in emptiness for the apostles." In the islands "noon jerks towards
its rigid, inert centre." *Echoless, empty, inert*—modifiers for Death (dare we
whisper its name?), the Great Negator. (In Western tradition, a "living

death" is synonymous with a destroyed ego.) Wherever Walcott travels, whenever he lets his rhetorical guard down, the Void is waiting with its shining, blank face.

He fights back the only way he knows ... by writing: "My palms have been sliced by the twine / of the craft I have pulled at for more than forty years." This compulsion can sometimes lead to bad writing, such as metaphors extended far beyond their initial freshness. "Here the wetback crab and the mullusc are citizens," he writes in poem XXVII, "and the leaves have green cards." Or, musing on the Holocaust, these lines, more suited for a John Belushi monologue:

> Brown pigeons goose-step, squirrels pile up acorns like
> little shoes,
> and moss, voiceless as smoke, hushes the peeled bodies
> like abandoned kindling, In the clear pools, fat
> trout rising to lures bubble in umlauts.
>
> (XLI)

When the compass swings north and Walcott attempts to re-create tropical stasis in Northern cities, inertia comes off as jadedness. Efforts to fuse literature and landscape often misfire: Boston city blocks become "long as paragraphs" and "... boulevards open like novels / waiting to be written. Clouds like the beginnings of stories." There are, however, moments of originality and rightness that make up for these lapses.

After self-imposed exile in cities like Boston and a Chicago "white as Poland," after returning to England, land of his "bastard ancestor" (significantly, it is the grandfather who is the bastard, not Walcott himself), he finally writes himself out of the Hole. Here is the conclusion of the fiftieth poem:

> These poems I heaved aren't linked to any tradition
> like a mossed cairn; each goes down like a stone
> to the seabed, settling, but let them, with luck, lie
> where stones are deep, in the sea's memory.
> Let them be, in water, as my father, who did watercolours,
> entered his work. He became one of his shadows,
> wavering and faint in the midsummer sunlight.
> His name was Warwick Walcott. I sometimes believe
> that his father, in love or bitter benediction,
> named him for Warwickshire. Ironies

are moving. Now, when I rewrite a line,
or sketch on the fast-drying paper the coconut fronds
that he did so faintly, my daughters' hands move in mine.
Conches move over the sea-floor. I used to move
my father's grave from the blackened Anglican headstones
in Castries to where I could love both at once—
the sea and his absence. Youth is stronger than fiction.

What impression does Derek Walcott want to leave us with? His insistence on the particular and personal precludes any suggestion that he'd like to be seen as statesman-poet in the tradition of Neruda. More likely, his intent is to frustrate all efforts at portraiture so that, closing the book, we can explain nothing except by referring to individual poems. With its wise artistry this collection also resists the presentation of a slick surface, shelf upon shelf of well-wrought urns polished to blinding perfection. "All the lines I love have their knots left in," Walcott writes, and this edition allows us a glimpse into the workshop. The early sonnet "A City's Death by Fire," for example, is a stilted portrayal of the Castries fire that is easily upstaged by "A Simple Flame" in *Another Life*. Certain images are recycled—an easel rifled across shoulders, a "galvanized roof with its nail holes of stars," the gull as a hinge in the sky, the pages of the sea. The last section of "Tales of the Islands" is incorporated verbatim at the end of "A Simple Flame."

Repetition and embellishment—these are also the devices of the storyteller. Walcott's rhetorical insistence works because we can hear him talking *to* us; we hear the words being strung on a breath. The story line—and I use "line" in a concrete sense, a thread running through fabric or a labyrinth—is held together by the authenticity of the storyteller's voice. Though we know we are seeing the world filtered through the teller, though we know he is weaving a spell, we trust him to tell the truth in his own way. "You have / a grace upon your words, and there is sound sense within them," said Alkinoos in praise of Odysseus, another castaway.

After reading the bulk of Derek Walcott's poetry, I am a little saddened, for I find the recent work a slight diminishment of his power, the flame turned a little lower. Still, he has surprised us before, and *Midsummer* augurs a fresh outburst. A *Collected Poems* forces a writer to start again with Nothing. Tabula rasa. And as the seasoned traveler knows, one of the most dangerous, and intoxicating, moments of any trip is takeoff.

STEWART BROWN

The Apprentice: 25 Poems, Epitaph for the Young, Poems, *and* In a Green Night

W alcott's poetry has always echoed with "Other men's voices / Other men's lives and lines."[1] This freely acknowledged willingness to appropriate styles, cadences, even attitudes from other poets has been variously explained as characteristic of a mind still culturally colonised or, on the other hand, as representing the humility of a major poet able and willing "to draw on the total heritage available to him as an alert and enquiring human being."[2]

There are grounds for both these views. As an English commentator notoriously observed at the time, "derivativeness, even pastiche, [was] common enough to be characteristic" of West Indian poetry right up to the period of Independence in the early '60s.[3] That urge to imitate was not, as that critic seemed to imply, some sort of congenital condition but was the cultural expression of a deeply ingrained and perhaps inevitable colonial outlook, which valued only that which had first been sanctioned by the 'mother country'.

The structuring ethos of the society was self-negating, dismissive of anything indigenous or locally instigated, especially if it were associated with folk values or a positive racial consciousness on behalf of the black population. The 'postcard verse'[4] collected in the early anthologies of West Indian poetry is characteristic of that mentality. The mellow fruitfulness of Vivian Virtue's Jamaican landscapes,

From *The Art of Derek Walcott*, edited by Stewart Brown. © 1991 by Stewart Brown.

> Mid the rusted brown of the star-apple boughs
> How the light south wind leaps and soughs
> In the gay days of March, the glad days of March,
> When the sky is a stainless violet arch,[5]

is typical of the genre, poets still, "imaginatively expatriates,"[6] as O.R. Dathorne put it, looking away from the West Indies for their mentors, their metres and their audience.

Any poet who would aspire to break the colonial die was taking on more than just literary tradition then. For the formally educated young colonial, effectively alienated by that education from such alternative traditions as his 'folk' society could provide, working in a language inextricably tied to the literature of the colonial power, and lacking any kind of intellectual community that might understand and support experiments in expressing a sense of national consciousness in forms and language appropriate to those concerns, the task must have seemed impossible. This was more or less Walcott's situation in the St. Lucia of his childhood, though in some ways he was fortunate, having that small band of "self civilising",[7] artistically inclined people—friends of his parents and a few of his peers— who were at least willing to listen to and discuss his ideas. More importantly his imagination was genuinely fired and sustained by his classical education and the literature it introduced to him. It was an education which, he was to assert later,

> must have ranked with the finest in the world. The grounding was rigid—Latin, Greek and the essential masterpieces, but there was this elation of discovery.[8]

Such a relish for the classic literature of Europe, supplemented by his,

> voracious appetite for literature ... you know you just ravage and cannibalise anything as a young writer ...[9]

which devoured first the 'moderns', then the Metaphysicals and subsequently Latin American, Russian, North American literatures constitute his access to that "total heritage" to which Mervyn Morris referred. Of course this cosmopolitan range of reference was more than just literary anthropology; it reflected his sense that history, such an encumbering and inhibiting force in many ways, had "made him a citizen of the world".[10] His family background and his island's history provided tangible links with many cultures and sanctioned his sense of legitimate access to the literatures of those cultures.

Much later in Walcott's career Joseph Brodsky, trying to understand the sweep of cultural reference in the body of Walcott's work, has argued that beyond such historical self-justifications, Walcott's ultimate claim to the empire of the world's literatures is his absolute commitment to poetry. That his sense of a "sacred duty to the Word",[11] beyond ties of race or political allegiance or personal love, bonds him to "Homer, Lucretius, Ovid, Dante, Rilke, Machado, Lorca, Neruda, Akmatova, Mandelstam, Pasternak, Baudelaire, Valery, Apollinaire ..."[12] Indeed, Brodsky asserts, "These are not influences—they are the cells of his bloodstream."[13]

In much of his early work, however, those cells sometimes threatened to clot into thromboses of ventriloquism. Just as in his early attempts at painting

> my hand was crabbed by that style,
> this epoch, that school ...
> ... this classic
> condition of servitude.[14]

so most of the poems in *In A Green Night* and the three self-financed, locally published booklets, *25 Poems* (1948), *Epitaph for the Young* (1949) and *Poems* (published while he was a student in Jamaica in 1951) are blatantly 'in the style of' various masters. The quest for a language and forms adequate to both his lived experience and his—seemingly contradictory—determination to make a poetry "legitimately prolonging the mighty line of Marlowe and Milton"[15] drove the young Walcott to test out the voices of his acknowledged masters as a means of identifying what styles might best serve the trauma of his situation:

> The whole course of imitations and adaptations was simply a method of apprenticeship. I knew I was copying and imitating and learning ... I knew I had to absorb everything in order to be able to discover what I was eventually trying to sound like.[16]

The journeyman apprentice, indentured to a particular artist or mastercraftsman whose techniques and mannerisms he would learn by a process of meticulous copying, only very gradually allowing anything of his own to enter the work, was a character familiar to Walcott from his study of painting. It is just such a relationship that he so lovingly recalls in 'Another Life' between Harry Simmonds, the eccentric, bohemian St. Lucian artist and his two art-besotted pupils, Walcott and 'Gregorias'—Dunstan St.

Omer. The transference from one art to another was natural enough and was sanctioned anyway by his equally beloved classical tradition in literature, which held imitation of master poets to be one of the routes to artistic fulfilment. Walcott seems to have taken to heart the advice of Longinus who declared that such imitation should not be "merely a copy of devices of arrangement and style but a positive emulation of their [the great poets'] spirit."[17]

So although there were no local literary masters the young Walcott would wish to emulate, the school anthology poets were "immediate experiences" and the technique of the apprentice—that working 'in the style of'—was both a challenge and a channel for the young poet's talent. Much later in his career Walcott offered one of his typically self-justifying prescriptions for the humility appropriate to a young poet by recalling his own apprentice period:

> Young poets should have no individuality. They should be total apprentices, if they want to be masters. If you get chance to paint a knuckle on a painting by Leonardo then you say "Thank God!" and you just paint a knuckle as well as you can.[18]

Just so the young Walcott had seen himself entering:

> ... the house of literature as a houseboy,
> [who] filtched as the slum child stole.[19]

Such a self-conscious apprenticeship constituted, in itself, an enabling mask which sanctioned the inevitable derivativeness of any young colonial writer's poetry[20] but at the same time furthered Walcott's career as the poet, the man of letters, in a society which placed small value on poetry as an end or art for itself but appreciated the spectacle of a local prodigy flaunting his colonial education and drawing praise from the metropolis or its repre-sentatives.

The real value of the early, colonially derivative Apprentice role lay in the distance it created between the poet—the mask wearer—and what the mask said. In a sense, of course, all writing is produced through such a mask, the I of a first person narrative is not even Barthes' "instance writing"[21] but an invention, a selection, a self-conscious—if sometimes self-deceived—projection of a character the writer invents to stand for himself. But the willed adoption of a distinctly other mask signifies something more cunning, more artful. As a strategy for dealing with the complexities of the Caribbean's ongoing history which would inevitably be the poet's theme if he was to write anything more than the postcard scrapes he so despised, the Apprentice persona allowed the young man to try out different positions on that history as well as different styles. Indeed the two were inextricably linked. Echoing Eliot's Prufrock, who must defend his vulnerability by making time "To prepare a face to meet the faces that you meet"[22] Walcott gives notice, in 'Prelude', the opening poem of *In A Green Night* and a survivor from his first collection *25 Poems*, that he will adopt the masks expected of him in the world from which the "steamers which divide horizons" came and to which he must, seemingly inevitably, direct his "accurate iambics":

> I go, of course, through all the isolated acts,
> Make a holiday of situations,
> Straighten my tie and fix important jaws.[23]

By accepting the role of Apprentice the historic pain which is his essential subject in the early verse—"the pain of history words contain"[24]—is deflected onto the various 'masters' and the young poet can examine it, manipulate it, start to come to terms with it almost in the way that a playwright investigates and manipulates his characters.

These words, "the pain of history words contain", encapsulate many of the historical and cultural contradictions of Walcott's situation in the St. Lucia of his youth. The dilemmas out of which Walcott wrote are metaphored precisely by the antagonism between his commitment to the language of English poetry—with all the cultural baggage that implies—and his similarly absolute commitment to the world he felt bound to recreate in his writing—the street and peasant life he could not enter except as an observer because he was not "black or poor" enough, which lived by a different language but which, none-the-less, provided the rhythms which constituted the pulse beat of [his] wrist."[25] It is his determination to learn the means by which he might do justice to that other life that is the heart of his apprenticeship, which distinguishes even his most derivative pastiche from the 'postcard verse' of his forbears in West Indian poetry. For above all else Walcott was determined to capture:

> the *feel* of the island, bow, gunwhales and stern as jealously as the fisherman knew his boat, and, despite the intimacy of its size, to be as free as a canoe out on the ocean.
>
> That apprenticeship would mean nothing unless life were made so real that it stank, so close that you could catch the

changes of morning and afternoon light on the rocks of the
Three Sisters, pale brown rocks carious in the gargle of sea, could
catch the flash of a banana leaf in sunlight, catch the smell of
drizzled asphalt and the always surprisingly stale smell of the sea,
the reek of human rags that you once thought colourful, but, God
give you that, in rage, a reek both fresh and resinous, all salted on
the page ...[26]

It is an aspect of that "life"—albeit a measured, tranquil, "Sabbath
afternoon" aspect of it—that is evoked in 'A Sea Chantey', in *In A Green
Night*, which pivots around the lines:

> Now an apprentice washes his cheeks
> With salt water and sunlight[27]

That "apprentice" is both the "ship boys" and, by implication, the poet
himself—an identification which is Walcott's metaphor for his avowed
commitment (as poet) to the life 'A, Sea Chantey' celebrates. Embracing the
Apprentice role and so making a virtue of his inevitable imitativeness frees
the young poet from the immediate problem of finding a form and a
language for the pain of that commitment; the master in whose studio he was
apprenticed has decided that for him. For the Apprentice then, "maturity"
will begin once he has completed "the assimilation of the features of [his
poetic] ancestors".[28] What I want to do in the rest of this essay is, very
briefly, to identify some of the "ancestors" to whom the Apprentice was
indentured in the early poems, and more importantly, to try to understand
why those writers were so attractive to Walcott at that stage of his career,
why he chose to use them as models in his self-conscious—and thus hardly
'derivative'—apprenticeship.

   To list all the authors that critics have heard echoing in Walcott's early
work is to compile a literary encyclopedia—from Matthew Arnold to
Wordsworth and Yeats via Hart Crane, Dante, Hopkins and Shakespeare.
But most of these are only mannered echoes, passing allusions. There are, it
seems to me, three distinct levels or intensities of influence evident in
Walcott's work as a whole, categories we might call; 'Literary Echoes', 'the
Colonial Apprenticeship' and 'the Workshop Contemporaries'.

LITERARY ECHOES

At one level there are these many voices that echo just occasionally in odd lines or cadences throughout his poetry, reflecting his "innocent"[29] literariness, or, more often, an acknowledgement of a debt, a way of paying respects to authors he has learnt from. For example, the echo of the opening lines of 'Piers Plowman' in the first line of 'The Schooner *Flight*', was, Walcott says, "put there deliberately: 'as this reminded me of that, so let it remind you also.'"[30] So, "In idle August, while the sea Soft"[31] pays tribute to, and invokes the associations of, "In a somer seson, whan softe was the sonne".[32]

THE COLONIAL APPRENTICESHIP

Walcott's allusiveness was not always so discreet however; in the second published volume of juvenilia—the long poem *Epitaph for the Young*—(hereafter referred to as 'Epitaph') other writers' lines, hardly amended, intrude into the narrative merely, it sometimes seems, to flaunt the young poet's knowledge of them. Walcott has said of 'Epitaph', that it was in many ways a conscious exercise in imitation, "all the influences are there: I mean visible, deliberately quoted influences."[33] It is the classic example of the second degree of imitation in Walcott's work; those poems written with another poet or poets—providing more or less "the complete formula".[34] But even in these poems the 'masters' were not chosen arbitrarily; they all spoke to Walcott's ambition and situation in various ways.

The Colonial Apprentice's first master, T.S. Eliot[35] was of the establishment and yet his work was experimental; he was both admired and suspected by the cultural masters at Walcott's school and in the literary world to which the young poet aspired. Eliot had broken the genteel, degenerate tradition of verse writing in his time but was also clearly in awe of Tradition; he was an 'outsider', a 'colonial', yet had somehow captured the imaginative centre ground. A radical in terms of his poetic methods and effects but beneath the bristling style essentially conservative in his attitudes, he had dramatised a personal anguish of faith against imagery drawn from what was traditionally considered an 'unpoetic' environment. In all these ways the appeal and relevance of the poetry and the man to the young Walcott's felt situation is clear.

The temperamental comparison between the two poets is underscored by biographical details included in a letter Eliot wrote to Sir Herbert Read,

> Some day I want to write an essay about the point of view of an
> American who wasn't an American, because he was born in the
> south with a nigger drawl, but who wasn't a Southerner in the
> south because his people were Northerners in a border state and
> looked down on Southerners and Virginians, and who therefore
> felt himself to be more a Frenchman than an American and more
> an Englishman than a Frenchman and yet felt that the USA up to
> a hundred years ago was a family extension.[36]

That schizophrenic self-image anticipates Walcott's sense of
isolation—"part white and Methodist"[37] in a community overwhelmingly
black and Catholic, but yet not comfortable in any other society, caught
between worlds with a language which set him apart and a dramatic sense of
himself as the outsider, the castaway. And just as that dislocation is basic to
the cast of Walcott's poetry so Eliot's sense of unease, of *outsiderness* may be
crucial to the view of the world that informs his poetry. His vision of 'The
Waste Land', one might infer, germinated in that very unease about his *place*
in the world.

True to his role as the Colonial Apprentice, Walcott adopted and
adapted Eliot's embattled world view. In 'Epitaph' Walcott was consciously
trying to make a 'Waste Land' of and for the Caribbean, transposing the
landscape of his burnt out cities, after the fire of 1948, with Eliot's broken,
haunted images. Chunks of various Eliot poems loom like proverbial
icebergs throughout the poem; as well as 'The Waste Land', 'Ash
Wednesday' echoes in 'Canto V', which moves from the shipwreck—a faith
become a "Broken three-master on the reefs of reason"—through the
humiliation of human vanity—"Man's only time of grace is utter weak-
ness"—to the belligerent reconciliation of the prayer to "Our Lady of
Fishermen", which is very reminiscent of section four of 'Dry Salvages' in
'Four Quartets':

> Protector and Maker of the weak
> Prevent us the necessity of coming to Thee
> Or the coming to Thee from necessity.[38]

But where 'The Waste Land' coalesces into a coherent vision, 'Epitaph', for
all its ambition and for all that it caught "the frustration of youth in the
Caribbean, the narrowness of island life and the deadening lack of
opportunity ..."[39], remains "a heap of broken images" that never quite come
together.

After *Poems* and 'Epitaph', Eliot's influence on Walcott's poetry is much less apparent; the apprentice had moved on to other masters. The influence persists, though, in the bleak imagery and allusive technique of the *The Castaway* poems and I suspect that Eliot's domestic sonnet 'Aunt Helen' may have provided a model for 'Tales of the Islands'. But after 'Epitaph' Eliot is essentially absorbed, has become one of the masters in the mature poet's archive of imagination.

Eliot, of course, had his own influences and some of these were adopted in turn by his apprentice. The most important was Baudelaire, whose sense of himself as being both *outside* the commonweal by virtue of his education and calling, yet crucially attracted to that milieu as the authentic life of his society, mirrors Walcott's feelings very well. Poems like 'Le Crépuscule de Soir' observe and understand the life of nineteenth century French society's outcasts without either pity or condescension:

> A travers les lueurs que tourmente le vent
> La Prostitution s'allume dans les rues;
> Comme une fourmilière elle ouvre ses issues;
> Partout elle se fraye un occulte chemin,
> Ainsi que l'ennemi qui tente un coup de main;
> Elle remue au sein de la cité de fange
> Comme un ver qui dérobe a l'Homme ce qu'il mange.[40]

> [Across those lights the wind tortures
> Prostitution is ignited in the streets;
> Like an ant-hill she opens her escapes,
> Spawning all over a secret path,
> Like an enemy's sudden attack;
> She stirs on the breast of the city of dung
> Like a worm that steals his meals from Man.][41]

That poem recalls some of the description of Castries low life and characters in 'Another Life', but more specifically it offered itself as the model for 'Kingston-Nocturne' in *25 Poems*.

> The peanut barrows whistle, and the ladies with perfumes
> And prophylactics included in the expenses
> Hiss in a minor key, the desperate think of rooms
>   With white utensils.

> Walking near parks, where the trees, wearing white socks
> Shake over the illicit liaison under the leaves,
> Silent on the heraldic sky, the statue grieves
>   That the locks
>
> Have still to be tested, and stores shut up their eyes
> At the beggars and hoodlums, when the skin breaks
> From the city and the owls, and maggots and lice,
>   Strike alight the old hates.[42]

Just as Baudelaire's poem has its companion piece in 'Le Crépuscule du Matin' so the Apprentice has his 'Kingston by Daylight'.

The other aspect of Baudelaire's work that spoke directly to the young Walcott was his honest exploration of the contradictions in his personality, particularly the antagonism between his "idealistic aspirations and a sinful nature".[43] Baudelaire's perverse relationship with his mulatto mistress Jean Duval also mirrors—with a nicely Walcottian irony—the young poet's relationship with Anna, his first love so affectionately recalled in 'Another Life'. Both women obsessed their respective poet's imagination and generated a self-consciously betraying art, and at the same time as both poets were celebrating the purity and fidelity of their love they were also indulging the baser aspects of their passions in the bars and brothels of their respective cities. So the pollen of the *Fleurs du Mal* blossoms in 'Letter to Margaret', in *Poems*,

> Pluck from the root
> This flowering evil of those divided by coins[44]

and in Chapters II–V of 'Tales of the Islands'. The guilty exploration of the 'dark' side of Baudelaire's nature provides the models for the most *explicit* passages of adolescent bravado or "confession" in 'Epitaph'. When, in 'Canto IX', which is prefaced by a quotation from Baudelaire's 'Le Voyage', the questing persona declares:

> I kick heels away from the white hairs of remission, am
> Divided between desire and dissolution,
> Between the advice of the red hag and the piety-pilfering
> sea[45]

he is embracing Baudelaire's "infernal experience"[46] as an adolescent rite of passage. Indeed the metaphor of the voyage of discovery, the central motif of

'Epitaph', is clearly derived from 'Le Voyage', the opening stanza of which is used as an epigraph to the whole poem. If Eliot and 'Four Quartets' provide the technical model for 'Epitaph', then Baudelaire and 'Le Voyage' emerge as its spiritual guides.

Baudelaire's influence, like Eliot's, is much more subtly manifested in the later work but the abiding influence seems to have been the particular significance of 'Le Voyage' for Walcott's imagination. Echoes of it are heard in several of Walcott's mature journeying-towards-truth poems. In 'The Gulf, for example, and particularly in 'The Schooner *Flight*', Shabine's soul is "a brigantine seeking its Ithaca"; he is another for whom:

> Chaque ilôt signalé par Phomme de vigie
> Est un Eldorado promis par le Destin:[47]

> [Each little island sighted by the look-out man
> Becomes another Eldorado, the promise of Destiny:][48]

But for him too,

> L'imagination qui dresse son orgie
> Ne trouve qu'un récif aux clartés du matin.[49]

> [Imagination, setting out its revels,
> Finds but a reef in the morning light.][50]

One wonders if that "l'homme de vigie" didn't resonate in the young man's imagination—himself a 'Man of Vigie', in Castries—whose vocation as a poet seemed to make him a kind of "look-out man".

That kind of punning would have been recognised by the third master of 'Epitaph for the Young', James Joyce, whose pubescent hero Stephen Daedalus provided a model for the kind of literary self portrait of the artist as adolescent rebel that is the narrative thread of the poem. Walcott recalls that at seventeen he was attracted by:

> the blasphemous, arrogant Stephen Daedalus ... my current hero
> ... [because] ... in the struggle and wrestling with my mind to find
> out who I was, I was discovering the art of bitterness. I had been
> tormented enough by the priests ... like Stephen I had my nights
> of two shilling whores ... and silently howling remorse. Like him
> I was a knot of paradoxes.[51]

So the poem contains passages of unashamed pastiche, flaunting "puns in the Joycean manner" as in the opening of 'Canto IX':

> In Buck Mulligan's mad tower, bulwarking all winds,
> Or stale as the flat sea repeating its wet vows, I
> Stephen, tremble at the drying hand of the withered sun,
> That is too old a hag to bother about the weather.[52]

Joyce—whose stature in Walcott's pantheon of great writers is acknowledged much later in his career in the poem 'Volcano'[53]—was in fact only one inflection of an Irish voice that constitutes a school to which the Colonial Apprentice was indentured. The other accents of that voice are those of Yeats and, in the early verse dramas, Synge. Walcott explained his identification with the Irish writers in an interview he gave in 1980:

> I've always felt some kind of intimacy with the Irish poets because one realised that they were also colonials with the same kind of problems that existed in the Caribbean. They were the niggers of Britain. Now, with all that, to have those outstanding achievements of genius whether by Joyce or Beckett or Yeats illustrated that one could come out of a depressed, depraved, oppressed situation and be defiant and creative at the same time ...[54]

If Joyce and Synge are openly 'cannibalised' by the Apprentice, Yeats' influence is less direct. In fact although one critic has spoken dismissively of Walcott's "theatrical borrowings" from Yeats and felt a crippling disjunction between a perceived racial anguish and "his harmonious pentameters, his stately rhymes, his Yeatsian meditations,"[55] it seems to me that Yeats serves more as a model of purpose and pose than of poetic technique. For although we know that Walcott had read Yeats keenly as a schoolboy there is little, apart perhaps from the Yeatsian self-dramatisation of the *hero* of 'Epitaph', in the three books of juvenilia that reveals anything substantially reminiscent of Yeats' several styles—and, as we have seen, the Colonial Apprentice was not shy to announce his imitations.

What Walcott seems to have drawn on in Yeats was, on the one hand his determination to create a specifically Irish literature that embraced the island's folk traditions, and on the other the idea of transposing—by an act of willed imagination—his own 'provincial' circumstances to a Classic other life; Yeats' work clearly legitimises Walcott's practice, Castries becoming Troy and Anna its Helen. And, in the context of Walcott's remarks about the resonances between the Irish and the West Indian experience, the compassion that could comprehend the beauty and capacity for good in the great houses of Ireland and their 'alien' aristocracy, in poems like 'Meditations in Time of Civil War' or 'Upon a House Shaken by the Land Agitation', can perhaps be seen to inform Walcott's controversial 'humanism' in 'Ruins of a Great House' and 'A Far Cry from Africa'.

Other early influences were less subtly assimilated. The two writers whose voices are most clearly emulated in *25 Poems* and *Poems* are W.H. Auden and Dylan Thomas. In his review of Walcott's first collection, broadcast on the BBC's 'Caribbean Voices' programme in 1948, Roy Fuller identified these two masters as the presiding influences on the apprentice work and made what was to become the conventional judgement, that of the two the example of Auden's "images drawn from contemporary experience; a verse that is capable of satire as well as love, flippancy as well as seriousness, ease as well as difficulty" might be beneficial to the young writer but that Thomas's "romantic ... stylised rhetoric" was a dangerous dead end.[56]

Just a generation older than Walcott and both intense, ambitious literary prodigies, acclaimed as poets of importance while still in their teens, Auden and Thomas were perhaps the most natural models for the Colonial Apprentice. Their opposed techniques appealed to distinct but equally fundamental aspects of his nature. Auden's classicism and technical virtuosity, made to serve the self-conscious image of himself as the rebellious intellectual, a spokesman for a disgruntled generation, tied in very neatly with Walcott's view of his own situation, as 'Epitaph' makes obscurely clear. In different ways Dylan Thomas shared many similarities of circumstance and personality with the teenage Walcott. Most importantly Thomas and Walcott shared a sense of being both *provincial* and yet uncomfortably distanced from the roots of the culture they felt to be their particular—provincial—inheritance. That distance was measured by the felt dislocation between the language of their poetry and a language that would be true to the experience of that culture's inner life and mythology. The provincialism bred in Thomas (as later in Walcott) a conviction never overcome that—notwithstanding the fame and the critical acclaim—he would always be an *outsider*, an intruder in the hallowed halls of metropolitan culture. So, trapped between two worlds—the Welsh-speaking heartland and the literary centre—and bespeaking an awe of God-in-nature that chimed true to the adolescent Walcott's spiritual self-shriving, the emotional appeal of Thomas's poetry is easy to understand.

Basically, then, the 'Audenic' apprentice—pieces are 'of the head' while the 'Thomasonian' are 'of the heart'. This head/heart opposition is

exemplified by the two poems most often cited as evidence of the influence
of Auden and Thomas on Walcott's early work, 'A Country Club Romance'
and 'A City's Death by Fire'. Auden's sharp suburban ballads 'Miss Gee' and
'Victor' are obvious models for 'A Country Club Romance':

> They were married early in August,
>   She said; 'Kiss me, you funny boy;'
> Victor took her in his arms and said;
>   "O my Helen of Troy."
>
> It was the middle of September,
>   Victor came to our office one day;
> He was wearing a flower in his button hole,
>   He was late but he was gay.
>
> The clerks were talking of Anna,
>   The door was just ajar;
> One said; "Poor old Victor, but where ignorance
>   Is bliss, et cetera."[57]

though despite their wry social commentary neither carries quite the edge of
personal pain that informs the satire of Walcott's poem. 'A Country Club
Romance' is a witty, cutting treatment of a very serious theme, and one close
to Walcott's experience as a "high brown" man of the Caribbean middle class
(one who, in 'Another Life', recalls his boyhood prayers that when he awoke
he would be white![58]). That theme is the "spite of shade" prejudice that
poisoned West Indian society and made such outcasts of individuals who
defied it.

The example of Auden's quirky and rather mechanically formal ballads,
distancing the teller from the subject whose tale is told—in very matter-of-
fact language and with a dry superior humour—provided the Apprentice
with a vehicle that enabled him to keep the anger that clearly fires the poem
under control and yet make his point most effectively:

> The Club was carefree as Paris,
> Its lawns, Arcadian;
> Until at one tournament, Harris
> Met her, a black Barbadian.
>
> He worked in the Civil Service,
> She had this job at the bank;

When she praised his forearm swerve, his
Brain went completely blank.

O love has its revenges,
Love whom man has devised;
They married and lay down like Slazengers
Together. She was ostracised.[59]

Of the several poems of overt social commentary or criticism in the juvenilia only 'A Country Club Romance' survived the ten years of consideration that informed Walcott's selection for *In A Green Night*. (The poem first appears as 'Margaret Verlieu Dies' in *Poems* and is considerably revised for the much smoother version in the major collection.) The particular reason why Walcott felt that this poem had enough in it to be rescued for the full collection while poems like 'O My Shameful, My Audacious', 'The Sunny Caribbean', 'The Cracked Playground' and 'Montego Bay—Travelogue 11', did not relates, I suspect, to that control of tone and emotion which Auden's handling of the ballad form demonstrated; for while the rage and anguish which characterises those discarded poems rings genuine enough, it also rings raw and naive against the restrained artfulness of 'A Country Club Romance'.

The borrowing from Dylan Thomas most often cited announces the debt in its very title; 'A City's Death by Fire', a survivor from *25 Poems* recalling Thomas's 'A Refusal To Mourn the Death, by Fire, of a Child in London'. But although the central issues of the two poems are similar the Apprentice echoes lines from all over Thomas's work to construct his poem, for example the lines,

> the hills were a flock of faiths
>
> ...
>
> All day I walked abroad among the rubbled tales
>
> ...
>
> Loud was the bird-rocked sky, and all the clouds were bales

all chime in Thomas's distinctive cadences. The justification of these overt borrowings is less apparent than that of the Audenesque style of 'A Country Club Romance', although perhaps the echoes of pulpit oration which sound in Thomas's poem might have been felt to be appropriate to Walcott's theme. The overall effect, however, is to distract the reader from what is otherwise a moving and important statement of personal dedication and renewed faith.

But it is in the nature of the role of the Apprentice that he suffers such lapses of judgement and it is too easy, with the advantage of thirty years hindsight, to underestimate the effect of Dylan Thomas's poems on a generation of impressionable, intense adolescents—there are certainly many worse sub-Dylan pastiches in the metropolitan journals and anthologies of the late 1940s and early 1950s. Dylan Thomas is in fact the master in whose school the journeyman apprentice seems to have tarried longest; 'In A Year', 'At Break of Mist', 'The Yellow Cemetery', 'As John to Patmos', 'Notebooks of Ruin' and 'Choc Bay' all owe much to Thomas's sonorous diction and distinctive mannerisms.

If Thomas's influence was the most pervasive in the early work, Auden's was the most meticulously copied. The classic expression of the Colonial Apprentice technique is certainly 'Berceuse' from *Poems*, which while it may be, as Frank Collymore judged, "as charming as one could wish for",[60] is such a straight take from Auden's famous 'Lullaby' as to induce schizophrenia of the inner ear in the reader!

> Darling as you bend to sleep,
> May your mortal breath remain
> Poised between the extreme deep
> Of the silence, or the pain.
> A bed and breath alone divide
> The body from the soul's release,
> In their dark judgement they decide
> Six feet of flesh, six feet of peace.[61]

In addition to 'Berceuse' and 'Margaret Verlieu Dies', poems like 'The Sunny Caribbean', and 'We Exiles' all bear Auden's imprint, one way or another. It is a nice irony, then, that a decade later, when Walcott was selecting his "poems 1948–60" for *In A Green Night*, that only one of the Audenesque poems was kept while four of the Thomas-school pieces survived.

Eventually the Apprentice must begin to *invent* his masters, to delineate the features and inflections of a style enunciated in voices which will be his own. Those voices are informed by a controlling intelligence still voraciously open to influence (though no longer prone to mimicry) by great literature whenever it is encountered, for Walcott has always contended that "maturity is the assimilation of the features of every ancestor", and in the "timeless, yet habitable moment" his great contemporaries are included among those ancestors". So Neruda, Cesaire, Brodsky and Lowell are all ancestors" as much as Marvell, Donne, Mandelstam and St. John Perse are.

In that context Walcott's apprenticeship was both inevitable and purposeful—a duty for one who aspired to be a great poet. He asserts in 'The Muse of History' that "Fear of imitation obsesses minor poets" but that:

> ... in any age a common genius almost indistinguishably will show itself, and the perpetuity of this genius is the only valid tradition, not the tradition which categorises poets by epochs and by schools. We know that the great poets have no wish to be different, no time to be original, but that their originality emerges only when they have absorbed all the poetry which they have read, entire, that their first work appears to be the accumulation of other people's trash but that they become bonfires ...[62]

THE CONTEMPORARIES

The voices that crackle in the bonfire that is Walcott's major poetry constitute the third level of influence bearing on his mature imagination, what we might call the Apprentice's 'workshop borrowings' from his contemporaries in that timeless yet habitable moment. For just as in a well established poetry workshop one member will—both consciously and unconsciously—borrow ways of seeing and saying from another member, so the mature Walcott has borrowed from those poets—alive and dead—whose work he both admired and drew a particular energy from. The image of the poetry workshop derives from some of Walcott's remarks about his relationship with these great poets. For example, when he says of his introduction to the Classic poets of his education that they evinced an,

> elation of discovery ... Shakespeare, Marlowe, Horace, Vergil— these writers weren't jaded but immediate experiences. The atmosphere was competitive, creative[63]

he might be speaking as a member of the best kind of poetry workshop where the writers' ideas, approaches and techniques spark off and inspire each other. Later in his career we might nominate such figures as Neruda, Pasternak, Márquez, Mandelstam, Lowell and Brodsky as members of this elite workshop, but in *In A Green Night* the influence of Yeats, as we have seen, and, I would argue, Marvell are best understood in these terms.

Much has been made of the parallels of personality and circumstance that link Walcott and Marvell and as we have seen Walcott was keen on such 'connections' but he 'discovered' Marvell and the Metaphysicals quite late on in his student career, as part of his undergraduate studies at the then University College of the West Indies in Jamaica. He was, by then, beyond the stage of making straightforward 'imitations' and he draws on 'The Bermudas', which provides the images around which 'In A Green Night' weaves its spiritual meditations and is a model for the language of several Walcott poems in that first full collection, in much more selective and subtle ways. 'In A Green Night' is by no means an apprentice work in the way that 'Prelude', 'A City's Death by Fire' or 'A Country Club Romance' are. It is, though, a mannered, highly wrought construction in the Metaphysical tradition; ambiguous, eliptical and dense with meanings that the reader must puzzle out or abandon. Helen Gardner's account of the problems some readers have always had with Metaphysical poetry has a familiar ring when we remember some responses to Walcott's early poetry in the Caribbean,

> It confuses the pleasures of poetry with the pleasures of puzzles
> ... [and] ... frequently employs curious learning in its com-
> parisons. It makes demands upon the reader and challenges him
> to make it out. It does not attempt to attract the lazy and its lovers
> have always a certain sense of being a privileged class, able to
> enjoy what is beyond the reach of vulgar wits.[64]

It was the Metaphysicals' technique of using metaphor as the prime vehicle of shape and meaning in their poetry that seems to have so greatly impressed Walcott, who has always, in Edward Baugh's words, "moved in metaphor as in his natural element."[65] The extended metaphors developed in poems like 'A Lesson for this Sunday', 'A Letter from Brooklyn', 'Laventille', 'The Gulf' and of course 'Another Life', owe more than a little to the Metaphysicals' manner of argument but are distinctively Walcott's in their language and movement.[66]

Walcott is continually adding voices to the list of those 'workshop contemporaries', asserting his status as one of the "great poets" who refuses to be obsessed by "fear of imitation". That determination was apparent even in those early works in which the young Walcott was consciously adopting a particular writer as his master—Eliot, Auden, Dylan Thomas—and attempting to produce poems in the style of those masters as a way of acquiring the tools and techniques that would equip him for his chosen career as the poet who would be both true to his place/people and to himself. That humility of spirit, that willingness to learn—to retain the apprentice's awe of his masters—also resonates in the mature poet's adaptation of the vision and techniques of peers—Lowell, Cesaire, Neruda, Brodsky—whose poetry seemed to him to deal most adequately with contemporary experience. These latter 'Workshop Contemporaries' are not crudely mimicked but subtly assimilated as resources of a voice that is, always, confronting the most serious and profound issues of his time. Overall, the humility of the Apprentice role enables the poet to indulge and justify his instinct, acknowledged in 'Midsummer VIII' to:

> ... let the imagination range wherever
> its correspondences take it.[67]

NOTES

1. Walcott, *Another Life*, p. 106.

2. Mervyn Morris, 'Derek Walcott', in Bruce King (*ed*), West Indian Literature, London, 1979, p. 144.

3. R.J. Owens, 'West Indian Poetry', in *Caribbean Quarterly*, Vol. 7; no. 3, December 1961, p. 121.

4. Walcott, in Edward Hirsh, 'An Interview with Derek Walcott', in *Contemporary Literature*, Vol. 20, no. 3, 1980, p. 283.

5. 'March Days' in J.E. Clare McFarlane (*ed*), *A Treasury of Jamaican Poetry*, London, 1949, p. 68.

6. O.R. Dathorne, Ed. *Caribbean Verse*, London, 1967, p. 9.

7. Walcott, in 'Meanings', in *Savacou*, no. 2, 1970, p. 45.

8. Walcott, 'Meanings', *op. cit.*, p. 51.

9. In Edward Hirsch, 'An interview with Derek Walcott', *op. cit.*, p. 282.

10. P.N. Furbank, 'In A Green Night', in *The Listener*, Vol. 68, no. 1736, 5 July 1962, p. 33.

11. Walcott, 'A Letter from Brooklyn', in *In A Green Night*, p. 53. (While this reference refers directly to the Word of God, elsewhere Walcott uses the phrase to refer to his sense of vocation as a writer.)

12. Joseph Brodsky, 'On Derek Walcott', *New York Review of Books*, 10 November, 1983, p. 39.

13. *ibid.*

14. Walcott, *Another Life*, p. 59.

15. Walcott, 'What the Twilight Says, an Overture', in *Dream on Monkey Mountain and Other Plays*, p. 31.

16. In Edward Hirsch, 'An interview with Derek Walcott', *op. cit.*, p. 282.

17. See Gerald F. Else, in Alex Preminger (*ed*), *The Princeton Encyclopedia of Poetry and Poetics*, Princeton, 1971, p. 379.

18. In Edward Hirsch, 'An interview with Derek Walcott', *op. cit.*, p. 419.

19. Walcott, *Another Life*, p. 77.

20. In his review of 'Young Trinidadian Poets' (*Sunday Guardian*, Trinidad, 19 June 1966, p. 5), Walcott commended the apprentice mentality in some of those whose work he was reviewing and advocated that all serious young poets should go through a period of consciously imitating the masters of the past, just as he had.

21. Roland Barthes, 'The Death of the Author', in *Image, Music, Text*, London, 1977, p. 145.

22. T. S. Eliot, 'The Lovesong of J. Alfred Prufrock', in *Collected Poems*, London, 1974, p. 141.

23. *In A Green Night*, p. 11.

24. Walcott, 'The Schooner *Flight*', in *The Fortunate Traveller*, p. 12.

25. Walcott, 'What the Twilight Says, an Overture', *op. cit.*, p. 15/16.

26. *ibid.*, p. 65.

27. Walcott, *In A Green Night*, p. 65.

28. Walcott, 'The Muse of History', in Orde Coombs (*ed*), *Is Massa Day Dead?* New York, 1974, p. 1.

29. P.N . Furbank, 'In A Green Night', *op. cit.*, p. 33.

30. In Nancy Schoenberger, 'An interview with Derek Walcott', in *The Threepenny Review*, Fall, 1983, p. 17.

31. Walcott, 'The Schooner *Flight*', in *The Star-apple Kingdom*, p. 3.

32. Line 1 of 'Piers Plowman'.

33. Robert Hamner, 'Conversation with Derek Walcott', in *World Literature Written in English*, Vol. 16, no. 2, November 1977, p. 411.

34. Keith Alleyne, 'Epitaph for the Young, a poem in XII cantos by Derek Walcott', in *Bim*, Vol. 3, no. 11, 1949, p. 267.

35. Although Eliot's influence is chiefly evident in 'Epitaph for the Young', which was published after *25 Poems*, it was in fact begun when Walcott was just 16, three years before the publication of *25 Poems*.

36. In Alan Tate (*ed*), *T.S. Eliot, The Man and His Work*, London, 1967, p. 15.

37. Walcott, 'What the Twilight Says, an Overture', *op. cit.*, p. 15.

38. Walcott, *Epitaph for the Young*, p. 27.

39. In Stanley Sharpe, *A West Indian Literature*, an unpublished MA thesis of the University of Leeds in 1952, p. 140. Sharpe was a contemporary

of Walcott's and his fascinating thesis is the first sustained account of West Indian literature.

40. Baudelaire, *Selected Poems*, New York, 1974, p. 80.

41. *ibid.*, p. 81.

42. Walcott, *Poems*, p. 26.

43. Edith Starkie in the Introduction to her edition of Baudelaire's *Selected Poems*, *op. cit.*, p. 19.

44. Walcott, *Poems*, p. 26.

45. Walcott, *Epitaph for the Young*, p. 27.

46. Edith Starkie in the Introduction to her edition of Baudelaire's *Selected Poems*, *op. cit.*, p. 19.

47. Baudelaire, *Selected Poems*, p. 96.

48. *ibid.*, p. 97.

49. *ibid.*, p. 96.

50. *ibid.*, p. 97.

51. Walcott, 'Leaving School', *op. cit.*, p. 13.

52. Walcott, *Epitaph for the Young*, p. 26.

53. Walcott, *Sea Grapes*, p. 62.

54. In Edward Hirsch, 'An interview with Derek Walcott', *op. cit.*, p. 288.

55. Helen Vendler, 'Poet of Two Worlds', *The New York Review of Books*, 4 March 1982, p. 23.

56. Roy Fuller, cited by Collymore, in his 'Review of *Poems*', in *Bim*, Vol. 4, no. 15, p. 224.

57. W.H. Auden, 'Victor, a Ballad', in *Selected Poems*, Harmondsworth, 1958, p. 48/49.

58. Walcott, *Another Life*, p. 617.

59. Walcott, *In A Green Night*, p. 31.

60. Frank Collymore, 'Review of *Poems*', *op. cit.*, p. 224.

61. Walcott, *Poems*, p. 23.

62. Walcott, 'The Muse of History', p. 25.

63. Walcott, 'Meanings', *op. cit.*, p. 51.

64. Helen Gardner, *The Metaphysical Poets*, Harmondsworth, 1957, p. 17.

65. Edward Baugh, 'Metaphor and Plainness in the Poetry of Derek Walcott', in *Literary Half-Yearly*, Vol. 11, no. 2, 1970, p. 53.

66. Helen Gardner, *The Metaphysical Poets*, *op. cit.*, p. 23.

67. Walcott, 'Midsummer VIII', in *Midsummer*, p. 218.

DAVID MIKICS

Derek Walcott and Alejo Carpentier: Nature, History, and the Caribbean Writer

The lexicographer's lizard eyes are curled in sleep.
The Amazonian Indian enters them.

Between the Rupununi and Borges,
between the fallen pen tip and the spearhead
thunders, thickens, and shimmers the one age of the world.
　—Derek Walcott, "Guyana"

The classics can console. But not enough.
　　　　　　　　　—Derek Walcott, "Sea Grapes"[1]

The choice to center a study of magical realism in Caribbean literature around the works of Derek Walcott may at first glance seem surprising.[2] Walcott, the Caribbean's greatest Anglophone poet, and its second Nobel laureate in literature (after Francophone poet St. John Perse), does make use of magical realist techniques, notably in the 1970 play *Dream on Monkey Mountain*; but he tends to shy away from the more flamboyant juxtapositions of fantasy and reality exploited by Alejo Carpentier, García Márquez, Wilson Harris, Carlos Fuentes, and others. Though not a full-blown magical realist, Walcott has frequently noted the importance to his work of writers like Carpentier and García Márquez. Among others, these two magical realists,

From *Magical Realism: Theory, History, Community*, edited by Lois Parkinson Zamora and Wendy B. Faris. © 1995 by Duke University Press.

Walcott has claimed, exemplify a prevailing regional aesthetic rooted in the cultural and historical reality of the Caribbean.[3]

Walcott's claim for magical realism as the authoritative aesthetic response to the Caribbean cultural context that defines his own work, as well as that of the Hispanophone writers, combined with his own occasional use of magical realist technique, makes him a pivotal figure for an attempt to define magical realism in a regional setting. Rather than claiming Walcott as a magical realist, I plan to demonstrate a family resemblance between Walcott and magical realist writers, notably Carpentier, and by doing so, to illuminate the picture of New World culture that is common to Walcott and his magical realist cousins. Specifically, I will argue that in Walcott magical realism forms one aspect of a much larger strategy of cultural mixing—a creolizing or transculturation—that is central to much of what Vera Kutzinski has called "New World writing."

Magic and reality may sound like a contradictory pairing. In literary history, however, the two terms seem to exist in oxymoronic or paradoxical cohesion, rather than antithesis. Magical realism finds itself especially at home in the novel, a form that claims realist authority through its grounding in ordinary life. Magical realists assert that the realist impulse, in order to fulfill itself, may require what seems at first glance to be a violation of everyday appearances by the rich and strange world of dreams. But this transgression presents itself as a neighboring of or intimacy between fantasy and empirical sobriety. Magical realism turns out to be part of a twentieth-century preoccupation with how our ways of being in the world resist capture by the traditional logic of the waking mind's reason an interest that Heidegger, Freud, and Wittgenstein share with literary and artistic modernism.

The magical realists' project to reveal the intimate interdependence between reality and fantasy is shared by the modernists, but magical realism and modernism proceed by very different means. Modernism tampered with the representational function of language, questioning the rightness of mimesis as such, because representation had obscured the reality of the writer's object. As Woolf, for example, argues in a polemic like "Mr. Bennett and Mrs. Brown," nineteenth-century realism obstructs the world that a truer, more accurately perceptive modernist writing must dedicate itself to revealing. Magical realism, unlike Woolf's modernism but like the uncanny, wills a transformation of the object of representation, rather than the means of representation.

Magical realism, like the uncanny, a mode with which it has strong affinities, projects a mesmerizing uncertainty suggesting that ordinary life may also be the scene of the extraordinary. Such dreamlike suspension on the border between the fantastic and the mundane offers a utopian, if evanescent, promise of transfigured perception, the hypnotic renewing of everyday existence.[4] Both the uncanny and magical realism narrate fantastic events not merely alongside real ones, but as if they were real. What seems most strange turns out to be secretly familiar. What is the difference, then, between the uncanny and magical realism itself? I will argue that magical realism is a mode or subset of the uncanny in which the uncanny exposes itself as a historical and cultural phenomenon. Magical realism realizes the conjunction of ordinary and fantastic by focusing on a particular historical moment afflicted or graced by this doubleness. Since magical realism surrounds with its fabulous aura a particular, historically resonant time and place, the theory of magical realism must supply an approach to history, not merely literary genre. The lucid fantasia that the magical realist mode offers is not an aesthete's intoxicant: magical realism appeals to Caribbean writers because it addresses the weight of historical memory that survives in the day to day life of the West Indies.

This idea of magical realism as a self-consciously historical form is suggested by Alejo Carpentier's influential discussion of *lo real maravilloso*, or marvelous reality. Carpentier gives birth to magical realism as a concept special to or necessarily implied by New World history. According to Carpentier's seminal formulation in his prologue to *The Kingdom of this World* (*El reino de este mundo*, 1949), the utopian imaginative freedom only dreamt of by the Old World surrealist becomes flesh in the New World, and especially in its Caribbean margin. Both Anglophone and Hispanophone Caribbean writers have followed Carpentier by asserting that the New World possesses an original aesthetic virtually embedded in its social and natural landscapes, a magical reality unavailable to the European artist or writer. Not the writer's style, but the historical scene that his or her writing reveals, provides the magic.

Fredric Jameson more explicitly formulates the historical basis of the magical realist aesthetic implicit in Carpentier's definition. For Jameson, magical realism relies on disjunctions among differing cultures and social formations, which coexist in the same space and time in the New World as they usually do not in Western Europe.[5] Jameson suggests that magical realist writing often stems from a place and time in which different cultures or historical periods inhabit a single cultural space (contemporary Eastern Europe and the South of Faulkner are Jameson's other examples).

Carpentier's prologue, like his novels, gives evidence for Jameson's reading by juxtaposing the relics of European conquest with the practices of

Amerindian and African cultures. We might infer that the uniqueness of the New World and its aesthetics derives from the dynamism of such cultural combinations: in the Haiti described in *Kingdom's* prologue, for example, the palace of Pauline Bonaparte appears along with the drums of *vodoun*. The cultural conflicts visible in such a mixture, the result of European imperialism, can also result in future-oriented macaronic fantasies of the kind that appear in Wilson Harris and Edward Kamau Brathwaite as well as in Carpentier. Walcott, like these writers, draws on the New World's meddling or mediation among cultures in conflict to turn a pessimism derived from historical violence into an optimistic hope for imaginative rebirth.

The Caribbean and Latin America mixing of cultures (African, European, Amerindian) can, then, become a source of invention whose energy derives from the conjunctions and cross-influences of radically different modes of thought and life. An example is the St. Nevis "tea meeting" described by folklorist Roger Abrahams, a rite that relies on the Africa-derived communal aesthetics of contributive interruption to provide a parody of cosmopolitan or overly Europe-centered rhetoric.[6] Participants in a tea meeting undergo elaborate coaching and preparation in order to deliver speeches in ornately literate style; yet each speaker's attempt at high propriety must yield to the continual freewheeling interruption of audience heckling and commentary. It is important to note that the parody involved in a tea meeting is ambivalent or dialogic in Bakhtin's sense and that the participants are seriously invested in the ideal of an eloquent, well-traveled sophistication even as they spoof it.

In the literary sphere, examples of creolization or cultural mixing analogous to the tea meeting appear in the works of the Barbadian poet Edward Kamau Brathwaite and the Trinidadian novelist Samuel Selvon. Both make expert use of dialect and folk culture within genres that obey the standards of a literary tradition derived from Europe. Walcott's own brilliant use of dialect in "high" literary forms equals Selvon's and surpasses Brathwaite's. Such mixing of cultures, I will suggest, also surfaces in the magical realist moments in Walcott's, and others', work.

The symbiosis of folk and high culture, along with the mixing of African, European Asian, and Native American strains forms a central part of the magical realist aesthetic, as Carpentier suggests in his essays. The magical realist novel of exploration, Carpentier's *The Lost Steps* (*Los pasos perdidos*, 1953) or Harris' *Palace of the Peacock* (1960), relies on such a geographical and historical fact of coexistence: South America sets alongside one another the prefeudal jungle, the modern capitalist city, and the feudal countryside. In *One Hundred Years of Solitude*, too, the magical realist compression of fantasy and mimetic narrative in which, for example, ghosts are a low-key realist feature of the Buendía household, finds its basis, particularly in the novel's early chapters, in the coincidence of two drastically different cultures that most readers would expect to belong to different eras: a folkloric magic with, as García Márquez has acknowledged, African roots[7] and rationalist scientific investigation. Similarly, the involuted, often incestuously repetitive character of the Buendía generations in *Solitude* finds its basis in a simultaneity of historical and social epochs.[8] Gypsies, necromancers, and the relics of Francis Drake take their place alongside United Fruit; and even Macondo's priest resorts to the pagan magic of levitation.

A juxtaposition of fantasy and reality akin to the instances I have cited from García Márquez provides the foundation for the central magical realist episode in Walcott's autobiographical epic *Another Life* (1973). In this scene Auguste Manoir, a merchant and "pillar of the Church" (168) in Walcott's native island, St. Lucia, is transformed into his dog, a snarling beast "more wolf than dog." Up to this point, the poem has been realistic in its narrative; the Manoir episode represents a sudden outbreak of the supernatural in a verisimilar context. Jameson's thesis of a cultural disjunction (in this case, that of Europe and Africa) as the foundation of magical realism seems to be borne out here, since Walcott's shift toward a magical realist mode occurs as a reaction to the European aspirations represented by characters like Manoir.

Let us take a closer look at the Manoir episode. Walcott has just been describing the Methodist church in St. Lucia. The Methodists' "Jacobean English" offers the poem's narrator a dialect associated with the figures of "Arnold, staid melancholy of those Sabbath dusks" and "those rigorous teachers of our youth, / Victorian gravures of the Holy Land" (166). The narrator then juxtaposes to this high-toned European belief a depiction of the African tribal religion that is the source of the werewolf myth, "an atavism stronger than their Mass." As Edward Baugh notes, Walcott's werewolf myth is related to the *jâ-gajé* (*gens engagés*) of St. Lucian folklore described by Daniel Crowley—humans who sell their services to the devil. "One step beyond the city was the bush" and its "obeah-man"; "One step beyond the church door stood the devil" (167),[9] Manoir's werewolf metamorphosis represents the revenge of Africa on Manoir. Manoir, in guarding his status as a pillar of the Christian church, has repressed the presence of Africa-derived magic in the West Indies.[10] Manoir's attempt to disguise the African roots of West Indian society is frustrated by the magical realist assertion of Africa's place beside Europe's in the New World.

Another Life at first glance seems to indulge in what I will call a classicizing strategy, an attachment to Europe similar to the one it attributes to Manoir. But the poem actually transforms classicizing into something wholly new and different from Manoir's mode, as Walcott sets his own use of classical and European tradition against the official or imperial exploitation of tradition that he associates with characters like Manoir. As it draws on classical motifs, *Another Life*'s style itself becomes an arena for the debate over the renewal of culture in the New World.

Yet Walcott's approach to classicizing style is still more complicated or mixed than I have indicated, since he can detect no clear or reliable distinction between an oppressive and a promising cultural inheritance. An example will illustrate. In lines like "The moon maintained her station, / her fingers stroked a chiton-fluted sea" (147), Walcott moves from a view of the empire as mundane or routinized ("maintained her station") to a classical ennobling of the colonial setting signaled by the adjective "chiton-fluted." As in the Manoir episode, such classicizing description—here of Castries, St. Lucia's port town, and Walcott's home—presents first of all an attempt to cover or disguise the reality of the New World with a European veneer:

> The moon maintained her station,
> her fingers stroked a chiton-fluted sea,
> her disc whitewashed the shells
> of gutted offices barnacling the wharves
> of the burnt town, her lamp
> baring the ovals of toothless facades,
> along the Roman arches ...
> her alternating ivories lay untuned,
> her age was dead, her sheet
> shrouded the antique furniture, the mantel
> with its plaster-of-Paris Venus, which
> his yearning had made marble, half-cracked
> unsilvering mirror of black servants,
> like the painter's kerchiefed, ear-ringed portrait: Albertina.
> (147)

The poet's elegantly poised description of the moon "strok[ing]" a "chiton-fluted sea" hints at a disharmony with its setting. The comparison of the sea to the ancient Greek chiton or tunic, familiar from classical painting and sculpture, offers a "whitewash[ing]" of the devastated landscape that it frames, as the rather jarring succession of images that follows indicates: the "gutted offices" and "toothless facades" present a discordant and grotesque, an "untuned," accompaniment for Hellenic grace. As the passage continues, it becomes clear that the classical images—the Roman arches, the cracked plaster-of-Paris Venus—are actually crumbling to ruins. The Europe-fixated aspiring of the young protagonist's imagination has denied this reality, transforming it to a marble worthy of his poetic heritage. But perhaps, as in the youthful Milton's tribute to Shakespeare, the authority of his precursors has immobilized the nascent poet and trapped him, for all his prodigious yearnings, in a place of poverty and loss. Fixed in a paralysis like that of his decrepit surroundings, the poet has been (in Milton's words) "made marble with too much conceiving." The chiton with which we began has waned, dwindling to a brilliant facade that conceals—but for only a moment—the disjunction between European tradition and Caribbean reality, as well as the gap between past and present.

Yet we can also find, in this same passage from *Another Life*, a hint of Walcott's inclination toward the West Indies' mixing of traditions, despite his yearning for a classicism that remains estranged, haughtily resisting a Caribbean translation. In this vein, Walcott suggests a likeness between the Venus and the portrait by his painting tutor, Harry Simmons, of the servant Albertina, which echoes a Delacroix portrait. Yet the comparison to the Greek goddess looks "half-cracked." Albertina, unlike Venus, here appears in traditional costume, kerchiefed and ear-ringed—that is, Africa-derived. But she also, of course, stems from Delacroix; and her very double-sidedness images a rough and equitable coherence of Europe and Africa, in contrast to the usual attempt to deny or restrict the African element. Simmons' portrait of Albertina therefore figures a more honest or answerable, a more indigenous, way of negotiating between Europe and the New World than the repressive sophistication of Manoir or the official classicism institutionalized in West Indian schools. The discord of traditions she represents is not so out of tune as the strained, and ultimately false, attempt to ignore such discord represented by the plaster-of-Paris Venus, which holds up an "unsilvering"— that is, false or foilless—mirror of its Caribbean setting. Walcott notes in his early manuscript that Albertina's "heroic," Europeanized features were combined in Simmons' portrait with her "honest" (i.e., realistically West Indian) costume, and that the young Walcott thus "saw that black woman could be beautiful as art."[11]

But the effort at an indigenous cultural syncretism figured in Simmons' Albertina, a reconciliation between old and new worlds that would avoid overreliance on the old, is not so easily achieved. Walcott in his notebook for *Another Life* reveals that the Europeanized aesthetic represented by Manoir, and by his own early identification with the British empire, remained a temptation for him in his writing of the poem: "I have not eradicated my hatred and longing for Europe."[12] At one point Walcott writes that in the West Indies "our values remain Victorian, protective"—the values of a vanished colonial world. "We seem to remember an imitative 'classic' landscape. Legacies of a marble museum, of Vergilian Latin and Athenian dialectic." Even the "Marxist-colonial" C. L. R. James, next to Frantz Fanon the most famous West Indian intellectual rebel, was, Walcott muses, "indoctrinated with the Graeco-Hellenic values of Arnold." "Our colonial adolescence even in the wrong climate and history was nourished like any young European's on bare ruined choirs, broken moonlit castles, on the inaccessible princess and the early death. Our spirits, if not our complexions, loitered palely around sunsets, darkening beaches and dramatic promontories looking seaward."[13]

Even as he indulges the memory of an adolescence steeped in lush, Victorian melancholy, Walcott in this notebook passage asserts the "wrong"ness of Victorian imagination and its cherished "Graeco-Hellenic" aura. Such fond European decadence seems incongruous with any potentially indigenous New World aesthetic. Yet Walcott's ambivalence about classical and late-Romantic tradition, his continued investment in the wispy Victorian plangency whose inappropriateness he derides, remains apparent in his notebook as he attempts, and then suddenly calls off, a classical invocation filtered through the English nineteenth century: "smoke: the leisure and frailty of recollection. I have an astigmatic memory. Assist me, mother of the Muses. Seaspray, noon-haze, the smoke of a green brush fire. Christ! No one needs that Denton Welch melody, that Palinuran-Tibullan languor, all elastic hexameters, the prose of convalesence [sic], the pallid, fevered hand."[14]

Walcott cannot, does not want to, entirely disdain the pale brow and hand of Victorian classicism, as *Another Life* will show. He will, instead, search for a way of using the classics that is sharply different from the colonial nostalgia he resists. Walcott's classicizing habit, in its aspiration to become native West Indian expression, follows Simmons' method in adapting Delacroix, rather than Manoir's loyalty to an essentially foreign Arnoldian piety.

Before discussing further Walcott's revisionary New World use of the classics in *Another Life*, I will mention one more colonial or official use of them. The invocation of the classical as a desperate attempt at the cosmopolitan status provided by Europe occurs in St. Lucia's Virgilian motto, "statio haud malefida carinis." In a memorable scene, Walcott depicts the line being drummed into the heads of St. Lucia schoolboys who, "solemn Afro-Greeks eager for grades,"[15] recite their rote responses in an accent influenced by the island patois. Interestingly, the motto, which means "a safe harbor for sheeps [ships]" (as the students answer, sheeplike), offers a negation—actually an unintentionally ironic reversal—of the *Aeneid's* description of the harbor at Tenedos, where the Greek navy hides while their horse is offered to the Trojans. The original line as it appears in Virgil, "statio male fida carinis" (untrustworthy harbor for ships), signifies not safety but trickery. In this imperial context, which relies on classical culture for ideological indoctrination, Walcott makes sure to amplify the phrase's original connotation of *male fida*, bad faith. The British empire, like the Trojans with their horse, connives at destruction, concealing its threat by distorting a Virgilian warning into a praise of safety and nondeception. Britain's addition of a *haud* ("not at all") in inventing the motto for its colony cannot mask the deceit necessary to Europeanize or classicize a culture like that of St. Lucia, which remains predominantly African in character.

Walcott responds to such manipulative uses of classical tradition in the official schoolroom context by imaginatively recasting the classics in the West Indies. In an early chapter of the poem, the young narrator, preparing for bed at dusk, remembers a classroom order from earlier in the day: "Boy! Who was Ajax?" (158). Already half asleep, he responds with a dreamlike catalog of St. Lucia characters, recalling Helen's catalog of warriors in the Iliad's book 3. This fantasy about the Homeric identities of contemporary Caribbean lives comprises the first crossing of dream and reality in the poem, a blurring of realms that will in a few pages generate the outright magical realism of the Manoir episode. Among Walcott's characters here is one Emanuel Auguste:

> Emanuel Auguste, out in the harbour, lone Odysseus,
> tattooed ex-merchant sailor, rows alone
> through the rosebloom of dawn to chuckling oars
> measured, dip, pentametrical. (160)[16]

In his notebook version of *Another Life* Walcott dwells at much greater length on the character of Emanuel Auguste, whom he remembers as a merchant seaman who "would quote his Shakespeare at length." Auguste remains both critical of his surrounding culture and faithful to his self-definition as a West Indian. "No one had a more painful love for his people," Walcott writes, "but he was experienced enough to let them know who they were. He never flattered or abused them," in spite of their abuse of him (he is jeered and interrupted on a feast day during his recital of Robert Service's "The Lifeboat").

Walcott, in his notebook, presents Auguste as a kind of model for the citation of European tradition. Auguste transforms this tradition, reinventing it as native performance. As a result of Auguste's recitals, Walcott writes, "I was drawn to grandeur, to a Shakespearean glory, to declamatory verse. I believed that these actors had inherited, in fact owned the literature which they recited. I never saw them as black or brown men trying to be English."[17] This notebook meditation on Auguste's character is important for our understanding of what Walcott is trying to accomplish when he depicts Auguste and others in the final published version of *Another Life* as analogous to characters in a European (Homeric) tradition. Through cross-cultural analogy, the poet tries to make Homer West Indian, just as Auguste made Shakespeare West Indian for the young Walcott: by appropriating and transforming the West Indies' European inheritance, rather than assuming it as debt or burden.

Anachronistic identification or analogy thus becomes one of Walcott's crucial ways of transfiguring a potential burden into an appropriated vision. The poet, in this choice of method, has a polemical axe to grind. Walcott's identification of St. Lucia's inhabitants with Homeric characters (a horse as Ajax, the "town's one clear-complexioned whore" as Helen, the "ex-merchant sailor" as a "lone Odysseus") represents an unofficial or private linking of the Caribbean with the ancient past, a way of bypassing the imprisoning choice between eager acceptance and contemptuous rejection of Europe—the opposites exemplified, respectively, by conservative and radical islanders. Walcott in *Another Life* speaks against those Caribbean rightists who affiliate themselves with Euroclassicism and "gild cruelty" by seeing "the colors of Hispanic glory / greater than Greece, / greater than Rome" in the conquest of the Aztecs. But he also condemns their leftist opponents, who reject the cruel oppression of tradition while staying frozen in its spell. Fixated on colonial injustice, the leftists "remain fascinated, / in attitudes of prayer, / by the festering roses made from their fathers' manacles" (286).

Walcott sees a dire inadequacy in the choice he is offered between the rebellious, bitter Caliban and the suffering, loyal Ariel as alternative role models for the New World.[18] As Walcott describes it, the New World exists in a fractured or mediated relation to the European tradition's Prosperos, rather than the direct relation that both Ariel and Caliban claim. As Walcott notes in an interview, Eliot's idea of the "unbroken arc" of tradition looks strangely inapplicable to "the education of the black in the Western world," in which "a sensibility ... has been broken and recreated."[19] The discontinuity of European empire with the African and Amerindian cultures that it has conquered reveals a historical violence that the Eliotic notion of tradition cannot smooth over. The European tradition in the New World shows signs of, not a continuous inheritance, but a turbulent persistence within revolutionary change. As the Guyanese novelist Wilson Harris writes, considering "the divide pre-Columbian/post-Columbian," "The question is—how can one begin to reconcile the broken parts of such an enormous heritage, especially when those broken parts appear very often like a grotesque series of adventures, volcanic in its precipitate effects as well as human in its vulnerable settlement?" Yet the very vulnerability inflicted by historical oppression, Harris continues, also leads to a "charg[ing]" of the New World landscape "with the openness of imagination," and thus a potential freedom from the past.[20]

In his effort to avoid the sterile, confining alternative between affiliating himself to and reacting against European tradition, Walcott in an important essay, "The Muse of History," identifies Whitman, Neruda, Borges, and St. John Perse as New World writers who overcome this restrictive dualism. These figures prove their difference, not by a Caliban-like cursing of the European past, but by a renewal of certain classical European themes as "instant archaism": "So [in Borges' 'Streetcorner Man'] the death of a gaucho does not merely repeat, but is, the death of Caesar. Fact evaporates into myth."[21] (Similarly, in *Another Life*, the merchant seaman Emanuel Auguste *is* Odysseus.) Exploiting anachronism to generate an "Adamic" vision of the New World, Walcott goes on, causes a primitive "wonder" (similar to Carpentier's *lo real maravilloso*), "an elation which sees everything as renewed," liberated from the oppression of the past, and yet which also sees the past that remains visible within the present, "the ruins of great civilizations."

New World ruins offer an ancient magic in the form of a wild, new freedom. The genuine difference of the New World situation—as Walcott expresses it in terms that ally him to Carpentier, Harris, and García Márquez—argues against the use of European or classical tradition as a means of either loyal affiliation or formative antagonism, since both loyalty and rebellion would imply the conservative, unbroken authority of European tradition. Instead, Walcott's tale of his "black Greek[s]" (294) in *Another Life*, as in his major epic *Omeros* (1990), acknowledges the fragmented afterlife of European tradition in the New World by inventing freely revisionary parallels between Homeric instances and the modern Caribbean.[22]

The release from a burdensome colonial inheritance by means of fantastic analogies between the present and the past, like Walcott's connection between the Homeric world and the contemporary West Indies, is only one way for New World writing to respond to the risks of history. Another way is that of Carpentier, who makes the magical realist mode a key strategy in his New World project of transculturation (that is, creolizing, or cultural mixing). To clarify the similarity between magical realism and other ways of transculturation in West Indian discourse, I will describe some specific affinities between Walcott and Carpentier.

As I have suggested, magical realism may transfigure a historical account *via* phantasmagorical narrative excess. The effect is to liberate history's destructive aspect into an imaginative sense of future. In such magical realist reinterpretation, the evidence of imperialist oppression remains visible in the forms of ruins whose decrepit appearance signals the pastness, as well as the persistence of imperialist power. The writer domesticates the memory of European rule, transforming it into a fantastically fertile subject for creative imagination. For example, the Spanish galleon in García Márquez's *One Hundred Years of Solitude*, its hallucinatory repose offering occasion for both the writer's and Macondo's fantasies, produces an imaginative freedom from the real cruelty of colonial history.

Yet, in the writers I have mentioned, and most notably in Walcott, the New World's colonial past is not always a magical ruin tamed by authorial fantasy. History may prove to be very much alive in its tenacious hold over both colonial masters and victims. Carpentier's narrative of the Haitian revolution, *The Kingdom of this World* (1949), provides an important case in point. In Carpentier's novel, fantastic Afro-Caribbean myth and natural landscape join forces in a battle against a cyclical, inevitably recurring historical violence that binds its victims to the colonial past even after the revolutionary achievement of independence. The malevolent power of history looks even more threatening as a result of the analogy between history and nature in *The Kingdom of this World*.

In *The Kingdom of this World*, Carpentier resists the demonic alliance that he has constructed between historical and natural forces. Walcott in *Another Life*, bearing the influence of his Caribbean precursor Carpentier, echoes Carpentier's doubleness by both grimly proclaiming a catastrophic bondage to the past and hopefully offering a natural wilderness as recourse against that past. Nature, for Walcott, figures a magically Edenic future that can stand against history. Yet such magic, in Walcott as in Carpentier, finally proves transient and powerless, forcing us to return to culture as the necessary site of poetic making.

In his notebook drafts of *Another Life*, Walcott develops his Edenic vision by drawing on Carpentier's idea of an aesthetic indigenous to the

Caribbean setting,[23] as well as the notion, reminiscent of García Márquez's Macondo in its early days, that in the New World "nothing [was] so old it could not be repeated."[24] (In the final version of *Another Life* this is transformed into the even more Macondoesque image of a world "with nothing so old / that it could not be invented" [294].) In this fantasy of the New World as paradise, social life matches a voluptuous, Edenic nature in its freshness and possibility—a dream that the later history of Macondo reveals as a delusion.[25]

Walcott's separation of history from natural landscape shows him to be an inheritor of Carpentier's anxious imaginative stance. For both Carpentier and Walcott, the turn from history and toward a wild, self-renewing nature seems a possible way to free the imagination from the oppressive nearness of the past. However, the nature that the protagonist quests after proves to be, in both *Another Life* and *The Lost Steps*, a solipsistic and oddly sterile solution to the question of New World writing. As both Carpentier and Walcott realize, an Edenic image of nature, though at first a deeply attractive prospect, proves futile exactly because it means denying the cultural complexities that make up the New World. In the next section of this essay, I explore further the attraction and the risk, for both Walcott and Carpentier, of the flight into nature conceived as an alien and incorruptible source.

> First, there was the heaving oil,
> heavy as chaos;
> then, like a light at the end of a tunnel,
>
> the lantern of a caravel,
> and that was Genesis.
> Then there were the packed cries,
> the shit, the moaning:
>
> Exodus.
> Bone soldered by coral to bone,
> mosaics
> mantled by the benediction of the shark's shadow,
>
> that was the Ark of the Covenant.
>   —Derek Walcott, "The Sea is History"

Carpentier's novels, like Walcott's poetry, demonstrate a creative unease with the confluence of history and nature in the New World. Such discomfort can culminate, in both writers, in a desire to escape history and to exalt instead the fierce power of a natural landscape that overshadows and shows up all human projects. This celebration of a sublime, apocalyptic nature occurs in Carpentier as a reaction against a history that claims omnipotence for itself. Thunder accompanies the propitiatory rituals announcing the Haitian slave revolt that provides Carpentier's historical subject matter, and nature itself seems complicit in the upheaval that, in Carpentier's words, "would bring the thunder and lightning and unleash the cyclone that would round out the work of men's hands."[26] The novel's conclusion, in which the ex-slave Ti-Noël is reduced once again to servitude under the new black masters of Haiti, drives home Carpentier's grim, implacable vision of history. For Carpentier, history offers a cycle of punishment as repetitive and irresistible as nature itself. But at the same time the novel's end teases us with the possibility of an apocalyptic release from repetition, the liberation that Ti-Noël might manage by mastering nature: "The old man hurled his declaration of war against the new masters.... At that moment a great green wind, blowing from the ocean, swept the Plaine du Nord, spreading through the Dondon valley with a loud roar."[27] Ti-Noël, in the novel's final pages, displays his conjuring power not only by raising a storm, but also by metamorphosing into a creature of nature, the man-bird of African-American folklore.[28]

The ending of Carpentier's *Kingdom*, then, suggests the possibility that an African magic associated with nature might escape colonial history. In fact, though, Ti-Noël's magic, like that of the arch-rebel Mackandal earlier in the novel, offers liberation only on the fictive level. The black man's real, historical status as victim will continue. Carpentier keeps in deliberate irresolution the distance between imagination and the historical facts that resist imagination's transformative magic. The magical realist technique of treating the fantastic as if it were real suggests a tempting, but too hopeful, promise of imaginative liberation: Ti-Noël as airborne saviour, a soaring half-god, half-beast bringing black freedom.

History and nature, joined through most of *Kingdom*, are uncertainly and hopefully disjoined at its conclusion. *The Kingdom of this World* finds the source of its marvelous, hallucinatory quality as narrative not only in the cycles of history, the terrible return of imperial oppression in the shape of Henri-Christophe and his successors, but also in the tantalizing and unrealizable project of a flight into nature as escape from history. The hope for escape is, I suggest, an important aspect of magical realist narrative, existing in tension with the historical basis of the mode itself as Jameson describes it.

The fragile wish for a separation of nature and history initiated in *The Kingdom of this World* continues in Carpentier's next novel, *The Lost Steps* (1953). Early on in the novel, the narrator stumbles into a stereotypical scene of revolution in the South American country he is visiting in his search for the origin of musical instruments. Carpentier's hero responds to the revolution by turning from history in order to pursue a reassuringly prehistorical prospect: the primal relation between humanity and music. He ignores the political uproar, the "magic situation" of violent disorder, and follows his scientific quest to the heart of the jungle.[29] As at the end of *The Kingdom of this World*, Carpentier's protagonist wishes for an imaginative empowerment, a magic, associated with the secrets of a nature that predates historical oppression. Tellingly, he wants to find the origin of music in human imitation of a natural phenomenon, the cries of animals.

The Lost Steps bears particular significance for a reading of Walcott because it focuses, like *Another Life*, on the predicament of a narrator whose writing stems from a personal history intimately bound up with his artistic capacity. (This emphasis on the autobiographical nature of creativity is shared by *The Lost Steps* and Wordsworth's *Prelude*, the most obvious poetic model for *Another Life*.) The narrator's journey in *The Lost Steps* is not just a scientific project; increasingly, it becomes a personal one, an effort to find a properly familial origin. In South America, he returns to the Hispanophone context of his infancy as well as to the maternal security provided by his girlfriend Rosario. The narrator, who feels that his life has turned stale and repetitious, believes that he can find the ideal therapy for his anomie in a landscape that transcends history, the supposed permanence or eternality of the New World wilderness. The wilderness will enable him to regain his creative powers as a composer as well: it presents a virtual blank slate for the artist as explorer. Motivated, then, by both artistic ambition and personal neurosis, Carpentier's hero proposes to himself the "Adam's task" of naming the New World in words and music. Yet the wilderness that the narrator discovers in *The Lost Steps* fails to offer the hoped-for empty canvas or blank page ready for Adamic telling. This nature recalls a history: most significantly, the chronicle of European explorers who, traveling long before Carpentier's narrator, confirm his most amazing perceptions:

> I turned toward the river. So vast was its stream that the torrents, the whirlpools, the falls that perturbed its relentless descent were fused in the unity of a pulse that had throbbed, from dry season through rainy season, with the same rests and beats since before man was invented. We were embarking that morning, at dawn,

and I had spent long hours looking at the banks, without taking
my eyes for too long from the narration of Fray Servando de
Castillejos, who had brought his sandals here three centuries ago.
His quaint prose was still valid. Where the author mentioned a
rock with the profile of an alligator high on the right bank, there
it was, high on the right bank.[30]

Throughout the narrator's journey into the jungle, he finds his point of view
already inscribed in the landscape by travelers like Fray Servando, his
precursor.[31] Such historical precedent presents both a comfort and a
frustration: a comfort because it seems to prove the permanence of the
explorer's vision, its duration over the course of centuries; a frustration
because it unavoidably places the narrator in the position of the belated
outsider, despite his longing to discard his Western cosmopolitan
perspective, to become one with the wilderness and its inhabitants. In *The
Lost Steps*, only an alienated character like the narrator can rightly perceive
the indigenous or native quality of the wondrous American real.[32] So it is for
Carpentier's readers: we sense the auratic thrill of magical realism as, wary of
its spell, we approach it from outside—from the cold realm of realist
expectation.

    Nor does the wilderness, finally, provide the unmarred, unchanging
stability that Carpentier's protagonist desires: at the end of the novel, he
makes a second trip into the South American jungle, and finds himself unable
to locate and return to the sights he encountered on his previous journey. As
Carpentier remarks in his essay "Conciencia e identidad en América"
("Conscience and Identity in America"), describing the journey up the
Orinoco that provided the autobiographical basis for his novel, the river stays
"immutable" and yet paradoxically ever-changing, in Heraclitean fashion.[33]
The fact that the Orinoco does change, despite its appearance of eternality,
indicates the elusiveness and, finally, the futility of the narrator's hope for a
secure and permanent origin. As Roberto González Echevarria writes, "The
attempt to return to th[e] source shows in *The Lost Steps* that no such unity
exists, that writing unveils not the truth, nor the true origins, but a series of
repeated gestures and ever-renewed beginnings."[34]

    The Lost Steps, then, by eliciting the reader's intimate identification with
Carpentier's first-person protagonist, makes the reader participate in a search
for origins that Carpentier then ironizes by submitting it to the presence of
colonial history. Not only does the protagonist repeat the postures of the
European explorers, he also stumbles on the absence of the meaningful
identity or grounded truth that outsiders always, and always vainly, hope to

find in the wilderness. Carpentier's irony is shared by Walcott, who, at the end of *Another Life*, first seeks nature as such a ground, as a possible way to overcome colonial history, and then shows what motivates this search: a desperate need to deny social and historical fact.

Walcott's most important theoretical statement, the "overture" to his 1970 volume *Dream on Monkey Mountain and Other Plays*, centers on a similar paradox, one clearly indebted to the shaky Heraclitean quality of Carpentier's marvelous real. In this overture, which bears the Nietzschean/Eliotic title "What the Twilight Said," Walcott, like Carpentier in *The Lost Steps*, asks if it is possible to see the New World through new, rather than old (whether European or African) eyes. Given his title, Walcott is perhaps reflecting here on the alternative between Nietzsche's affirmation, his desire for a dawn that would follow the twilight of European *ressentiment*, and the early Eliot's nocturnal despair over cultural decline. In fact, a Janus-faced reaction to the project of transfiguring culture, suggesting both Nietzsche's hope and Eliot's pessimism, becomes visible in the course of Walcott's essay. Poised between home and exile, Walcott reflects in "What the Twilight Said" on his ambiguous position as a black West Indian drawn toward Europe, a character allied to, yet distant from Caribbean culture.

In "What the Twilight Said," Walcott largely occupies himself with his experience as director of the Little Carib/Trinidad Theatre Workshop from 1959–76, a time during which he confronted both the facts of West Indian society and the temptation to aestheticize these facts by turning the social into a kind of folkloric Eden. Significantly for my theme, Walcott expresses this temptation as an inclination toward magical realism. Walcott begins the essay by reflecting on his own aestheticized perception of the West Indies' endemic poverty as a magic reality, ripe for cinematic or theatrical rendering in the Vincente Minnelli colors of the gorgeous tropics: "One walks past the gilded hallucinations of poverty with a corrupt resignation touched by details, as if the destitute ... were all natural scene-designers and poverty were not a condition but an art.... In the tropics nothing is lovelier than the allotments of the poor, no theatre is as vivid, voluble and cheap."[35]

Despite the essay's epigraph, a quotation from Beckett's *Waiting for Godot* in which Pozzo speaks to the foreigners Vladimir and Estragon of "what *our* twilights can do" (emphasis mine), Walcott begins "What the Twilight Said" from the point of view of a traveler or distant observer alienated from the West Indian scene.[36] The traveler occupies a fortunate position, since the West Indian setting, like Carpentier's marvelous real, reveals its magic only to the stranger. As the essay continues, Walcott considers and rejects a possible (and highly popular) alternative to the role of distant, abstracted stranger encountering a foreign magic. Instead of choosing exile, one might proudly accept Caribbean culture, including its deprivations, as one's own. In Caribbean drama, writes Walcott, this embrace of the popular means "the cult of nakedness in underground theatre, of tribal rock, of poverty, of rite." One problem with such a primitivist solution, according to Walcott, is that it remains tied to the past. The claim for an impoverished native culture as properly West Indian remains "an enactment of remorse for the genocides of civilization." Resentful leftism portrays Afro-Caribbean culture as the victim and avenger, and therefore the antagonistic mirror, European civilization.[37] At its grimmest, Walcott's essay meditates on what he sees as the inevitable fact that any "authentic" expression of Caribbean folk culture cannot be self-directed, but must instead react to a European perspective. Before anything else, the islands' authenticity is a consumer item for the neo-imperialist powers that economically dominate the region.

Walcott presents a second, related argument in "What the Twilight Said" against the primitive-folklorist approach to Caribbean culture, the simplistic proclaiming of African origins touted by the "witchdoctors of the new left with imported totems" (35).[38] The New World has permanently transformed Africa, as it has Europe and Asia; the syncretism of these new conditions displays itself in Walcott's own "generation," which "had looked at life with black skins and blue eyes." "We are all strangers here" (9–10), in the rich and strange Caribbean, and this setting's newness demands, not an impossible return to the African roots that have been irrevocably changed, nor a continuing protest against the slavemaster that can only perpetuate the old roles, but a future-directed artistry, "a new theatre ... with a delight that comes in roundly naming its object" (26). The imagery that Walcott uses to describe his goal of an innovative, future-directed theater in the Caribbean suggests, once again, an Edenic picture of nature. In order for this theater to "Roundly name its object"—like Adam in the garden—"for imagination and body to move with original instinct, we must begin again from the bush" (25–26). Ironically, of course, the image of the bush suggests Africa, the origin that in Walcott's argument hampers originality. Walcott's irony hints that the idea of a newly Edenic beginning must prove deceptive since, despite the author's wishes, it allows the past to have its voice.

Since "we ha[ve] no language for the bush" (37), no means to recapture the positive value of "the African experience" (37), Walcott in his career as a theatrical director and playwright struggles against the poisonous contagion of mythical African origins: "The myth of the organic, ineradicable tsetse, the numbing fly in the mythically different blood, the myth of the uncreative, parasitic, malarial nigger, the marsh-numbed imagination that is happiest in mud.... After a time invisible lianas strangle our will." During the work of preparing a stage production, "every night some area in the rapidly breeding bush of the mind would be cleared, an area where one could plan every inch of advance by firelight" (33–34). The irony is pungent: the director, after militantly clearing the bush for his theatrical project, renders the landscape barren. His artistic purism in Crusoe-like isolation, "wrecked on a rock while hoping that his whirlpool was the navel of the world" (36).[39] As we shall see, Walcott writes into the conclusion of *Another Life* a similarly strong implication of the alienated solipsism hidden within the desire for Edenic artistry.[40]

"What the Twilight Said" finally recovers from the implications of such authorial isolation, which were themselves earlier defined as a temptation toward an Edenic-solipsistic New World vision, through its display of socially concerned ironies. Walcott depicts a scene in which the playwright/director and his actors climb upward to see themselves in the landscape of Walcott's youth, the famous promontory of St. Lucia called the Morne:

A band of travellers, in their dim outlines like explorers who arrived at the crest of a dry, grassy ridge ... with the view hidden, then levelling off to the tin-roofed, toy town of his childhood. The sense of hallucination increased with the actuality of every detail, from the chill, mildly shivering blades of hill-grass, from their voices abrupted by the wind, the duality of time, past and present piercingly fixed as if the voluble puppets of his childhood were now frighteningly alive.... [S]ome turned towards the lush, dark-pocketed valleys of banana with their ochre tracks and canted wooden huts from whose kitchens, at firelight, the poetry which they spoke had come, and further on, the wild, white-lined Atlantic coast with an Africa that was no longer home, and the dark, oracular mountain dying into mythology... It was as if they had arrived at a view of their own bodies walking up the crest, their bodies tilted slightly forward, a few survivors. (38)

This passage noticeably allies itself to a central aspect of magical realist and uncanny aesthetics, the sense of a world that looks all the more fantastic because of its extreme or hyperreal "actuality." The *unheimlich* landscape at once both invites and alienates: "The sense of hallucination increased with the actuality of every detail." This double vision of the self, a Pisgah sight of both past (Walcott's personal history) and future (his artistic goals), goes beyond self-concern to suggest a tableau of the New World as visionary frontier.

But the communal character of this vision does not alleviate the artist-observer's estrangement from his native landscape and its population: "Knowing the place could not tell me what it meant," Walcott writes, "I watched them but was not among them." Finally, he adds that "we would have to descend again" from this inspired "achievement" (38) to more mundane difficulties. And it is important to note that the retrospective author describes the vision itself as a "dying into mythology," not a living future. The theater company's ascent of the Morne, then, may be no closer to a dawn of living creation than the earlier solipsistic picture of a search for the individual "body['s]" "original instinct" and for an Edenic landscape, vacant of the social, to surround it. In both cases, the artist's isolation seems built into the structure of his perception, and his ambition to "roundly name [his] object" by demonstrating his native relation to it therefore appears enmeshed in a vicious circularity.

The descent or "dying," the sense of a culture of tragic "survivors," that occurs at the end of Walcott's "What the Twilight Said" stands in ironic counterpoint to the conclusion of the play that this "overture" introduces, *Dream on Monkey Mountain* (1970). The hero of *Dream*, Makak, climbs back to his mythical home at the play's end after beheading the white goddess who has imprisoned him in his role as a black messiah. Now, after violently freeing himself from an oppressive past, Makak returns, Noah-like, to "walk with God" back to the mountain of his origins: "Now this old hermit is going back home," he proclaims, "back to the beginning, to the green beginning of this world" (326).

The exalted conclusion of *Dream on Monkey Mountain*, replete with Christological significance, provides an obvious contrast to the sad decline of Walcott's own darkening vision at the end of "What the Twilight Said." *Dream*'s notion of a "green beginning," an origin that liberates the hero by freeing him from the cultural symbolism of master and slave, oppressor and oppressed, proves impossible in the autobiographical world depicted in "What the Twilight Said," which like *The Lost Steps* implies that every "new" beginning conceals an obsessively self-conscious return to the past. The liberating potential of magical vision, then, seems to decrease for Walcott as it becomes subject to the artist-observer's consciousness of the central role that his own alienated perspective plays in this magic. Such self-consciousness remains largely absent from *Dream on Monkey Mountain*, but it is prominent in "What the Twilight Said" and *Another Life*.

Walcott's search for Edenic origin as escape takes an even more compromised or ambivalent form in *Another Life* than it does in "What the Twilight Said." At the end of *Dream*, Makak's beginning is "green" because it remains at one with the natural landscape of his island, the mountain; it is a beginning because he has divested himself of the weight of the imperialist past. Similarly, in *Another Life* Walcott the poet-narrator begs to

> begin again,
> from what we have always known, nothing,
> from that carnal slime of the garden ...
>
> by this augury of ibises
> flying at evening from the melting trees,
> while the silver-hammered charger of the marsh light
> brings toward us, again and again, in beaten scrolls,
> nothing, then nothing,
> and then nothing. (286–87)

The beginning that Walcott vaguely, if resonantly, suggests at the end of *Dream on Monkey Mountain* becomes explicit in *Another Life*. But this flight into nature, repeatedly promised in *Another Life*, is just as repeatedly withdrawn. In the passage cited above, Caribbean nature, by giving the poet a life and a writing all its own (the "beaten scrolls"), offers an alternative to those "who remain fascinated ... / by the festering roses made from their fathers' manacles, / ... / who see a golden, cruel, hawkbright glory / in the conquistador's malarial eye" (286)—that is, those who fetishize historical oppression as the product of either heroic mastery or wretched vulnerability. Nature instead offers a blankness or innocence, a nothing," ready for the Adamic mission of the writer: naming.

Tellingly, Walcott gives as one of his epigraphs to *Another Life* the passage from *The Lost Steps* in which the narrator endows himself with "Adam's task" of name-giving (188). Yet, also tellingly for Walcott's purposes, the Carpentier passage reveals what we have already seen: the difficulty, really the futility, of this Edenic task, as Carpentier's narrator likens himself in this same passage to the Europe-obsessed South American artists who will not even attempt to describe their native environment.[41] Indeed, there is something empty in the "nothing" that remains after the New World landscape has been denuded of its cruel and complex history. It presents an ironic vacuity, as hopeless as the "vacant eyes" of the artists who, in the Carpentier passage, turn away from America and toward Europe.

Carpentier's magical America is not just the outcome of a mixing of cultures. In a passage like this one, the New World's auratic charm also conveys the writer's effort to evade the fact of such mixing and come out into a pure landscape, cleared of history.

Walcott shares with Carpentier the impulse to purge his writing of historical *conciencia* by identifying it with an Edenic New World landscape. Early in *Another Life*, however, Walcott takes a different daring turn. He asserts the implication of the Caribbean landscape in the historical events that took place in it, rather than separating out the natural scene as he will later on. After evoking the history of European empire taught him by his "choleric, ginger-haired headmaster" in St. Lucia ("a lonely Englishman who loved parades, / sailing, and Conrad's prose"), Walcott suddenly describes the most famous incident associated with St. Lucia's major landmark, the Morne:

> The leaping Caribs whiten,
> in one flash, the instant
> the race leapt at Sauteurs,
> a cataract! One scream of bounding lace (213)

In 1651 the Carib Indians of Grenada, surrounded and outnumbered by the British, leapt off a steep hill that later became known as the "Morne des Sauteurs" (Leapers' Hill).[42] Walcott follows his description of the Caribs' leap with breathless, relentlessly enjambed lines depicting a kind of poetic self-annihilation to match the Caribs' suicidal charge: he presses Pegasus' hoof back into the earth whence it sprouted.

> I am pounding the faces of gods back into the red clay they
> leapt from the mattock of heel after heel ...
> and I have wept less for them dead than I did
> when they leapt from my thumbs into birth, than my
> heels which have never hurt horses that now pound them
> back into what they should never have sprung from,
> staying un-named where I found them
> in the god-breeding, god-devouring earth! (213)

As Walcott sees it here, the return to mute nature figured in the Caribs' leap surpasses the artist's effort to represent this mass suicide. The Indian warriors transcend the aesthetic by jumping back into the unrepresentable. Their action overwhelms the poetic artistry that would depict it as history because it digs deeper than history, literally embedding culture in the natural fact of landscape. In the face of this desperate indigenous intensity, poetry yields.

Walcott's surrendering of poetic artifice to nature seeks to establish a presence still marked in the landscape: the miraculous yet historically genuine event of the Caribs' self-sacrifice. Strong and enraptured, the writer submerges his word in the rushing vocables of the self-naming, suicidal *sauteurs*:

> yet who am I, under
> such thunder, dear gods, under the heels of the thousand
> racing towards the exclamation of their single name,
> Sauteurs!
>
> ... I am one
> with the thousand runners who will break on loud sand
> at Thermopylae, one wave that now cresting must bear
> down the torch of this race, I am all, I am one
> who feels as he falls with the thousand now his tendons harden
> and the wind god, Hourucan, combing his hair. (214)

The mass of warriors are a breaking wave. This moment of oneness, the immersion of the poetic self in the currents of a history seen with and as nature, points toward a Whitmanian general embrace. With his cross-referencing of the New and the Old World in the passage I have just cited, Walcott erases the divisions among American, African, and European ancestry that have been a constant theme in his work.[43] The advancing Caribs look like the runners at Thermopylae, and the entire passage ends with a mixing of European and American—the mention of the Amerindian god Hourucan in the context of ancient Greece. As with Borges' identification of the gaucho as Caesar, or Walcott's of Emanuel Auguste as Odysseus, a fabulous historical analogy here obscures the actual history of colonial conquest, beginning a luminous, revisionary reworking of the cultural energy that passes from the classical to the contemporary. Along with the transfiguring of history into natural landscape—also a trick of magical realism in its lush, paradisal moments—comes the disappearance of the poet's alienated point of view, his prison of colonial inheritance. With the *sauteurs'* flight, the oppression of the past lifts and frees us into imagination.

Walcott's claim in this passage that "I am all, I am one" with a mass of historical individuals looks back to Whitman, as I have suggested, but also to one of Whitman's descendents, Pablo Neruda. In his exalted and tremendous poem *The Heights of Machu Picchu* (*Las alturas de Machu Picchu*), Neruda prophetically invokes the monumental relics of the Inca site Machu Picchu, identifying himself with the oppressed masses who survive within or below its ruined scene.[44] The poet's self-identification with a past people—Walcott with the Caribs, Neruda with the Incas—demands the finding of a historically resonant and indestructible place (the Morne, Machu Picchu). In both cases, culture lives on as nature. As González-Echevarría notes, Neruda's *Canto general*, the longer poem that enfolds *The Heights of Machu Picchu*, begins by conflating human history and natural landscape.[45] Walcott's passage, with its Genesis-inflected mention of the Caribs as "red clay" being "pounded" back into earth by the poet-potter as he searches after the power of origins, echoes this opening moment of *Canto general*. Neruda, like Walcott and like Carpentier's narrator in *The Lost Steps*, seeks the birth of humanness out of natural fact: "Man was earth, a vessel, the eyelid / Of the quivering clay, a shape of potter's earth, / Carib spout, Chibcha stone."[46]

Yet if Walcott, like Neruda, plays a prophetic role by assuming the bardic voice of creation, he also backs away, later on in *Another Life*, from Neruda's overwhelming descent toward excruciating empathy with an ancestral people ("Tell me everything, chain by chain, / Link by link, and step by step, / File the knives you kept by you, / Drive them into my chest and my hand").[47] Like Carpentier, Walcott turns from Neruda's impulse toward incarnate solidarity with the primitive or ancient. The final two sections of Walcott's poem attempt to focus the diffident, nervous consciousness of a narrator not sure how to identify, much less identify with, the history that surrounds him, yet who responds to it with an attentive care. In the penultimate section of *Another Life*, Walcott invokes the Wordsworthian "child" who

> puts the shell's howl to his ear,
> hears nothing, hears everything
> that the historian cannot hear, the howls
> of all the races that crossed the water,
> the howls of grandfathers drowned
> in that intricately swivelled Babel,
> hears the fellaheen, the Madrasi, the Mandingo, the Ashanti,
> yes, and hears also the echoing green fissures of Canton,
> and thousands without longing for this other shore
> by the mud tablets of the Indian provinces ...

see, in the evening light by the saffron, sacred Benares,
how they are lifting like herons,
robed ghostly white and brown,
and the crossing of water has erased their memories.
And the sea, which is always the same,
accepts them. (285)

Walcott's beautiful recollection of the African and Asiatic voices driven to the new shores of the Caribbean[48] does not, this time, give us a rough courage that runs with the masses toward historical suffering and glory, but instead a subtle persistence allied to the nature imaged in the seashell and "the sea, which is always the same." Nature effortlessly assimilates, and erases, its crowds of human inhabitants, soothing them into oblivion. Here, then, a fluid, all-forgiving cosmos distances the poet from Caribbean history, rather than stamping it into place as a monumental memory, as in the *sauteurs* passage. One central subtext for Walcott is Wordsworth's celebration, in the *Prelude*, of the infant memories borne by a maternal nature that persists beneath the strata of revolutionary violence and biographical trauma.[49]

Like Whitman more than Wordsworth, Walcott uses nature to welcome the human masses into a healing depth of unborn process: "The crossing of water has erased their memories. / And the sea, which is always the same, / accepts them." Walcott, in an interview with Edward Hirsch, speaks of "the erasure of the idea of history" in Caribbean nature, "in the surf which continually wipes the sand clean, in the fact that those huge clouds change so quickly."[50] This therapeutic forgetting, nature's promise of healing human history through obliteration and mutability, makes Walcott want "to teach [him]self the poetry of natural science."[51]

In the notebooks for *Another Life*, Walcott presents his wish for a poetics of nature devoid of the human by championing a fellow solitary, "the figure of Crusoe" (a favorite Walcott character in other poems as well). Walcott invokes a Crusoe who has become "tired of the gift," the quintessentially human capacity of being "articulate." "He has learnt the indifference of his dog, but their separate emptinesses are terrible. Empty his mind as monotonously as he wants he cannot become a dog since he has more than a dog's desires."

Walcott presents Crusoe's impulse toward a doglike state of inarticulate emptiness as an alluring ascetic project, a Stevensian pursuit of poverty that aims to empty out the self's intellective wiles. When Friday arrives, Crusoe loses his mission, returning to human language and to the "commonplace sanity" and "self-righteous"-ness that accompanies it. For Walcott, the

Crusoe we see with Friday has been infected by "a puritanism that has learnt something from experience, when, unlike most men, he once really understood nothing."[52] With Friday's appearance, then, Crusoe loses the crude, reductive stability of his earlier devotion to "nothing."

For Walcott's Crusoe, nature promises a potential solace or refuge from humanity. But the final pages of *Another Life* question the viability of this refuge more radically than elsewhere in Walcott, by way of the solitary figure of the poet. In *Another Life* the poet wishes for himself the inhuman "nothing" that he grants the lone Crusoe in his notebook. Near the end of the poem, Walcott wants only the inarticulate, pure "nothing" of a nature devoid of human culture, "the real / rock I make real." Here the isolated self alone within stony, unyielding landscape represents an escape from the master–slave conversation of Crusoe and Friday, whose relation seems an infernal model for the whole of colonial history:

> Inured. Inward. As rock,
> I wish, as the real
>
> rock I make real,
> to have burnt out desire,
> lust, except for the sun
>
> with her corona of fire.
> Anna, I wanted to grow white-haired
> as the wave, with a wrinkled
> brown rock's face, salted,
> seamed, an old poet,
> facing the wind
>
> and nothing, which is,
> the loud world in his mind. (290)

Like Oedipus or Lear, the poet is supported by his daughters: "balanced ... by the weight of two dear daughters."[53] Walcott calls on the aged, self-imposed isolation of these two tragic heroes, both hoping for the peace that might come about through a quieting of the destruction that their own stubborn wills have brought about. In addition to Shakespeare and Sophocles, in this densely allusive section of the poem we can hear the voices of at least four other texts that convey, in varying tones, the desire for peace, for a respite from the cruelty of will: Ginsberg's *Howl*, Eliot's *Ash Wednesday*, and Stevens' "The Snow Man" and "The Rock."

A reduction of Edenic possibility to the aridity of bare rock, Walcott's nature remains a strenuously deliberate projection. The poet hopes that "inured" will rhyme with "inward," that his "tireless hoarse anger" will be ossified, as rock, into impermeable Stoic stasis. But as Walcott well knows, such a wish to mimic the assurance of the rock's solidity marks a necessary falling short, a hopeless effort to evade the contingency and confusion of human culture. (The immediately preceding section on imperialist history has raised the stakes beyond the personal by reminding us that, for Walcott, the will has a malignant historical form.)

Walcott's evacuation of cultural and historical subject matter, his strategy for securing the self by shoring it up alone with nature, will not last. In the final section of *Another Life*, he returns to his autobiographical story, and with it to the people of St. Lucia. Now, in an abrupt reversal, the social seems "stronger" than nature. Suddenly, the wave is no longer a phenomenon that can transcend, save, or provide escape from the human, as it has been throughout the poem. Instead, it represents the writer's "desertion" of his "folk's" culture:

> Forgive me, you folk,
> who exercise a patience
> subtler, stronger than the muscles
> in the wave's wrist ...
>
> forgive our desertions. (293)

The embrace of the popular culture of St. Lucia aims at a "patience" that, the poet hopes, will succeed where a rigid, Stoic self-torment has failed. The acceptance of the folk marks out a third way, beyond both the isolation of the solitary Crusoe and the torment that occurs between Crusoe and Friday. But Walcott shifts his ground yet again when he follows his celebration of the people's strength with a vision of the artist's autonomous mastery: as godlike creator, he fashions his own world, independent of any popular basis. The invocation of Walcott's painter friend Gregorias (Dunstan St. Omer) here removes the presence of the island's culture entirely in the interest of quasi-Edenic artistic freedom:

> We were blest with a virginal, unpainted world
> with Adam's task of giving things their names
> with the smooth white walls of clouds and villages
> where you devised your inexhaustible,
> impossible Renaissance. (294)

The dissonance between this dream of the artist "devising" in an unpopulated, paradisal wilderness and the embrace of the "folk" that directly precedes it forces us to juxtapose the conclusion of *Another Life* to more pessimistic versions of the same theme, like the guilty aestheticizing of island poverty in "What the Twilight Said" or the passage from the notebook for *Another Life* in which Walcott writes that he sought out the poor "not only to depict and record, but to be like them": "Yet the more he learnt, the wider the crack between them grew."[54] The palinodic acceptance of the "folk" near the end of *Another Life*, in its sentimental need for "forgive[ness]," is less assured as poetry than the earlier and later images of artistic isolation that surround it. There seems to be an insurmountable division between the artist, who lives within the European tradition, and the folk culture that supplies the object of his depiction and that he also, in his peculiar way, inhabits. The permanent fact of such divisions, as I have argued, provides the foundation of Walcott's art and unites him with Carpentier and other New World magical realists. Like Borges' hero in "The South," he stands aloof, frightened and entranced by his image of the folkloric powers that surround him. Walcott's work, like Carpentier's and García Márquez's, conjures with an elusive grammar that at once joins and disjoins realism and fantasy, Europe and Africa, high and low culture, traveling artist and indigenous folk.[55]

NOTES

1. All citations of Walcott's poetry refer to his *Collected Poems 1948–1984* (New York: Farrar, Straus and Giroux, 1986).

2. A case for the kinship between the English-speaking Caribbean and the phantasmagoric world of the Latin American novel could perhaps best be made with reference to the novels of the Guyanese writer Wilson Harris, whose hallucinatory narratives are contemporary with García Márquez's. For a treatment of Harris in terms of magical or marvelous realism, see Selwyn Cudjoe, *Resistance and Caribbean Literature* (Athens, Ohio: Ohio University Press, 1980), pp. 255–57. Walcott's "Guyana," from which I draw an epigraph for this essay, joins Harris to Borges as "the surveyor" and "the lexicographer," respectively (Harris worked as a surveyor in Guyana). The point of the conjunction is Walcott's frequently voiced desire for an indigenous New World style of writing, one suited to its unique geographical and cultural landscape. On the question of "New World writing" I have been influenced by Vera Kutzinski's admirable *Against the American Grain*

(Baltimore: Johns Hopkins University Press, 1987), though I hope to show in Walcott's work some of the tensions and resistances to cross-cultural juxtaposition that Kutzinski tends to play down. So far the most advanced study of Walcott's work is Rei Terada's *Derek Walcott's Poetry: American Mimicry* (Boston: Northeastern University Press, 1992).

3. See the interview with Sharon Ciccarelli, in *Chant of Saints*, ed. Michael Harper and Robert Stepto (Urbana: University of Illinois Press, 1979), in which he states the similarity he perceives between himself and "Spanish-American poets" on the basis of a shared regional culture (306), noting that "I probably am a total stranger to the African, whereas I am not a stranger to [García] Márquez, or Fuentes, or Paz" (307). Walcott also notes that he is "interested in writers like [García] Márquez who have an instinctive way of handling the natural and the legendary in close proximity" (307).

4. Compare what Rosalind Krauss, paraphrasing Fredric Jameson, calls the utopianism of "Van Gogh's clothing of the drab peasant world around him in an hallucinatory surface of color." Krauss, "The Cultural Logic of the Late Capitalist Museum," *October* 54 (1990): 11, and Jameson, "Postmodernism, or the Cultural Logic of Late Capitalism," *New Left Review* 146 (1984): 59.

5. See Fredric Jameson, "On Magic Realism in Film," *Critical Inquiry* 12, 2 (Winter 1986): 301–25. In addition to Jameson, I am also relying for my version of the aesthetics of magical realism on its closeness to the category of the "marvellous," defined by Tzvetan Todorov in *The Fantastic* (1970; Columbus: Ohio State University Press, 1973) as the rendition of exotic or supernatural events as if they were real.

6. See Roger Abrahams, *The Man-of-Words in the West Indies* (Baltimore: Johns Hopkins University Press, 1983).

7. See Vera Kutzinski, "The Logic of Wings: Gabriel García Márquez and Afro-American Literature," *Latin American Literary Review* 13 (January–June 1985): 133–46. For example, the flight of Remedios the Beauty (*One Hundred Years of Solitude* [1967; New York: Bard/Avon, 1970], pp. 22–23) stems from African folklore. See also Rosa Valdés-Cruz, "El realismo mágico en los cuentos negros de Lydia Cabrera," in *Otros mundos, otros fuegos* (East Lansing: Michigan State University Press, 1975), pp. 206–9, and Mireya Camurati, "Fantasia folklórica y ficción literaria," in the same collection, pp. 287–91.

8. For the incest theme as a return of the past, see, for example, *Solitude*, pp. 145, 217; for the themes of hereditary memory and the sense of a continual degeneration combined with continual repetition, pp. 166–67 and 177. For Father Nicanor's levitation, see pp. 84–86.

9. Crowley's article "Les êtres surnaturels à Ste. Lucie," *Le Caraibe* 8 (June-July 1955), is cited in Edward Baugh, *Derek Walcott, Memory as Vision: Another Life* (London: Longman, 1978), p. 11. It is, I believe, significant in this context that Carpentier in his Prologue to *The Kingdom of this World* dwells on lycanthropy and that Mackandal and Ti-Noël undergo animal metamorphoses in the novel.

10. Interestingly, in the early manuscript versions of *Another Life* (1964–65), which is largely in prose, Walcott presents the werewolf story as a mere fable that he refused to believe even in his youth. Further references to the two notebook manuscripts, now in the collection of the University of the West Indies in Mona, Jamaica, will be designated as Notebook 1 and Notebook 2.

11. Notebook 1 (September 11, 1965): 38. Compare Simmons' reading of George Campbell's poem on the black child that occurs near the beginning of the poem (149).

12. Notebook 1 (September 30, 1965): 10. Critics have sometimes accused Walcott of an excessive attachment to, and too-perfect mastery of, European poetic tradition; see especially Helen Vendler's review of *The Fortunate Traveller* in the *New York Review of Books*, March 4,1982: 23-27

13. Notebook 1 (September 30,1965): 4.

14. Ibid., 8.

15. Cited from "Homecoming: Anse La Raye," in *Collected Poems*, p. 127. Walcott frequently makes use of Odyssean images and even Homeric epithets in his poetry; see, for example, the title poem of *Sea Grapes* (in *Collected Poems*, pp. 297–98).

16. In this section of the poem Walcott succeeds admirably in his adaptation of Robert Lowell's manner. For a sharp assessment of the Lowell–Walcott connection, see, Calvin Bedient's valuable "Derek Walcott, Contemporary," *Parnassus* (Fall–Winter 1981): 31–44.

17. Notebook 2 (November 12, 1965): 76–78. Walcott (76) implicitly contrasts Auguste's mode with the elevation of an "embalmed yet corruptible tradition," as if it were the Host or the fragments of the true cross—an image that carries over into the final poem (183–84).

18. The use of the Ariel and Caliban figures as emblems of the colonial's relation to the colonizing Prospero has a long history including the works of José Enrique Rodó (most famously), O. Mannoni, Aimé Césaire, Roberto Fernández Retamar, and others. The related issue of the ritual posing of white against black as rival and independent essences, a strategy that ties both white and black to an oppressive past, is discussed in Frantz Fanon's *Black Skins, White Masks*, trans. Charles Lam Markmann (1952; New

York: Grove Press, 1967) and developed in Abdul janMohamed's *Manichaean Aesthetics* (Amherst: University of Massachusetts Press, 1983).

19. See Sharon Ciccarelli's interview with Walcott in *Chant of Saints*, p. 303.

20. Harris' 1964 address, "Tradition and the West Indian Novel," is cited in Cudjoe, pp. 255–56.

21. Walcott, "The Muse of History," in *Is Massa Day Dead?*, ed. Orde Coombs (Garden City, N.Y.: Anchor/Doubleday, 1974), p. 2.

22. The practice of introducing the classical as analogous to the modern finds its most influential modern instance in the practice of Pound, Joyce, and Eliot. Interestingly, it appears as willful failure in one of the magical realist texts that Walcott cites in *Another Life*, Carpentier's *Lost Steps*, Harriet de Onís (1953; New York: Bard/Avon, 1979). In Carpentier, the narrator's chimerical attempt to identify the Greek Yannos as an Odyssean character signals the overextended and obsessive aspect of his personal quest for primitive origins (the origin of music and his own discontent). In Carpentier's novel, classical parallelism represents just another version of the ironic and futile search for origins.

23. "We have still not invented a language natural to our landscape, for fear of irregular syntax and bad pronunciation" (Notebook 2: 82, December 20, 1965 entry).

24. Notebook 2: 110, June 10, 1966 entry.

25. For the distinction between the earlier Edenic and the later decadent Macondo, see Lois Parkinson Zamora, *Writing the Apocalypse* (Cambridge: Cambridge University Press, 1989), pp. 25–32.

26. Cited in Roberto González Echevarria, *Alejo Carpentier: The Pilgrim at Home* (Ithaca: Cornell University Press, 1977), p. 136. González Echevarria's consideration of nature and history in Carpentier prompts my (rather divergent) reflection on the same issue here.

27. Alejo Carpentier, *The Kingdom of this World* (*El reino de este mundo*), tr. Harriet de Onís (1949; Harmondsworth: Penguin, 1980), p. 112.

28. See ibid., pp. 26–27, 108–12.

29. See *The Lost Steps*, pp. 55, 88–91.

30. Alejo Carpentier, *The Lost Steps*, p. 102. In his essay "Conciencia e identidad en América" ["Conscience and Identity in America"], Carpentier, in a similar vein, writes that "the conquistadors saw very clearly the aspect of marvelous reality [*el aspecto real maravilloso*] in American things." Here Carpentier alludes to Bernal Diaz's mention of Amadis de Gaula as a precursor text for his own vision of America. In *La novela latinoamericana en*

vísperas de an nuevo siglo y otros ensayos (Mexico City: Siglo XXI Editores, 1981), pp. 130–31, my translation.

31. See González Echevarria, "Carpentier y el realismo mágico," in *Otros mundos, otros fuegos*, pp. 221–31.

32. Rosario, for example, remains too immediately or emotionally present, too natively allied to the context of the jungle, to feel its magic. See *The Lost Steps*, pp. 99, 104.

33. "For me, the Orinoco started to become the water of Heraclitus, unchanging, present, always renewed, and it harmonized with the saying of Heraclitus that 'you can bathe in the same river, but never twice in the same water,'" "Conciencia e identidad," in *La novela latinoamericana*, p. 106.

34. González Echevarria, *The Pilgrim at Home*, p. 212.

35. Derek Walcott, *Dream on Monkey Mountain and Other Plays* (New York: Farrar, Straus and Giroux, 1970), pp. 3–4.

36. Samuel Beckett, *Waiting for Godot* (New York: Grove, 1954), p. 24. Walcott is attentive to the irony that Vladimir and Estragon are more "native" to the scene of Godot than is Pozzo; Beckett's play profoundly questions the idea of a native landscape or home. In more general terms, Beckett's exile from Ireland is not unlike Walcott's from St. Lucia.

37. Walcott's notion of the danger involved in bondage to the past, specifically to the history of colonial oppression, is indebted to Fanon, but divorced from Fanon's revolutionary optimism; it will play an important role, as I will argue, in his response to Neruda in *Another Life*.

38. See also p. 27, with its reference to "reactionaries in dashikis" who "screamed for the pastoral vision, for a return to nature over the loudspeakers." Walcott's hostile relation to the 1970 Black Power revolt in Trinidad is very noticeable in "What the Twilight Said"; his 1982 play *The Last Carnival*, by contrast, sees the revolt as a tragedy rather than a misguided farce.

39. Walcott has often used the Crusoe image in his poems: see, for an early example, "Crusoe's Island."

40. Bedient, p. 34, wonderfully describes Walcott's tendency in his poems to wish for disconnection and isolation. See also Vendler, p. 26.

41. "That night," Carpentier writes shortly after the lines that Walcott cites, "as I looked at them [the artists] I could see the harm my uprooting from this environment, which had been mine until adolescence, had done me" (71).

42. See Baugh, p 45.

43. For an early example, see the well-known "A Far Cry from Africa."

44. See the final section of Neruda's poem, along with Emir Rodriguez-Monegal's essay on the Whitmanesque and the prophetic (rather than materialist) quality of *Las alturas de Macchu Picchu*: "El sistema del poeta," in *Pablo Neruda*, ed. Rodriguez Monegal and Enrico Mario Santi (Madrid: Taurus, 1980), pp. 63–91.

45. See González Echevarria, *The Pilgrim at Home*, pp. 160–61.

46. The translation of the Neruda passage is by Anthony Kerrigan (from Pablo Neruda, *Selected Poems* [New York: Delta, 1970]).

47. Translation by John Felstiner from his *Translating Neruda: The Way to Macchu Picchu* (Stanford: Stanford University Press, 1980), p. 239

48. Many Indian laborers were imported into the West Indies, mostly as cane-cutters, by Great Britain in the later nineteenth century to make up for the loss of slave labor; and Chinese merchants and workers are also common in the islands.

49. The other major echo in the passage I have just cited is Walcott's heartbreaking variation on a line of the Aeneid's book 6, which portrays the dead souls reaching out in "longing for the farther shore" of Elysium (Aen. 6–314: "tende-bantque manus ripae ulterioris amore"). In general, Virgil represents imperium in the poem; Homer's *Odyssey*, here as in other Caribbean works, represents the promise of freedom offered by the New World voyage. Walcott's interest in the Odyssean analogy for New World experience is evident in his work; I have already pointed to one salient example, the title poem of *Sea Grapes* (in *Collected Poems*, pp. 297–298).

50. Edward Hirsch, "The Art of Poetry XXXVII: Derek Walcott" (interview), *The Paris Review* 101 (1986), p. 214. I am indebted to Edward Hirsch for additional information concerning his conversations with Walcott.

51. Notebook 1 (August 4,1965): 20.

52. Notebook 1 (August 7,1965): 23.

53. Walcott here recalls the late Wordsworth poem that begins with the poet leaning on his daughter and citing Samson Agonistes: "A LITTLE onward lend thy guiding hand ...."

54. Notebook 1 (August 4, 1965): 21.

55. I would like to thank the University of Houston for a Research Initiation Grant enabling me to do much of the research for this piece, and the University of the West Indies (Mona, Jamaica) for their assistance. Lois Parkinson Zamora and Elizabeth Gregory offered helpful editorial guidance. Finally, Derek Walcott graciously gave me permission to quote from his manuscripts.

GREGSON DAVIS

"With No Homeric Shadow": The Disavowal of Epic in Derek Walcott's Omeros

A la fin tu es las de ce monde ancien

Bergère, ô tour Eiffel le troupeau des ponts bêle ce
matin.
—Guillaume Apollinaire

The ghost of Homer sings. His words have the sound of the
sea and the cadence of actual speech.
—Marianne Moore

The American poet Marianne Moore opens a famous poem with words
that appear, at first reading, both disingenuous and radically subversive:

POETRY
I, too, dislike it: there are things that are
important beyond all
this fiddle.[1]

After this brusque disavowal of poetry—of her own love for her cherished
vocation—she proceeds at once to attenuate, if not recant, her opening

From *The South Atlantic Quarterly* 96, no. 2 (Spring 1997). © 1997 by Duke University Press.

broadside in a tone of mitigation: "Reading it, however, with a perfect contempt for it, one / discovers in / it after all, a place for the genuine." The rest of the poem provides a veritable catalogue of images, instances of what Moore regards as "genuine." In fine, the reader is first seduced by an apparently sincere confession of dislike that is implicitly collusive ("I, too, dislike it"); but no sooner has this complicity between poet and audience been reinforced by a gnomic declaration ("there are things that are important beyond all / this fiddle") than we are led to an immediate counterassertion or correction—a statement of preference for a truly authentic brand of verse ("a place for the genuine"). We are led, in other words, to revise our reading of the first line and to hear it, in retrospect, as tongue-in-cheek and ironic. In our revised perception we come to realize that the ostensible disavowal of poetry is not, after all, a blanket dismissal, but rather the first move in a dialectical maneuver the culmination of which is, paradoxically, a profession of faith. "Perfect contempt" turns out to be, surprisingly, a proposed way of "reading" poetry with a discriminating eye for quality. The poem evolves, in effect, into an avowal of what the poet judges to be genuine in the realm of the poetic. She has chosen this rhetorical pathway (disavowal–qualification–avowal) as a subterfuge to guide us to the special place that she has marked out for herself—a place she calls, in the final strophe, "the imaginary garden" of poetry.

Moore's pseudo-disavowal is given a totalistic cast: she archly claims to "dislike" poetry in general. The paradoxical rhetoric of (dis)avowal in Derek Walcott's *Omeros* represents an analogous move, but one by which poetic genre rather than poetry *tout court* is foregrounded. The genre in Walcott's case is the epic. Although this Caribbean poet has explicitly rejected the epic label in published interviews, it is his generic disavowals in *Omeros*—his internal "performative" exclusions—that will be our focus here. As Oliver Taplin has pointed out, Walcott's poem provokes the reader by its length and ambition, as well as the very names of its characters, to make comparisons with Homeric epic.[2] Why then does the narrating voice conspicuously disavow the Greek-epic paradigm at more than one fulcrum point in the poem? Or, to rephrase the question in more narrowly rhetorical terms, what does the narrator gain from invoking Homer while disowning the Homeric genre? This rhetoric of inclusion / exclusion has aesthetic, linguistic, and philosophical implications, among others. Walcott's version of the gambit so brilliantly epitomized in Moore's poem appears to yield an egregious paradox (what Taplin calls "denial" and "contradiction"). Here, I shall attempt to establish a *formal* as well as a literary-historical context for the performance of disavowal.

To begin with the literary-historical background to the strategy of disavowal, literary scholars who work in the Greco-Roman tradition conventionally refer to the move as *recusatio* (refusal), and there is by now a voluminous critical literature dissecting the device as practiced most notably by the major Augustan poets: Horace, Vergil, Propertius, and Ovid. The Latin poets, for their part, modeled their conventional (dis)avowals on topoi derived from Greek poets of the Hellenistic period such as Callimachus, who strove to find a "place for the genuine" ostensibly by eschewing Homeric manner and matter. In this Hellenistic and Roman line of tradition, epic grandeur is bypassed, even obliquely denigrated, in favor of small-scale, "light" composition. The internal critical discourse of these Greek and Roman poets in the shadow of Homer is framed in generic terms: the epic is set up as the generic "other" against which the non-epic composer defines his craft. A single, well-known example of the Latin convention may suffice by way of illustration, namely, Ovid's second book of love poems, the *Amores*, which begins with a programmatic reformulation of his generic choice:

> Once, rashly, I sang of war in heaven and giants
> with a hundred arms. My diction soared to the occasion—
>
> the cruel vengeance of Mother Earth, and the piling
> of Pelion upon Ossa upon Olympus.
>
> But while I was busy with Jupiter standing on a storm-cloud,
> thunderbolt at the ready to defend his heaven,
>
> Corinna slammed her door. I dropped the thunderbolt
> and even forgot the Almighty.
>
> Forgive me, Lord. Your weapons couldn't help me.
> That locked door had a far more effective bolt.
>
> I returned to couplets and compliments, my own weapons,
> and broke down its resistance with soft words.[3]

In Ovid's humorous, even parodic, version of the rhetorical convention, the speaker stages an abrupt abandonment of grand themes—metaphorized in Jove's thunderbolt—under the irresistible impact of erotic passion. He opts for light elegy, rather than heavy epic, as the genre best suited to amorous themes. The metaphor of "thundering Jove," incidentally, is appropriated from the prologue to Callimachus's *Actia*, a Hellenistic text that served as a kind of aesthetic manifesto for an entire generation of Latin poets. The author of the *Amores* is echoing this defining text while reenacting the drama of generic choice in his own programmatic poem.

It would be easy to multiply examples of rhetorical disavowals in ancient and modern European lyric, for the convention is nothing short of ubiquitous in poetry of all periods. What is of interest here is how it functions in the major composition of a contemporary poet who delights in manipulating traditional motifs as a sophisticated means of articulating his own aesthetic. Walcott's move is best clarified by comparison with its deployment in the work of other poets, ancient and modern (insofar as these epithets circumscribe a Eurocentric lyric tradition). As the Apollinaire epigraph indicates, even supposedly iconoclastic precursors of modernism like this poet utilized, consciously or unconsciously, the complex dialectic of rejection and reassimilation: "In the end you are tired of this ancient world. // Shepherdess, O Eiffel Tower, the flock of bridges is bleating this morning."[4] Immediately after bluntly disavowing antiquity (and, by implication, its outmoded generic repertoire) in his first line, the radical poet of "Zone" proceeds, in the second, to invert the ancient pastoral convention that opposes city to country, on his way to defining his own modernist voice. Despite the dismissive opening, this double move is a standard formal ploy in the antique discourse of self-definition. "Self" in such contexts refers, of course, to the artistic persona that is constructed through the performance of writing/reading.

In comparing homologous enactments of disavowal, it is important to consider the contours of the disavowed: the shape and dimensions of the "other" set up as a generic foil to the poet's articulation of his/her project. As our glance at Moore's "Poetry" revealed, the other may, at one extreme, be conceived with such amplitude that all inauthentic "fiddle" is strenuously differentiated from the genuine article; for Apollinaire, the dividing line is drawn so as to exclude (ostensibly) the entire Greco-Roman tradition ("ce monde ancien"). Walcott's frequent deployment of this foil is supremely elastic, so it provides a useful gauge of his virtuosity as it is exercised from the more ample to the more narrow generic horizons.

In his exquisite long poem *Another Life*, Walcott deferentially ascribes grandeur of style (a standard feature of epic discourse) to the visual opus of his friend, the painter whom he calls Gregorias:

> Provincialism loves the pseudo-epic,
> so if these heroes have been given a stature

> disproportionate to their cramped lives,
> remember I beheld them at knee-height,
> and that their thunderous exchanges
> rumbled like gods about another life,
> as now, I hope, some child
> ascribes their grandeur to Gregorias.[5]

Striking in this formulation of the conventional poetry/painting comparison is the way in which the postcolonial poet is represented by the infant who hears the dominant European voices as grown-up "thunder" emanating from gigantic figures. (Ovid's metaphor comes to mind.) In the very act of establishing the sound as distant thunder, the speaker expresses the hope that his artist friend will have succeeded in reaching an equivalent resonance, so to speak, in the rival medium of painting. This move of displacement (from Walcott, the aspiring poet, to the artist "Gregorias") is a common feature of the classical convention whereby another contemporary poet and friend is often put forward by the speaker as more suitable for the task of imitating the grand style. Thus the speaker in *Another Life* is already engaged in a process of self-reflection concerning the formation of an authentic voice that has declined to emulate the epic thunderbolt. The effort by Walcott's speaker to hold European canonic grandeur at a distance while acknowledging its power parallels (though perhaps subliminally) the stance of Ovid and the Augustans vis-à-vis Greek models. Both contemporary postcolonial poets and postclassical Latin poets strive to legitimate their own unique voices by claiming distinctness from a remote, Olympian epic manner.

At several sutures in the fabric of *Omeros* a narrative thread appears that is nominally incongruent with Walcott's mode of rewriting the Homeric version of the Helen of Troy myth. This alternating (and alternate) narrative is ascribed to a character named Dennis Plunkett, a former British sergeant-major who has retired to the island of St. Lucia. An amateur historian, Plunkett adopts a project (for him an obsession) that involves discovering suggestive analogies for the grand enterprise of the Trojan War in events of Caribbean colonial history, such as the 1782 naval conflict between the British and the French known as the Battle of Les Saintes. Plunkett's desire to write a history of St. Lucia along epic lines is rooted in a quasi-literary impulse to read historical parallels in verbal coincidences and wordplays, such as the fact that St. Lucia had acquired the sobriquet the "Helen of the West Indies" because it was a notorious bone of contention between rival colonial powers in the archipelago. Although the narrator appears to distance himself from Plunkett's project (which, ironically, he describes as an attempt to reduce history to metaphor), it is nevertheless given a marked prominence in the poem, thereby posing the tantalizing question of the relationship between the two, generically different narrative strategies. The poet/narrator perhaps comes closest to framing the question in a passage that, openly averring both the convergence and the divergence of the two narrative agendas, takes up the reinvention of the Greek Helen as a Black St. Lucian housemaid:

> Plunkett, in his innocence,

> had tried to change History to a metaphor,
> in the name of a housemaid; I, in self-defence,
> altered her opposite. Yet it was all for her.

> Except we had used two opposing stratagems
> in praise of her and the island; cannonballs rolled
> in the fort grass were not from Olympian games,

> nor the wine-bottle, crusted with its fool's gold,
> from the sunken *Ville de Paris*, legendary
> emblems; nor all their names the forced coincidence

> we had made them. There, in her head of ebony,
> there was no real need for the historian's
> remorse, nor for literature's.[6]

What is ostensibly disavowed here is, in fact, a move that is made by both narrative orders (historiographic and literary). Homeric names, and the stories they carry, are shamelessly exploited by both composers, the speaker concedes. This acknowledgment of an underlying convergence, however, also encompasses a disavowal, for the poet/narrator, who has claimed that "forced coincidences" are unnecessary ("there was no real need"), now candidly criticizes a "stratagem" he has also intermittently employed elsewhere in the poem. The rhetorical leverage he gains by this admission and juxtaposition is subtle and effective, allowing him to have his cake and eat it too by an oblique denigration of a pseudo-historian's use of Homeric names as a stratagem of praise without any apparent consciousness that the epicizing of St. Lucia and the ennobling of an actual maid are inherently specious.[7] The well-known Aristotelian dictum that poetry is "more philosophical than history" is latent in the juxtaposition.

Walcott's use of an ersatz historiographer as a generic foil may seem highly contrived and artificial to the reader unfamiliar with its conventional character. An example from a Latin poet whose work mediates Greek models may help to elucidate the rhetorical technique at work in *Omeros*. In addressing a lyric poem to his friend and patron Maecenas, Horace positions him as a potential composer of historical narrative who, he asserts with false modesty, is better equipped than himself to handle epic themes adequately:

> You would not wish me to tune the lyre's gentle strains
> to the drawn-out wars of savage Numantia, nor harsh
> Hannibal, nor the Sicilian sea ruddy
> with Punic blood
>
> nor the wild Lapiths, the wine-distraught Hylaeus,
> and the earth-born brood subdued by Heracles' might
> that caused the gleaming demesne
> of ancient Saturn
>
> to tremble at the danger: surely you, Maecenas,
> would better relate in a historian's prose the wars
> of Caesar, and alien kings dragged by the neck
> through Roman streets;
>
> for my part my Muse has wished me to relate
> Licymnia, my mistress: her sweet songs, her gleaming
> eyes, her constancy throughout our truly
> mutual passion.[8]

In accordance with the ancient convention of the separation of stylistic levels, the Horatian disavowal emphasizes the disparity between historical and lyric discourse by presenting the subject matter—love rather than battles—as the determining factor in the poet's choice of the gentle lyric strain. Walcott's placement of Plunkett operates like Horace's of Maecenas, setting in relief the poet/narrator of *Omeros*, although the generic status of this poem is deliberately left vague and undefined. With the "historical epic" voice of Plunkett contrapuntal to that of the narrator, however, all those "forced coincidences" are an integral part of the polyphonic composition.

An important aspect of the form being delineated here is what we might call the reintegration of a disavowed term. Taplin has shrewdly remarked that although Walcott rejects the epic theme of "battles," *Omeros* contains copious references to figurative "lances."[9] The reintegration, at the figurative level, of matter ostensibly excluded by the speaker is also thoroughly conventional in the *recusatio*.[10] In the work of the Augustan poets, for instance, it is standard for the "recusing" poet to eschew military matter ("kings and battles," in Vergil's summation in the prelude to *Eclogue* 6), but then to reincorporate such matter via metaphor. Thus Ovid, in the poem quoted earlier, reclaims some previously abandoned weapons by transferring them to the erotic sphere: "I returned to couplets and compliments, my own weapons, / and broke down its resistance with soft words." By a similar subterfuge in "Zone," as we have seen, Apollinaire repudiates ancient pastoral in language that figuratively transfers the bleating of sheep to the bridges of modern Paris.

In his many appropriations of epic subject matter, Walcott reveals that he is not actually renouncing "epic" so much as redefining it and, in the process, demonstrating the fundamental fluidity of the whole concept of genre. This metaphorical reclamation of an "epical" allure that is strenuously denied on the literal surface is nowhere more transparent than in the passage in which the griot characterizes the suffering of his people in the Atlantic slave trade:

> But they crossed, they survived. There is the epical splendour.
> Multiply the rain's lances, multiply their ruin,
> the grace born from subtraction as the hold's iron door
>
> rolled over their eyes like pots left out in the rain,
> and the bolt rammed home its echo, the way that thunder-
> claps perpetuate their reverberation.[11]

In the reverberation of the "thunderclap" analogy we may perhaps hear the distant echo of epic disavowals.

In its use of generic foil *Omeros* conjures up many reincarnations of the epic bard.[12] Since the very name is a signifier for the entire epic tradition (including the Homeric poems), we may conceptualize it in terms similar to those Claude Lévi-Strauss used to describe myth: the figure of Omeros consists of all its variants, a rhapsode figure comprising non-European as well as European instances, such as the African griot who recounts the past experiences of the tribe. Late in the poem, the speaker reports a dialogue with a vagrant bard whom he recognizes as a reincarnation of Homer: "'I saw you in London,' I said, 'sunning on the steps / of St. Martin-in-the-Fields, your dog-eared manuscript / clutched to your heaving chest.'" The bard's reply to the recognition of his timeless identity ends with a disclosure: "a drifter / is the hero of my book."[13] There is an implied convergence between the epic singer / writer and his theme, between the wandering Odysseus and the drifting epic bard who, like Phemius or Demodocus in the Homeric intertexts, does the circuit of the Mycenean courts. Drifting is also a metaphor that relates to the sea and its currents, of course, so the motif of the sea as "fluid" epos is once again emphasized.[14]

It is in the context of such strategic redefinitions of Homeric themes that the speaker utters a startling, even explosive, disavowal in reference to the unnamed book carried by Omeros: "'I never read it,' / I said. 'Not all the way through.'" It is significant that the initial denial is immediately corrected with "not all the way through," alerting the reader to the hyperbole endemic to virtually all variants of the disavowal gambit—hyperbole that also prepares us, as it does in Moore's poem, for the explicit reading instructions soon to be vouchsafed—here, by Omeros. Responding to the speaker's objections to the divine apparatus in the *Iliad* and the *Odyssey*, Omeros is made to say, "Forget the gods ... and read the rest." The brusque, charged exchange between the two poets culminates in a revelation that not only negates the hyperbole of "I never read it" but replaces it with a description of Walcott's peculiar relationship to the Homeric text: "I was the freshest of all your readers."[15] Clearly, what occurs through this sleight of hand is that Walcott's own reading of Homer—an underlying aesthetic agenda of the poem—acquires legitimacy, even authentication, from the mouth of "Homer" himself. The poet's stance of disavowal allows him to reposition himself vis-à-vis the tradition, to stake out a claim for the "genuine" and thereby authenticate the aesthetic that governs his reading and, by extension, his rewriting of a canonic text.

The rhetorical structure of "generic disavowals" has a philosophical underpinning that may be framed in terms of the writer's quest for an originary poetic language. Walcott exposes this deeper structure in the same self-reflexive passage in which he compares (and discriminates between) Plunkett's project and the poet's—his own:

> Why not see Helen

> as the sun saw her, with no Homeric shadow,
> swinging her plastic sandals on that beach alone,
> as fresh as the sea-wind? Why make the smoke a door?[16]

The question pinpoints the epistemological predicament that constrains all writers, wistfully proposing a "way of seeing" that is an unattainable ideal, given the nature of language: a Helen seen "with no Homeric shadow." In the next subsection, the speaker pursues a self-interrogation that, like all "rhetorical" questions, contains its own answer:

> When would my head shake off its echoes like a horse
>
> shaking off a wreath of flies? When would it stop,
> the echo in the throat, insisting, "Omeros";
> when would I enter that light beyond metaphor?[17]

The desire for a pristine linguistic universe, the "light beyond metaphor," arguably subtends the poem as a whole. From a broader perspective, we may plausibly infer that this desire is ultimately the source of the dynamic of all generic disavowals. In Walcott's poetics, the nexus between the desire to transcend metaphor and the motif of disavowal is by no means confined to the text of *Omeros*. An extremely lucid instance of that nexus is already manifest on the surface of the early poem "Greece." Here, in the compass of two brilliant strophes, the speaker represents himself as climbing a seaside cliff and discarding "a great book" in a purifying gesture that enables him to utter words denuded of intertextual echoes—the very project he reposes, almost poignantly, in *Omeros*. The Homeric corpus, with its burden of echoes, is precisely what is being discarded here:

> The body that I had thrown down at my foot
> was not really a body but a great book
> still fluttering like chitons on a frieze,
> till wind worked through the binding of its pages
> scattering Hector's and Achilles' rages
> to white, diminishing scraps, like gulls that ease
> past the gray sphinxes of the crouching islands.
>
> I held air without language in my hands.[18]

The cathartic gesture of discarding the Homeric poems leads to the repossession of a pristine, unmediated bond with things ("air without language"), as the poet begins to write, transcribing substantives directly from nature and thereby reinventing the names of things: "Now, crouched before the blank stone, / I wrote the sound for 'sea,' the sign for 'sun.'"[19] This reinventing of lexemes captures the creative vision that may perhaps be most parsimoniously formulated in semiotic terms, namely, the Saussurean axiom of the "arbitrary" nature of the sign, which, along with its corollary the "empty signifier," is strenuously denied by most poets, who endorse the "necessary fiction" that words can and do refer to things in an unmediated relation to which a genuine poet has access. As Walcott phrases it, "I learned what a noun is, writing this book. No one is Adam. A noun is not a name you give something. It is something you watch becoming itself, and you have to have the patience to find out what it is."[20] At the level of discourse as well as at the microlevel of vocabulary, the quest for "the original story," as it is termed in "Greece," is predicated on discarding all prior texts. The reader, no less than the writer, is aware that exorcising a vision of a universe, and a fortiori a linguistic universe, from text (*hors-texte*) is a doomed enterprise, but it is energetically pursued nonetheless by any writer who desires to create Moore's "imaginary gardens with real toads in them."[21]

  Walcott's inflection of the quixotic quest for the full signifier ("the sign for 'sun'") may be aptly compared with that of Wallace Stevens. Among the many texts in Stevens's lyric corpus that perform a gesture of disavowal as a precondition for recuperating a lost linguistic plenitude, perhaps the most elucidating for our purposes is "The Man on the Dump." Stevens's speaker represents himself as a post-Romantic poet who finds himself on the dump—a symbolic site on which all prior (Romantic) images of the moon have been discarded. From this vantage point he is empowered to see (and write) the moon "as the moon," thus recouping the putative integrity of the linguistic sign:

> Between that disgust and this, between the things
> That are on the dump (azaleas and so on)
> And those that will be (azaleas and so on),
> One feels the purifying change. One rejects
> The trash.
>   That's the moment when the moon creeps up
> To the bubbling of bassoons. That's the time
> One looks at the elephant-colorings of tires.
> Everything is shed; and the moon comes up as the moon
> (All its images are in the dump) and you see
> As a man (not like an image of a man),
> You see the moon rise in the empty sky.[22]

The fresh vision (and the language in which it takes shape) is here predicated on a prior refusal, on discarding the encrustations of the quintessential Romantic sign, the moon. Whether or not "The Man on the Dump" constitutes a conscious intertext for a recurrent strand in the fabric of Walcott's *Omeros*, it is illuminating to compare those passages in which Walcott reaches for the "light beyond metaphor." In this regard, the words attributed to the persona named Afolabe summarize succinctly, even gnomically, the insight that underlies and informs the rhetoric of disavowal. The narrative context is a dialogue between the African Afolabe and his Caribbean descendant Achille—a dialogue cast in a dreamlike, Vergilian (read: mediated Homeric) underworld. Achille has spoken of the means by which he has been transported to his ancestral homeland "by a swift, // or the shadow of a swift." The attentive reader, immediately recognizing the muse of Omeros in the recurrent emblem of this seabird, is thereby alerted to the implications of Afolabe's aphoristic response: "No man loses his shadow except it is in the night, / and even then his shadow is hidden, not lost."[23] Walcott's "Homeric shadow" is never lost in *Omeros*; it is only sporadically occluded. Paradoxically, however, it is most present at those very moments when its absence is most fervently proclaimed as the object of the poet's desire.

NOTES

The South Atlantic Quarterly 96:2, Spring 1997. Copyright © 1997 by Duke University Press.

1. Marianne Moore, "Poetry" (longer version), in *The Complete Poems of Marianne Moore* (New York, 1981), 266–67.

2. Oliver Taplin, "Derek Walcott's *Omeros* and Derek Walcott's Homer," *Arion* 1 (1991): 213–26.

3. *Ovid's Amores*, trans. Guy Lee (New York, 1968), 59–60 (ll. 11–22).

4. My translation. The French text of these opening lines of "Zone" is from *Guillaume Apollinaire: Oeuvres poétiques*, ed. P. Adéma and M. Décaudin (Paris, 1956), 213.

5. Derek Walcott, "The Divided Child," in *Another Life* (New York, 1973), 41.

6. Derek Walcott, *Omeros* (New York, 1990), 270–71 (6.54.2).

7. Walcott's own words, as quoted in a *New York Times* interview, make the point incisively: "One reason I don't like talking about an epic is that I think it is wrong to try to ennoble people.... And just to write history is

wrong. History makes similes of people, but these people are their own nouns"; *New York Times*, 9 October 1990, C13.

8. Horace *Carm.* 2.12; my translation. For the unorthodox ascription of Licymnia (the beloved) to the speaker rather than the addressee, see Gregson Davis, "The Persona of Licymnia: A Revaluation of Horace *Carm.* 2.12," *Philologus* 119 (1975): 70–83.

9. Taplin, "Walcott's *Omeros* and Walcott's Homer," 223–24.

10. For a discussion of key Greco-Roman examples of such "incorporation," see Gregson Davis, *Polyhymnia: The Rhetoric of Horatian Lyric Discourse* (Berkeley and Los Angeles, 1991), 30–36.

11. Walcott, *Omeros*, 149 (3.28.1).

12. Cf. Taplin, "Walcott's *Omeros* and Walcott's Homer," 215.

13. Walcott, *Omeros*, 282, 283 (7.56.3).

14. See Marianne Moore's review of Ezra Pound's *Cantos* (from which my epigraph is taken), in *A Marianne Moore Reader: Poems and Essays* (New York, 1961), 149–66.

15. Walcott, *Omeros*, 283 (7.56.3).

16. Ibid., 271 (6.54.2).

17. Ibid., 271 (6.54.3).

18. Derek Walcott, "Greece," in *The Fortunate Traveller* (New York, 1981), 35–36.

19. Ibid., 36.

20. *New York Times*, C13.

21. Moore, "Poetry," in *Complete Poems*, 267.

22. Wallace Stevens, "The Man on the Dump," in *The Palm at the End of the Mind*, ed. Holly Stevens (New York, 1972), 163–64.

23. Walcott, *Omeros*, 138 (3.25.3).

PAULA BURNETT

"The Theatre of Our Lives": Founding an Epic Drama

Antonio: His word is more than the miraculous harp.
The Tempest, II.i.90

From his earliest days as an artist, Walcott's vision of a Caribbean aesthetic led him not just to epic poetry but to epic drama, the topic of this study's final chapters. First it may be useful to pause on the thinking behind his theater practice (revisiting some questions of ideology mapped in the first half of the book). That practice has much in common with Brecht's concept of epic theater (investing the term with a deliberately antiheroic meaning), but Walcott has developed Brechtian ideas in his own personal and particularly Caribbean way. As a term from classical literature, epic is associated first with poetry; in the Western tradition it has not been usual to apply it to drama. The plays of Shakespeare, for instance, are usually classified as comedies, tragedies, and some hybrids between these two categories variously known as romances, tragicomedies, and histories, not epics, although a number of the plays might be called epic. The way plays such as *Antony and Cleopatra* or *Coriolanus*, for instance, deal with the connection between the individual and the collective invites such a term (Cleopatra's private desires, for instance, are carefully shown drawing her country's political fortunes in their wake). Adaptations, such as that of the Antony and Cleopatra story, to the modern

From *Derek Walcott: Politics and Poetics*. © 2000 by the Board of Regents of the State of Florida.

technology of film, adaptations that invite a populist label of "epic," underline the complex relationship between epic and romance. Both tend to be concerned with nonmimetic representation—with narrative remote from everyday life—but for different ends: where the objective of romance is escape from reality, the objective of epic is the reintegration of the reader-spectator into the real political world. The unusual combinations of effect Walcott has sought in some of his plays have led them sometimes to be regarded—and dismissed—as romance, when, if they had been understood as epic in intent, they might have earned a different kind of attention and respect.

Where epic poetry, associated with the classics, had, in the European tradition, acquired an aura of remoteness from the ordinary people, the term "epic" in this century has been repopularized through its application to the new art of film. From the earliest days of cinema, the designation of epic was attached to certain kinds of drama with an ambitious scope of representation, usually of events regarded as originating the contemporary nation or cultural group, such as Griffith's *Birth of a Nation* made in 1915, which Woodrow Wilson likened to "writing history with lightning,"[1] or the films of Eisenstein, narrating the key events of the Russian Revolution. The term "epic" was subsequently applied to the stage: Brecht promoted the idea of an epic theater,[2] borrowing Eisenstein's concept of the new style of representation—his montage approach, in which each episode could signify independently, and his provocation of the audience to think and act rather than to empathize.[3] After reading Marx's *Capital* in 1926, Brecht saw him as the ideal audience for his drama.[4] He rejected the aesthetic of psychology, demanding an intellectual response more in tune with sociology and philosophy: "The sociologist is the man for us," he wrote; "This is a world and a kind of drama where the philosopher can find his way about better than the psychologist."[5] In an early attempt to summarize his concept of epic theater, Brecht wrote:

> The essential point of the epic theatre is perhaps that it appeals less to the feelings than to the spectator's reason. Instead of sharing an experience the spectator must come to grips with things. At the same time it would be quite wrong to try and deny emotion to this kind of theatre. It would be much the same thing as trying to deny emotion to modern science.[6]

This is a crucial qualification: Brecht's idea of epic is not anti-emotion, but against unthinking emotion, the kind that bolsters the status quo by suppressing critical thought. The emotion that results from full political consciousness—the kind, for instance, that Brecht seeks to provoke with Mother Courage's silent scream—he saw as altogether different.[7]

Brecht's "anti-metaphysical, materialistic, non-Aristotelian drama," which sought to teach the spectator a new "practical attitude, directed towards changing the world," was much discussed in the 1950s when Walcott was grounding himself as a dramatist and director.[8] The anti-mimetic stance was one that Walcott's early drama reflected, although some of his more recent plays have returned to a more conventional Aristotelian approach. In Brecht's phrase, "the Aristotelian play is essentially static; its task is to show the world as it is. The learning-play ["Lehrstück"] is essentially dynamic; its task is to show the world as it changes (and also how it may be changed)."[9] From his early plays on, Walcott explored different models of didactic theater, ranging from the dialectical materialist episodes of *Drums and Colours* to the generic and symbolic approach of the folk morality play in *Ti-Jean and His Brothers*. His objective has certainly been to change the world, but where Brecht's notion of change is pinned firmly to the relations of production in the materialist world—to the political order—Walcott's has always been concerned primarily with the symbolic order that validates the political order. He has identified the most pernicious injustice suffered by his people as one of cultural representation, of which material injustice is a product. To address the latter without the former would be pointless. He therefore, while in exemplary Brechtian manner drawing attention to the means and control of production (for instance, by writing the cocoa-dancers into the story of *The Last Carnival*), focuses on key moments of cultural production, transmission, and interaction. Walcott's equivalent to a Brechtian symbolic moment—such as that in *Mann ist Mann*, in which a spurious "elephant" is marketed as a commodity—is perhaps a scene such as that in *The Last Carnival*, in which a mimetic Eurocentric tableau re-presents the past hegemony of European art in a deconstruction of the indigenous creole culture of Trinidad in 1970. Where Brecht lays bare the bones of materialism, Walcott exposes first the skeletons of *culture*.

Walcott has never sought a theater of elaborate mimetic effect, and even when representing what Brecht would have called bourgeois drama (in some of his musicals or in plays such as *Remembrance* or *Viva Detroit*), he does so for political ends, as Brecht does in *The Threepenny Opera*.[10] As with the public response to this play, the tendency of some spectators to read his plays within a dominant type rather than as an anti-type is a problem common to much ironic representation. Like Brecht, Walcott typically gives trenchant exposure to the materialist causes of action, taking on capitalism principally in its imperialist manifestation, and he is less interested in the Freudian psychology of his characters as individuals than in their interaction with society, both as products of the social order and as transmitters of it. However, in a theatrical tradition still largely wedded to mimesis, the unconventional nature of the effects sought can be alienatory without being productively so, as Brecht intended. As Brecht was acutely aware, to appreciate epic theater, the spectator needs to become an "expert," schooled in "complex seeing," a perceptiveness blunted by the linear manipulation of the spectator in conventional theater, who is led through a carefully controlled sequence of responses.[11]

Walcott parts company with Brecht, however, and with the modern Western tradition in general, over his metaphysical strategy. Brecht's antimetaphysical position reflects the scientific rationalism of the modern West, but for Walcott the refusal of mimesis as method entails its replacement with a symbolic method drawing on myth. Like Brecht, he draws on mythic forms such as the folk fable, but unlike Brecht he does not just use them dialectically but takes the metaphysical seriously. In the act of disenchantment, he re-enchants, with the fundamental mythic gest (to borrow Brecht's term) of the refusal of death in a return to life, enacted as a recurrent motif in his drama. As a result, his drama is ultimately not Brechtian, although it draws on Brecht's ideas, nor is it traditionally mimetic. It offers a new model: a postcolonial theater that is politically oriented but reconnects to drama's ancient root in sacred ritual in order to reach its ideological objective.

Although Brecht subsequently replaced the term "epic" with "dialectical," in response to persistent misunderstandings, he did not significantly alter his meanings. Elizabeth Wright sums up what his epic theater signified:

> By "epic," Brecht is broaching a definition which transcends the traditional concept of the genre. The epic (das Epische) is not only not tied to a particular genre, but it can also be found in other genres, taking with it its connotations of narrative distance. The drama thereby surrenders the old characteristic quality of suspense, together with its concomitant effect of luring the audience into purely subjective identifications and the final granting of emotional release. Instead the stage begins not only to narrate but also to comment and criticize from a viewpoint not necessarily tied to the immediate action.[12]

The theater of illusion was to be replaced by a new relation between drama and audience, the distance of "Verfremdungseffekt" [alienation or estrangement] provoking the audience to think rather than feel, and in particular to think historically in order to make informed choices about action in the future. The past, particularly as conceived post-Foucault, becomes a primary subject: in Wright's phrase, "the re-writability of the text of history offers a model for the theatre."[13] Brecht regards the author not as originator but simply as someone who "produces from the materials of history."[14] Walcott, too, is concerned with representing history not only in his poems but also in his plays. Proceeding from a lively awareness of the role of the grand narratives, which ignored the existence of communities like his own and portrayed the past in order to maintain the hegemonic center, he began from his earliest days as a dramatist to write alternative histories for his own people, reflecting different starting points, choices, and assumptions. This takes place within a developing critique challenging the value of history as discourse; he deconstructs the dominant account, replacing the grand narrative with a socially aware local alternative—but then affirms that history is not as important as it claims to be. The apparent ambivalence is a dialectical strategy resulting in the mythic approach: to overemphasize history would be to lock the present to a tragic past and, disastrously, the future to revenge, when what he wishes to assert is the possibility of renewal and of fresh beginnings. In Christian terms, it connects with the difference between the ethic of justice in the Old Testament and the ethic of redemption in the New. While it invests in the ideal, it does not repeat the old utopianism of the bourgeois theater of illusion.

Myth and history have gone hand in hand in Walcott's dramatic works. Where some of his early drama, most notably *Drums and Colours*, shows a very Brechtian approach to history, Walcott was already developing his own style with the mythic folk play: both *Ti-Jean and His Brothers* and *Drums and Colours* were first performed in 1958. As his career has progressed, he has never entirely abandoned the history play, his most recent one, *The Ghost Dance*, integrating the two dimensions of history and myth to an unprecedented degree. Walcott has gone beyond Brecht in understanding the role of myth in society and its radical potential in art. Walcott, like Brecht, believes in the transformative power of art, but unlike Brecht he regards that power as essentially metaphysical.

This has implications for kind and form. Brecht used comedy for social change: for him, according to Wright, the "target of comedy is the historical irrelevance and inauthentic modes of living of a society stuck with an outworn set of beliefs long after history has moved on."[15] His perception that the comic process could be introduced anywhere led to his refusal of comedy and tragedy as absolute categories of narrative. In his own practice as a playwright, he blurred the genres, as Wright explains, allowing the historical context to determine whether a sequence of events was to be regarded as comic or tragic. The categories, in Wright's terms, "are not to be regarded as mutually exclusive, as essences which can be reconciled, as in tragicomedy, but as something intertwined in an ambivalent way: the comic combines with the serious when their connection with social and historical realities is revealed. The literary separation of them into two genres is itself an ideological act."[16] This is particularly helpful in an evaluation of Walcott's practice as dramatist. He, too, typically intertwines comic and tragic elements in an ambivalent way, for ideological reasons, as the plays considered below demonstrate. He identifies the predominance of comedy as a feature of his cultural milieu. His 1970 essay "What the Twilight Says," which delineates a marked sense of his separation from the actors and the mass of the people, explores his relationship with his company and through them with the culture of his community, describing how his actors were "humanists" whose "genius is not violent, it is comic." Rehearsing Genet's *The Blacks*, they "cannot enjoy its mincing catamite dances of death," because "their minds refuse to be disfigured." Yet Walcott as their director wishes to lead them into a "truly tragic joy."[17] But he differs from Brecht in that his ideological position is not tied to the materialist world. For him, the world of "reality" matters not "in vacuo" but because of its connection to a transcendent metaphysical "reality." Philosophically, then, Brecht's works of skeptical rationalism are remote from the metafiction informed by Walcott's faith; but both, as artists and socialists, use a similar practice in devising theater pieces that will, they hope, help to transform the world.

Brecht's lasting importance, according to Wright, derives from his diversification of theatrical language, using folk forms and language to dialectical ends: he "de-literalized the language of the stage, drawing upon the dialects of his own region in order to create a new language of the theatre that was neither purely regional nor purely classical."[18] The terms could be applied to Walcott's forging of a new language for Caribbean theater, which draws on the Creole continuum as well as on the whole literary tradition in English. His signal contribution has been to explore ways in which textuality can deliver simultaneously in the theater both the accessibility of informal language and the depth of poetry.

The founding of a theater is an act not only of great vision but of great willpower. As children, Derek and his twin brother, Roderick, had, like most children, been play-makers; as adults both became dramatists.[19] In a very small island, with a tiny, fragmented community and little access to formal theater, it would be difficult to overestimate the originality of such choices. What formal theater there was in the region was dominated by the Western tradition, with an indigenous regional theater barely budding. In the 1930s and 1940s, Marcus Garvey, C. L. R. James, and Roger Mais, among others, had initiated local drama with an ideological objective, as part of the anticolonial movement, but to two boys growing up in St. Lucia in the 1930s and 1940s, these must have seemed remote, with films (mainly American) providing their only regular exposure to formal drama. But by 1994, according to Errol Hill, Derek had written thirty-eight dramas, Roderick twenty-six, with both of them writing musicals and screenplays alongside their stage plays.[20] Walcott, looking back from middle age, has written, "When one began twenty years ago it was in the faith that one was creating not merely a play, but a theatre, and not merely a theatre, but its environment."[21] The dream was that the theater was to build the society it would serve and which would sustain it.

The lead from the older generation had been crucial. The boys' mother, Alix Walcott, was a keen amateur actor who recited Shakespeare about the house.[22] The family's commitment to art had been beleaguered from the start, because it had to be asserted defensively against the island's disapproving Catholic majority:

> My mother's friends, those who had survived my father, had been members of an amateur dramatic group, some cultural club which had performed Shakespeare and given musical concerts, when my father was their "moving spirit." ... Their existence, since most of them were from a religious minority, Anglican, Methodist, or lapsed Catholic, had a defensive, doomed frailty in that steamy, narrow-minded climate. Perhaps because of this they believed in "the better things of life" with a defiant intensity, which drew them closely together. Their efforts, since the pattern would be repeated for my brother and me, must have been secretly victimized.[23]

Where the lead of the parental generation is often resisted in the antiauthoritarian phase of adolescence, the boys were able to follow in their seniors' theatrical footsteps perhaps partly because these were already in an antiauthoritarian mode. Both twins went on to find themselves with early plays, selected to represent St. Lucia in the 1958 festivities for federation, banned by the Catholic Church: Derek's *The Sea at Dauphin* was considered antireligious, and Roderick's *Banjo Man* immoral. As a result, the St. Lucia Arts Guild withdrew from the festival, although Derek's play *Drums and Colours* became its centerpiece.[24]

But more importantly, as well as being surrounded by a small group of educated people committed to active drama and knowledgeable about world theater, the boys identified with the island majority, who in their daily lives engaged in informal drama, in their storytelling, their entertainments, and their community rituals: "being poor," said Walcott, "we already had the theatre of our lives."[25] A band of evangelists surrounded on a street corner were "the shadows of his first theatre," as was the Christmas masquerade of the devil and his imps who "would perform an elaborate Black Mass of resurrection at the street corners."[26] This is where Brecht said his theater was to begin: "The epic theatre wants to establish its basic model at the street corner, i.e. to return to the very simplest 'natural' theatre, a social enterprise whose origins, means and ends are practical and earthly"; but that street life in Walcott's experience was from the outset not just earthly but myth-inflected, bound up with his community's expression of spirituality, as his choice of examples demonstrates.[27]

St. Lucians lived a theatrical life, with "everything performed in public": "The theatre was about us, in the streets, at lampfall in the kitchen doorway, but nothing was solemnised into cultural significance."[28] Walcott has described it as a "simple schizophrenic boyhood" with its two lives, "the interior life of poetry, the outward life of action and dialect."[29] What the oral tradition offered was the example of spontaneous creativity to set against the literary tradition's notion of text. Narration exhibited a primary formalism, a primary theatricality:

> Best of all, in the lamplit doorway at the creaking hour, the stories sung by old Sidone, a strange croaking of Christian and African songs. The songs, mainly about lost children, were sung in a terrible whine. They sang of children lost in the middle of a forest, where the leaves' ears pricked at the rustling of devils, and one did not know whether to weep for the first two brothers of every legend, one strong, the other foolish. All these sank like a stain. And taught us symmetry. The true folk tale concealed a structure as universal as the skeleton, the one armature from Br'er Anancy to King Lear. It kept the same digital rhythm of three movements, three acts, three moral revelations, whether it was the tale of three sons or of three bears, whether it ended in tragedy or happily ever after. It had sprung from hearthside or

lamplit hut door in an age when the night outside was a force, inimical, infested with devils, wood demons, a country for the journey of the soul, and any child who has heard its symmetry chanted would want to retell it when he was his own storyteller, with the same respect for its shape. The apparent conservatism of West Indian fiction, whether in fiction or in theatre, is not an imitative respect for moulds but a memory of that form.[30]

To a young dramatist with "a mind drenched in Elizabethan literature," to whom "the Jacobean style, its cynical, aristocratic flourish came naturally," the long-refined graces of the oral tradition with its simple, effective formalism offered a vital example.[31]

Fired by this twin heritage and the independence movement's politics, the young Derek Walcott saw the need for founding a local theater—first island-based and then regional—and from the outset conceived of his own role not only as a poet but as an initiator of drama. In 1950, he and his brother established the St. Lucia Arts Guild, which performed both canonical plays of world theater and new local drama by themselves and others. Derek was active with the undergraduate drama group while at Mona, the Jamaica campus of the then University College of the West Indies,[32] and in 1959 he founded the Trinidad Theatre Workshop, a group that met and rehearsed for seven years before making its first public performance.[33] Walcott remained dedicated to this group for twenty years. It was only after a personal crisis that he decided to make the move that most contemporaries with literary ambitions had made years before, the migration to a northern metropolis. After settling in Boston, he continued to involve himself regularly with playmaking, not only as a dramatist but as a director, both in America (for *The Ghost Dance*, for instance) and in the Caribbean, and he has made an occasional foray elsewhere to assist in the rehearsal of his work, for instance, residing at Stratford-on-Avon while *The Odyssey* was in rehearsal.

His life as a man of the theater has thus been central to his aesthetic project. Although it has rarely been his only activity (he has continually written nondramatic poetry and necessarily been involved in other activities such as his journalism for the *Trinidad Guardian* to support his family), it has been a crucial determinant on where the middle decades of his life were lived, and it came to represent a symbolic choice. Walcott's name became a byword among Caribbean artists for the possibility of remaining at home and becoming an artist. He was the living proof that to stay in the region did not have to mean sacrificing the chance of a wider reputation—although at the time there must often have been doubts as to whether, if he had gone to London or stayed in New York in the 1950s, his worldwide reputation might not have got under way earlier. He was ambitious, but from the beginning he was clear that his primary ambition was to create for the Caribbean. What he secured for himself by staying there was the continual renewal of his aesthetic commitment to the region, and to his epic project to create an art worthy of it. His sustained involvement in theater was vital to his staying in touch with the community at large; it prevented him from becoming a remote and mannered poet. He came to see the pathos of actors of his company who strove for what they called "better speech when theirs had vigour that was going out of English."[34]

Drama was central to Walcott's idea of a Caribbean aesthetic for several reasons. First, where written poetry required not only literacy but literary awareness and was an art that few would appreciate, drama could appeal to all the people regardless of educational opportunities, excluding no one. It could be a genuinely popular art form, which poetry in print would never be. The immediacy of shared performance—the orality of the language, the scope for sound of other kinds, particularly song, and the expressive potential of the visual element, via the human figure as actor, dancer, and musician in the milieu of setting and lighting—attracted Walcott as idealist and visual artist as well as wordsmith. The scenic design invited a dramatist with a highly developed visual sense to conceive of the staging as a vital signifier, intrinsic to the action. It lent itself naturally to symbolic expression. The text came into being with its role as visual sign part of the conception, not applied later by a design team, as in so much metropolitan theater. In addition, the cooperation of the performers and their presentation to a responding audience in the shared space of performance (whether in the open air or an enclosed space) offered a model of community, the kind of community which art itself could help to build. Even the creation of the drama's backbone, the text, participated in this collectivity, as the company of players developed the playwright's initial draft with him in rehearsal. The theater offered the experience of a shared (and radically unclosed) art, unparalleled in any other art form; only the theater united all the arts in a collectively produced display. It was also local and particular, made for the home community in a sense that the poetry was not. The poetry was an outreach art, a means of communicating first with the Caribbean community, isolated across the region, but also potentially with a worldwide readership, wherever English was understood, but the drama was conceived essentially for the Caribbean, couched in a verbal, visual, and symbolic language directed primarily to the insider.

This drama was to be epic in two senses. First, it was, in the Brechtian sense, to use nonmimetic methods to raise political awareness. Secondly, it was to perform the social role of epic poetry. The events of a cruel history and the discourse of imperialism had conspired to produce a people with low self-esteem and little regard for either their individual or collective identity; the task for the new art was to remedy that lack. As Walcott wrote: "Colonials, we began with this malarial enervation: that nothing could ever be built among these rotting shacks, barefooted back yards and moulting shingles; that being poor, we already had the theatre of our lives.... If there was nothing, there was everything to be made. With this prodigious ambition one began."[35] Epic poetry had been the worldwide form through which a people sustained a sense of their identity, but in the absence of a continuing ancient tradition of oral poetic performance, drama was the most crucial art form precisely because of its popular appeal. Walcott's focus, in his Nobel lecture, on the *Ramleela*—doubly epic as "the epic dramatization of the Hindu epic the *Ramayana*"[36]—draws the world's attention to a miraculous cultural survival from India to Trinidad of a community ritual, creolized and vigorous in its new location: "The performance was like a dialect, a branch of its original language, an abridgement of it, but not a distortion or even a reduction of its epic scale. Here in Trinidad I had discovered that one of the greatest epics of the world was seasonally performed, not with that desperate resignation of preserving a culture, but with an openness of belief that was as steady as the wind bending the cane lances of the Caroni plain."[37] It was a case not for nostalgia or elegy but for "celebrations of a real presence."[38] Walcott intends irony, of course, in his use of the phrase "I had discovered ..."; discovery in the "New" World is an indication of prior ignorance rather than of innovation. The *Ramleela* had always been there, since the East Indians had come to Trinidad, just as the Americas were there before Columbus. He develops the irony: "I had recently adapted the *Odyssey* for a theatre in England, presuming that the audience knew the trials of Odysseus, hero of another, Asia Minor epic, while nobody in Trinidad knew any more than I did about Rama, Kali, Shiva, Vishnu, apart from the Indians, a phrase I use pervertedly because that is the kind of remark you can still hear in Trinidad: 'apart from the Indians.'"[39] It is a judicious reminder that the Western literary tradition has its roots in just such orally transmitted folk rituals and that the "European" tradition should be traced beyond Europe, to Asia. It is also a tart reminder that marginalization of one group by another is not confined to the old dominant cultures. What it shows above all is that the Antillean culture of today is a composite of anciently diverging cultures coming together once more.

There were other folk forms on which to draw. The folktales about Ti-Jean, which are part of the eastern Caribbean patois heritage, are adapted to the stage in Walcott's early play, *Ti-Jean and His Brothers*. His brother Roderick has used the St. Lucian festivals of the Rose and Marguerite rival groups in his drama.[40] The Trinidadian carnival is another public theatrical ritual that Derek Walcott has used on stage, but for him it is problematized by commercialization and state exploitation, resulting in commodification and debasement. In his intention as dramatist and director to "transform the theatrical into theatre,"[41] carnival is the prime example of Caribbean society's theatricality and has been accepted by many artists as the starting point for indigenous drama, but Walcott pinpoints carnival as a symbol of the rule of illusion that the Brechtian artist aims to destroy: "this was a society fed on an hysterical hallucination, that believed only the elaborate frenzy now controlled by the state. But Carnival was as meaningless as the art of the actor confined to mimicry."[42] He identifies the consequences for their theater: "as their society avoids truths, as their Carnival is a noise that fears everything, too many of the actors avoid the anguish of self-creation."[43]

As the basic figure for his study of Caribbean drama, Kole Omotoso juxtaposes Walcott's strictures about carnival with Errol Hill's claim that carnival offers the basis of a national theater, although with the disclaimer, "The history of Caribbean drama and theatre, and consequently its future, cannot be predicated on the opposite views of Errol Hill and Derek Walcott."[44] He contextualizes Hill's claim in relation to Eric Williams's rise to power in Trinidad and sets Walcott's remarks on carnival against the background of the then new phenomenon of ministers of culture supporting, the "folk" arts (seen as entertainment) to the exclusion of the "serious" arts (such as Walcott's theater). He not only suggests that Walcott's position set out in the essay is a "bitter poetic lamentation" at the lack of official support—which is to reduce a serious discussion to a materialist level—he misrepresents Walcott's position as positing "the Caribbean-colonial condition which underlines its incapacity to create anything for itself."[45] Walcott in fact quotes the now notorious passage from Froude, which claims of the West Indies that there are "no people there in the true sense of the word, with a character and purpose of their own," in order to demonstrate the cultural hegemony of imperialism, which can shake the confidence of those trying to be the region's artists.[46] Caricaturing Walcott's argument, Omotoso concludes that it is "an extreme position which cannot be validated without doing grave injustice to the oral history of the Caribbean" and goes on to characterize Walcott's Trinidad Theatre Workshop as a "failure, in spite of what looks like a heroic effort," because it was "transplanting theatre as it was understood in the West into the Caribbean" and "ignores some important aspects of the expression of the play-consciousness of the Caribbean."[47] Hill's position is clear and straightforward and is well understood; Walcott's is complex, though not inconsistent, and is often misrepresented, though not often as seriously as here.

His remarks in "What the Twilight Says," far from being a repudiation of folk culture, come out of a lifelong commitment to its value. It is the appropriation by government of folk culture and its commercialization in the name of tourist attraction that Walcott so strenuously opposes; what then passes for folk culture he sees as essentially folk culture traduced. He addresses himself in a kind of meditation:

> You despise the banal vigour of a future, where the folk art, the language, the music, like the economy, will accommodate itself to the center of power, which is foreign, where people will simplify themselves to be clear, to be immediately apprehensible to the transient. The lean, sinewy strength of the folk dance has been fattened and sucked into the limbo of the nightclub, the hotel cabaret, and all the other prostitutions of a tourist culture: before you is the vision of a hundred Havanas and mini-Miamis, and who dares tell their Tourism Boards and Cultural Development Committees that the blacks in bondage at least had the resilience of their dignity, a knowledge of their degradation, while their descendants have gone both flaccid and colourful, covering their suffering with artificial rage or commercial elation?[48]

His grief for the lost integrity of the folk forms drives the attack: "Their commercialization is now beyond anger, for they have become part of the climate, the art of the brochure."[49] The hypocrisy of intellectuals who now "found values in [carnival] that they had formerly despised" and "apotheosised the folk form, insisting that calypsos were poems," is attacked for the dishonesty of the position espoused, not because the position itself is untenable. The "[W]itch doctors of the new left with imported totems" are opportunists, anathema to one who has a long track record in building art out of folk forms.[50]

Walcott's use of the term "hallucination" is part of a chain of recurrence designed to dominate the essay. "Hallucination" describes a way not only of seeing but of experiencing the world: it is a trope of transformation, but negatively coded, the "reality" that we infer from it, as its opposite, being presumed preferable. It is a dangerous illusion of the kind

Brecht set out to destroy, bearing a complex relation to imagination and to art, as in Walcott's opening exploration of the twilight-transformed ghetto as "the gilded hallucinations of poverty ... as if ... poverty were not a condition but an art. Deprivation is made lyrical, and twilight, with the patience of alchemy, almost transmutes despair into virtue."[51] In such a context, the attack on carnival comes to seem very different from the polar opposite of Hill's faith in it. Motivated by a belief very close to Hill's, Walcott is in fact protesting against the appropriation of the folk forms to support the new hegemonies, as he makes clear:

> In these new nations art is a luxury, and the theatre the most superfluous of amenities. Every state sees its image in those forms which have the mass appeal of sport, seasonal and amateurish. Stamped on that image is the old colonial grimace of the laughing nigger, steel-bandsman, carnival masker, calypsonian, and limbo dancer. These popular artists are trapped in the state's concept of the folk form, for they preserve the colonial demeanour and threaten nothing. The folk arts have become the symbol of a carefree, accommodating culture, an adjunct to tourism, since the state is impatient with anything which it cannot trade.[52]

Walcott saw that what was needed was a revolutionary art, not one that perpetuated the old illusions. If folk forms were used to prop up the colonial subservience, they had failed. If they were to meet Brecht's criteria, they must be used in ways that recovered their original energy. In using carnival in *Drums and Colours* and *The Last Carnival*, and in using the characters and forms of the folktale in *Ti-Jean and His Brothers*, Walcott was not using the folk arts for bourgeois ends; on the contrary, he was entering into their essence in order to make them signify as new.

With such folk elements, epic drama could also establish a popular mythology and could reconnect the people to self-knowledge and to pride by modeling history as not just a site of humiliation but as the locus of dignity, survival, and heroism. As John Berger observes, "A people or a class which is cut off from its own past is far less free to choose and to act as a people or class than one that has been able to situate itself in history."[53] But as Walcott saw it, for Caribbean people the past was a double-edged sword that could wound in unexpected ways and had to be handled with care.

Walcott's first choice of a subject for historical drama, suggested to him by his brother, was *Henri Christophe*,[54] written in 1949, which drew on the story of heroic revolution in the francophone Caribbean—which was in a sense his history directly as a St. Lucian—and which the Marxist writer and philosopher C. L. R. James had introduced as drama to the region. His choice also indicated a vision of a regional identity that embraced the whole geographical area, extending across linguistic and political boundaries. It signaled that the symbolic moments of the region's history belonged to all of its inhabitants, regardless of their ethnic, cultural, or political identity. Also, by focusing on the region's direct legacy of the French Revolution, Walcott was in a sense sidestepping British rule, at that date still firmly entrenched in his homeland, thus subtly marginalizing the British history in the region, although of course his use of English as his artistic vehicle was an acknowledgment of that history. France, however, was not his topic; his subject was the heroic antislavery revolution of Haiti that resulted in the Americas' first republic. He has described how at the age of nineteen he was "drawn ... to the Manichean conflicts of Haiti's history" out of a sense of identification and envy from his prerevolutionary St. Lucia: "The parallels were there in my own island, but not the heroes: a black French island somnolent in its Catholicism and black magic, blind faith and blinder overbreeding, a society which triangulated itself medievally into land baron, serf, and cleric, with a vapid, high-brown bourgeoisie."[55] The heroes were tragic figures to him then, in the mold of Webster's heroes with their magnificent decadence. Dessalines and Christophe were "men who had structured their own despair": "Their tragic bulk was massive as a citadel at twilight. They were our only noble ruins." They enacted a revolution against the plantocracy which was like a heresy, contaminated with the sin of pride. In a crucial parallelism, the forty-year-old Walcott describes himself as a young poet matching two tropes of power, secular and divine:

> He believed then that the moral of tragedy could only be Christian, that their fate was the debt exacted by the sin of pride, that they were punished by a white God as masters punished servants for presumption. He saw history as hierarchy, and to him these heroes, despite their meteoric passages, were damned to the old darkness because they had challenged an ordered universe.... Those first heroes of the Haitian Revolution, to me, their tragedy lay in their blackness.... Now one may see such heroes as squalid fascists who chained their own people, but they had size, mania, the fire of great heretics.[56]

If they failed, because of divine intervention to destroy their presumption, as he saw it then, they were heroes, though tragic ones. The later gloss on their fascism—"the corruption of slaves into tyrants"—was not how the nineteen-year-old saw it: if they had defied the old order, they deserved his admiration. His was a revolutionary desire; by modeling in his play the heroism of the Haitian Jacobins, to use James's term, he hoped to stir his own somnolent people to similar vision and courage. He tells how he apprenticed himself to the contemporary revolutionaries of French Caribbean origin: "the young Frantz Fanon and the already ripe and bitter Césaire were manufacturing the homemade bombs of their prose poems, their drafts for revolution."[57] But they were both "blacker" and "poorer," and he envied the clarity of their position, seeing his own as complicated, even compromised, by a bourgeois and mixed-race heritage. *Henri Christophe* was an important play, for Walcott and for the Caribbean. With its high style, its blank verse, and its history-given tragic closure, it demonstrated that the region's history could provide the theater with subjects of a high seriousness, a grandeur that was unfamiliar. The fact that the heroes in question were slaves who became statesmen meant that they subverted the usual (Aristotelian) notion of the "great" man as the focus for tragedy. Walcott chooses to quote from his play in the later essay; the passage he selects is that in which Christophe answers the Archbishop's imputation of his guilt before God with a statement of pride, ending: "I am proud, I have worked and grown / This country to its stature, tell Him that."[58] The evident admiration for the courage of the defier of authority is fundamentally metaphysical. As he says, "The theme has remained: one race's quarrel with another's God." Christophe's surviving citadel clinches it with a symbol: "a monument to egomania, more than a strategic castle; an effort to reach God's height. It was the summit of the slave's emergence from bondage. Even if the slave had surrendered one Egyptian darkness for another, that darkness was his will, that structure an image of the inaccessible achieved. To put it plainer, it was something we could look up to. It was all we had."[59] Christophe's moral stature is like that of Faust, or Milton's Satan. Although the Walcott of 1970 distances himself from the revolutionary power of the vision, it remains with him as the core epic struggle, of man against God, which, for Walcott, courts atheism but always returns to faith. Christophe prefigures a range of antiauthoritarian heroes in his plays, heretical challengers, culminating in Odysseus.

The Haitian Revolution was revisited by Walcott in his play for the inauguration of the West Indies Federation in 1958, *Drums and Colours*. It was, according to Omotoso, a "major achievement" particularly "given the time it was written": "The scope and leadership which this epic gives to the direction of West Indian theatre has not been equalled by another historical play from the West Indies."[60] Although written in the early 1980s, the substance of the claim is still valid. This was a play with a given historical program, commissioned to represent the region's past. Gordon K. Lewis has identified the peculiar difficulty of this: "There is no first principle of reference, no great martyrology to inspire the new generations. When therefore the West Indian playwright is asked, as in the Federal Festival of 1958, to produce a pageant-play on the region's history he has no one great single event, like the Haitian war of liberation or the Cuban Ten Years War, to use as the central *motif* of his production."[61] That the region should be characterized by an absence of martyrs may seem a particularly tragic irony, given its history, and Lewis's comment indicates another obtuseness that Walcott's solution to the "problem" shows up. Why, after all, desire to represent four hundred years of history by a monolithic image? Although the federation was made up of former British colonies only, Walcott declined the narrow political definition of the region and its history (always geographically absurd) by including the Spanish and French empires as well. This play has an obviously epic scope (in the conventional sense), broader than that of *Henri Christophe*, its approach to history not nostalgic but representing the past for the sake of the future. In John Berger's phrase, the past "is not for living in; it is a well of conclusions from which to draw in order to act."[62] The play was clearly motivated by an ideology of racial and cultural pluralism, and by egalitarianism: at the originary moment of the new community symbolized by federation, art, it promised, could help to bring about the transformed society. This was a Brechtian position. Brecht's project is "to provoke the audience to want to change the social reality that goes on producing distorted objects, including persons," according to Wright: "For Brecht knowledge is that which results in a process of continual transformation of the world as we know it."[63] Walcott proceeds by selecting examples from history that hold up to the light the dystopian image of the world as it has been. The drama follows the Brechtian epic principle by demystifying the exploitative social relations of the past, determined by imperialism, but it also models the kind of egalitarian pluralism that a collective society can deliver. In a development of Brecht typical of Walcott, it also flirts with a comedic utopianism, offering an image of the desired world in the hope that life, on the mimetic principle, may eventually mirror the aesthetically represented ideal.

Epic's need for heroes would seem to be at odds with egalitarianism. The Western epic with its roll-call of "great" men has been deeply implicated in art's co-option to the perpetuation of oppression; one might ask, for example, whether the notion of revolutionary heroes is incompatible with egalitarian objectives. After citing Froude's assertion that "[t]here has been no saint in the West Indies since Las Casas, no hero unless philo-Negro enthusiasm can make one out of Toussaint," Walcott writes of his own generation's experience of the revision of history: "My generation since its colonial childhood had no true pride but awe. We had not yet provided ourselves with heroes, and when the older heroes went out of fashion, or were stripped, few of us had any choice but to withdraw into a cave where we could scorn those who struggled in the heat ... [I]t is this fever for heroic examples that can produce the glorification of revenge. Yet revenge is a kind of vision."[64] Walcott mentions his play *Henri Christophe* in "What the Twilight Says" but not the play that most tested his and the region's ability to provide historic examples of the hero, *Drums and Colours*. *Drums and Colours* focuses on four protagonists who were prime movers in history; two were the heroes of imperialism and are shown in decline, and two were martyrs to the anti-imperial struggle: one seeing the integrity of the cause destroyed by the instinct for revenge, the other making the nonviolent stand of heroic self-sacrifice. Alongside these historic heroes, the play reflects Walcott's lifelong preoccupation with other kinds of hero. His particular contribution to epic has been the exploration of the Everyman hero, a plebeian who is a kind of antihero in that he models an anarchic, antiauthoritarian stance.

Walcott's initial position is an anti-imperialist stance, which he explores in anticapitalist and antiwar terms in accordance with Marxist thinking. But in that a Marxist ideology has been claimed by regimes just as authoritarian and repressive as those of Western capitalist imperialism, Walcott's position is also interrogative of such abuses. Hegemony of the right or the left is challenged in the name of the individual—the ethical test always comes down to what one individual does to another as manifest of a system—but what might seem a very American focus on individualism is tempered by a very Caribbean sense of community. In aesthetic terms, this moves the focus away from a single protagonist, the hero, toward the group. Here the drama leads the poetry; long before he defined the group focus of *Omeros*, for example, or even the "alphabet of the emaciated" in *Another Life*, Walcott created the multicultural group of interventionist carnival maskers, symbolizing the ordinary people of the Caribbean, who preside over *Drums and Colours*. Later plays, such as *The Last Carnival* and *The Ghost Dance*, avoid giving prominence to a single hero but explore the interwoven stories of a number of individuals. There is a focus on ordinary people's relations with the "great" events recorded in the history books and an awareness of the small-scale situations in which political decisions are commonly executed. Power is shown in its effects on the people, the anonymous ones exposed to the world's gaze by their re-creation in the drama. The stoicism, and faith in goodness, of the sufferer becomes a heroic subject. As noted, in *Dream on Monkey Mountain* the history of racist contempt that lies behind the naming of Makak (macaque) of "Monkey" mountain is turned back on itself, as the scorned "Nobody," the old, poor charcoal-burner, rediscovers his real name, Felix Hobain ("Felix" meaning "happy"). The trickster-hero, surviving by his wits and his compassion, whether Anansi or Ulysses, is a recurrent figure in the plays, long before Walcott's dramatization of the *Odyssey* itself. Odysseus founds the reversal of negative identity: by naming himself to the Cyclops as "Nobody," he secures his heroic survival and return to his own.

As well as pioneering the revisioning of a tragic history as heroic, and the presentation of the "little man" as revolutionary emblem of the collective egalitarian experience, Walcott has also initiated another approach to epic with his focus on the artist. In "What the Twilight Says," he models the artist as hero, writing of his company of actors as "heroes ... because they have kept the sacred urge of actors everywhere: to record the anguish of the race."[65] He also projects himself as a heroic figure, as one of the company of artists who began as "new Adams" and,[66] with irony, as a sacrificial, godlike figure, one of the "self-appointed schizoid saints," confessing, in 1970, to having been guilty of an "egotism which can pass for genius."[67] Although the self-projection of the creator in the work can serve Brecht's purpose of reminding the audience of the fictionality of the representation, Walcott's preoccupation with the artist as figure is Romantic as well as Brechtian. In fact, the artist as fictional persona participates equally powerfully in both dimensions, the individual and the collective, drawing on the inner self for his art but doing so for the sake of and with the help of the community, the "I-an-I" group. In the drama, the representation of the artist as persona in a shared performance gives trenchant symbolic meaning to this Janus-like role. In *The Last Carnival*, for example, Victor (named significantly to indicate the power of art, the "fountain" of his surname) is the artist as inspired solitary— in the post-Romantic Western tradition—but his art is developing toward community, as in his tableau for carnival, while the son who succeeds him dedicates himself to the collective art of carnival design, creolizing the family tradition.

As the artist exemplifies the way in which the individual and the community in an ideal society can unite, so sexual love demonstrates in a different dimension how two can be one. The creative encounter of difference is at the root of creolization, both in Caribbean art and personal relationships. In his concern to hold up the hope of the "republic of love"[68] (which is essentially egalitarian, available to all), Walcott tends to incorporate in his dramas a narrative element of sexual romance that may seem populist in a rather naive way if its symbolic function is not appreciated. The appeal of the Don Juan myth to Walcott is that it embodies just that hope, as his play adapting Tirso de Molina, *The Joker of Seville*, demonstrates. The epic poems of the Renaissance, by Tasso or Spenser or Ariosto, led by Dante, use earthly love as a figure of its divine equivalent, in accordance with Christian Platonic thought. For Walcott, too, sexual love is an epic subject that can serve as metaphysical allegory.

Both art and sexuality are transformative. They represent a creative response to the world and can deliver the magic of metamorphosis, capable of reinventing as positive that which appeared locked in to a tragic negative. As already noted, the tone of epic is usually composed of a blend of the tragic and the comic. (Brecht's revision of the genres is something rather different.) Traditional epic often sets up an "eros"/"thanatos" opposition—love, symbolizing the comedic, against war, symbolizing the tragic. Heroism can be shown in either field. Walcott's epic work tends toward open-ended closures, in *The Last Carnival*, for example. *The Ghost Dance* has an apparently tragic ending of a Brechtian ambivalence. A festive play such as *Drums and Colours* weaves comedy and tragedy in a tense web, conjuring an upbeat ending, yet the late plays of Shakespeare that evince a similar pattern are known as his "romances," in a literary discourse in which "romance" has come to be used faintly pejoratively. Since "romance" in this context is applied to comedy, and since it is normally characterized as in opposition to realism, this would seem to associate tragedy with mimesis. A complex question of philosophy underlies the distinction. Walcott, writing from within a mythic tradition—that of redemption—which is essentially comedic, is challenging, by his art, the modern Western rationalist skepticism, which is characterized by a nihilistic perception of the human condition, finding its artistic manifestation in tragedy. Several of his plays present a mythic action, of apparent death followed by a return to life. In such refusals of tragic closure, Walcott is most conspicuously at odds with mainstream metropolitan tradition. This is culturally derived; it is in the name of his people's habit of faith that he addresses any audiences who wish to hear. Even the terrible history of the Native Americans as narrated in *The Ghost Dance* is placed in a strongly positive context.

This metaphysical optimism, unfamiliar as it is in "serious" metropolitan drama, can be an obstacle to the appreciation of his plays by northern audiences. In the Caribbean, ironically, the pattern is reversed: many of the plays have tended not, after all, to reach a broad popular audience because of their high seriousness. In response, Walcott has sought to avoid the high-brow label by populist devices, sometimes risking the integrity of his piece by his concern for its entertainment value. As a result, some of his least Brechtian plays have been some of the weakest. Yet there is a growing list of popular successes, not least—surprisingly perhaps, given the modern disregard for the classics—The Odyssey. Also, although most of the plays were devised with a Caribbean audience in mind, they increasingly find international audiences. Some originally staged in the Caribbean are being performed not only in diverse anglophone communities but also in places such as Sweden and Italy.[69]

It may be that epic is most popular when closest to romance, as the success of The Odyssey may indicate, both as Homer's poem and as Walcott's play. Although superficially one of his least Brechtian plays, it is actually a skillful politicization of the mythic story. Brecht might have been surprised at the part Walcott has made myth play in his dialectical theater. Some of his most memorable gests (the Brechtian term) are those which signify mythically. Also, to the three levels of language that Brecht identifies—"plain speech, heightened speech and singing"[70]—Walcott adds from the inception of each drama as text a concept of visual representation, reciprocal to the verbal sign, and commonly symbolic in function. The dramatist who is also a painter has this advantage, but both Brecht and Walcott bring their experience as poets to their theatrical writing. Brecht, after listing six of his own plays as involving the "application of music to the epic theatre," said, "music made possible something which we had long since ceased to take for granted, namely the 'poetic theatre.'"[71] Walcott has from the beginning regularly used music and song in his plays and has written a number of musicals. He has also made prominent calls for the restoration of poetry to the theater. His own practice, which began with quasi-Jacobean verse, has moved on to combine the fluidity of colloquial speech with profound poetry often of an inspired simplicity, in a way that has become the hallmark of his epic theater. It is particularly Walcott's use of poetry in the theater that carries the dramatic experience over into widely different cultural milieux.

Brecht found the audience of his time frustrating, saying it "hangs its brains up in the cloakroom along with its coat,"[72] but while Walcott may be disappointed at the lack of response, to date, to much of his dramatic work, he would probably not be much concerned, unlike Brecht, at audiences being unaware of his political subtleties, confident that, if anything, in performance (and securing that objective is the first hurdle) the language and the mythic patterns work their "magic" directly on the unconscious.

NOTES

1. Rees, ed., *Dictionary of Modern Quotations*, 351.

2. Willett dates Brecht's first use of the term in print to May 1927 and cites a contemporary letter from Professor Fritz Steinberg: "It wasn't Marx who led you to speak of the decline of the drama and to talk of the epic theatre. It was you yourself. For, to put it gently, 'epic theatre'—that's you, Mr Brecht." Willett, ed., *Brecht on Theatre*, 22.

3. Brecht met Eisenstein on his visit to Berlin in 1929. Brecht's conception of the relation between early film and theater is instructive; in 1930 he wrote:

> It is conceivable that other kinds of writer, such as playwrights or novelists, may for the moment be able to work in a more cinematic way than the film people. Up to a point they depend less on means of production. But they still depend on the film, its progress or regress; and the film's means of production are wholly capitalist.... To the playwright what is interesting is its attitude to the person performing the action. It gives life to its people, whom it classes purely according to function, simply using available types that occur in given situations and are able to adopt given attitudes in them. Character is never used as a source of motivation; these people's inner life is never the principal cause of the action and seldom its principal result; the individual is seen from outside. Literature needs the film not only indirectly but also directly. (Willett, ed., *Brecht on Theatre*, 48)

As for the question of the hero, Brecht identified Chaplin as "in many ways ... closer to the epic than the dramatic theatre's requirements" (Willett, 56). Brecht was well aware that its dependence on capital would tend to make film reproduce the worst aspects of the old theater of illusion; sound films, he said in 1935, were "one of the most blooming branches of the international narcotics traffic" (Willett, 90).

4. Marx was "the only spectator of my plays I'd ever come across. For a man with interests like his must of necessity be interested in my plays, not because they are so intelligent but because he is—they are something for him to think about" (Willett, 23–24).

5. Willett, ed., *Brecht on Theatre*, 21, 24.

6. "Schwierigkeiten des epischen Theaters," November 1927, Willett, ed., *Brecht on Theatre*, 23.

7. In 1952, Brecht reiterated the point: "It is not true, though it is sometimes suggested, that epic theatre ... proclaims the slogan: 'Reason this side, Emotion (feeling) that.' It by no means renounces emotion, least of all the sense of justice, the urge to freedom, and righteous anger." Willett, ed., *Brecht on Theatre*, 227.

8. Brecht uses the phrases specifically about his drama *Die Mutter*, but they are applicable to his ideas of epic theater in general. Willett, ed., *Brecht on Theatre*, 57.

9. Ibid., 79.

10. Brecht says *The Threepenny Opera* "is concerned with bourgeois conceptions not only in content, by representing them, but also through the manner in which it does so. It is a kind of report on life as any member of the audience would like to see it ... at the same time, however, he sees a good deal that he has no wish to sec." Willett, ed., *Brecht on Theatre*, 43.

11. Ibid., 44.

12. Wright, *Postmodern Brecht*, 31.

13. Ibid.

14. Ibid., 1.

15. Ibid., 50

16. Ibid.

17. Walcott, "What the Twilight Says," 22–23.

18. Wright, *Postmodern Brecht*, 3.

19. "He and his brother were already creating their own little theatre, 'little men' made from twigs enacting melodramas of hunting and escape, but of cowboys and gangsters, not of overseers and maroons." "What the Twilight Says," 20.

20. Banham, Hill, and Woodyard, *Cambridge Guide to African and Caribbean Theatre*, 181, 183.

21. Walcott, "What the Twilight Says," 6.

22. "Meanings," *Savacou* 2, 1970. When an interviewer described his mother as "walking round the house quoting *The Merchant of Venice*," Walcott interrupted: "Well, yeah, not quoting, standing up and doing it. Not walking around. She was performing, you know." Walcott, *Desert Island Discs*, BBC Radio 4, June 14, 1991.

23. Walcott, "Leaving School," 26.

24. Banham, Hill, and Woodyard, *Cambridge Guide to African and Caribbean Theatre*, 177.

25. Walcott, "What the Twilight Says," 4.

26. Ibid., 20.

27. Willett, ed., *Brecht on Theatre*, 126.

28. Walcott, "What the Twilight Says," 4, 7.

29. Ibid., 4.

30. Ibid., 21–22. The original edition has "if to weep," not "whether to weep."

31. Ibid., 11, 12.

32. Omotoso, *The Theatrical into Theatre*, 155.

33. Ibid., 159. For the history of Walcott's theatre, see Bruce King, *Derek Walcott and West Indian Drama*, and Judy Stone, *Theatre*.

34. Walcott, "What the Twilight Says," 32.

35. Ibid., 4.

36. Walcott, *Antilles*, 65.

37. Ibid., 68.

38. Ibid.

39. Ibid., 66.

40. Banham, Hill, and Woodyard, *Cambridge Guide to African and Caribbean Theatre*, 183.

41. Walcott, "What the Twilight Says," 30.

42. Ibid.

43. Ibid., 22.

44. Omotoso, *The Theatrical into Theatre*, 12.

45. Ibid., 51.

46. Walcott, "What the Twilight Says," 16–17.

47. Omotoso, *The Theatrical into Theatre*, 52.

48. Walcott, "What the Twilight Says," 23–24.

49. Ibid., 33.

50. Ibid., 30–31.

51. Ibid., 3–4.

52. Ibid., 7.

53. Berger, *Ways of Seeing*, 33.

54. Walcott, "Meanings," 45.

55. Walcott, "What the Twilight Says," 10–11.

56. Ibid., 11–12.

57. Ibid., 11.

58. Ibid., 12.

59. Ibid., 13.

60. Omotoso, *The Theatrical into Theatre*, 145.

61. Lewis, *The Growth of the Modern West Indies*, 393, cited in Omotoso *The Theatrical into Theatre*, 120.

62. Berger, *Ways of Seeing*, 11.

63. Wright, *Postmodern Brecht*, 24, 25.

64. Walcott, "What the Twilight Says," 17–18.

65. Ibid., 5.

66. Ibid., 6, 7.

67. Ibid., 28.

68. Walcott, "The Ghost Dance." Since the dramatic texts given detailed analysis in the remainder of this study are mainly unpublished, or drafts, revisions, or performance scripts of published texts, it seems less confusing if quotations are consistently *not* annotated. The main text indicates when a published version is under discussion.

69. Walcott's *The Last Carnival* was performed in Swedish in Stockholm in the autumn of 1992. *Ti-Jean and His Brothers* (as *Ti-Jean e i suoi Fratelli*) was staged for the Sixty-Seventh Theatre Festival of San Miniato, Pisa, in July 1993.

70. Willett, ed., *Brecht on Theatre*, 44.

71. Ibid., 84–85.

72. Ibid., 27.

JAHAN RAMAZANI

The Wound of Postcolonial History:
Derek Walcott's Omeros

From an early age Derek Walcott felt a special "intimacy with the Irish poets" as "colonials with the same kind of problems that existed in the Caribbean. They were the niggers of Britain."[1] Passionately identifying with Yeats, Joyce, Synge, and other Irish writers, Walcott shared especially in their conflicted response to the cultural inheritances of the British empire— its literature, religion, and language. At school, Walcott recalls, Joyce's Stephen Dedalus was his "hero": "Like him, I was a knot of paradoxes," among other things "learning to hate England as I worshipped her language."[2] His best known lyric, "A Far Cry from Africa" (1956), elaborates the poem of ambivalence toward imperial and anti-imperial bloodshed, building on Yeats's simultaneously anticolonial and anti-anti-colonial stance in works such as "Easter, 1916" and "Nineteen Hundred and Nineteen."[3] As Yeats used a series of counterbalanced questions to dramatize his inner divisions after the Easter Rising, Walcott forty years later responds to the Mau Mau rebellion with a spiral of questions that "turn" on each other with ever stronger torque:

> I who am poisoned with the blood of both,
> Where shall I turn, divided to the vein?
> I who have cursed

From *The Hybrid Muse: Postcolonial Poetry in English.* © 2001 by the University of Chicago.

The drunken officer of British rule, how choose
Between this Africa and the English tongue I love?
Betray them both, or give back what they give?
How can I face such slaughter and be cool?
How can I turn from Africa and live?

Another thirty-four years later, in his Caribbean epic, *Omeros* (1990), Walcott is still puzzling out what it means to love the English language yet hate English imperialism. As a character within his own narrative, Walcott travels to Ireland, literalizing his revisitation of Joyce and Yeats as precursors, and there—struck anew by the shared postcolonial problem of linguistic and literary inheritance—he memorably declares Ireland "a nation / split by a glottal scream."[4]

An epic divided to the vein, a poem split by a glottal scream, *Omeros* asks how the postcolonial poet can both grieve the agonizing harm of British colonialism and celebrate the empire's literary bequest. Walcott's pervasive figure of the wound can help us to understand his answer to this question, as the figurative site where concerns with imperial injury, literary archetype, and linguistic heritage most graphically intersect. "This wound I have Stitched into Plunkett's character," ventures the poet early in *Omeros*. Conflating wound and suture, Walcott suggests that the odd surgery of poetry may have to disfigure a character with wounds to repair historical injuries. "He has to be wounded," continues the poet defensively. Why must the poet stitch some kind of wound into all of his major characters, from Philoctete, the emblematic black descendant of slaves, to Plunkett, the representative white colonial; from the lovelorn Achille to Hector, Helen, even himself? Because, the poet explains, "affliction is one theme / of this work, this fiction," as indeed of Afro-Caribbean literature and much Third World literature in general (28). That the wound trope is central to *Omeros* suits preconceptions of postcolonial writing as either "victim's literature" or "resistance literature." But Walcott's use of the figure—for example, attaching it here to the white colonial Plunkett—frustrates the assumptions it elicits. Indeed, this seemingly unsurprising motif continually turns strange and unpredictable in Walcott's hands; this strangeness starts with his willingness to embrace the motif after having denounced the literature of Third World suffering for decades.

In examining Walcott's elaboration of the wound in *Omeros*, I trace the complex genealogy of its primary bearer, the black fisherman Philoctete. Appropriating the classical type of the wound-tormented Philoctetes paradoxically enables Walcott to give new voice to the suffering of Afro-

Caribbean peoples under European colonialism and slavery.[5] In this character, Walcott fuses still other literary prototypes of North and South, Old World and New. The astonishing hybridity of Walcott's black victim exemplifies the cross-cultural fabric of postcolonial poetry and contravenes the widespread assumption that postcolonial literature develops by sloughing off Eurocentrism for indigeneity. Repudiating a separatist aesthetic of affliction, Walcott turns the wound into a resonant site of interethnic connection within *Omeros*, vivifying the black Caribbean inheritance of colonial injury and at the same time deconstructing the uniqueness of suffering. Hybrid, polyvalent, and unpredictable in its knitting together of different histories of affliction, Walcott's radiant metaphor of the wound helps to dramatize poetry's promise as one of the richest and most vibrant genres of postcolonial writing.

Perhaps the most ambitious English-language poem of the decolonized Third World, Walcott's massive *Omeros* is written in long rolling lines—typically of twelve syllables—grouped in loose terza rima stanzas; alludes abundantly to Homer, Joyce, and Aimé Césaire; and ranges from precolonial Africa to eighteenth-century Saint Lucia, from the nineteenth-century United States to contemporary Ireland. Interwoven with its story of Philoctete's wound are plots of a Saint Lucian Achille and Hector struggling over a beautiful Helen, of an English Plunkett and Irish Maud seeking peace in the Caribbean, and of a composite poet—part Walcott, part blind pensioner—striving to tell the history of his island. Of Afro-Caribbean poems in English, only Kaman Brathwaite's *The Arrivants* (1967–69) is a work of comparable scope, size, and aspiration, Brathwaite's fragmentary trilogy also revisits the trauma of the Middle Passage and looks back to Africa, bases characters on inherited literary types and intermingles West Indian creole with literary English. But whereas an epic poem of Caribbean "wounds" or "hurts of history" might be expected of Brathwaite, professional historian and poet of New World African dispossession and survival, Walcott in the 1960s and 1970s declared his hostility to Afro-Caribbean literature about "the suffering of the victim."[6] While many Caribbean writers of this period chronicled the inherited devastation of European slavery and colonialism, Walcott, accusing Brathwaite among others of being absorbed in "self-pity," "rage," and "masochistic recollection," called instead for an artistic celebration of the Adamic potential of the New World African: perpetual exile was, in his view, the condition for a new creativity.[7]

In Walcott's poetry of this period, the wound or scar is often the figurative locus of such criticisms. Toward the end of his grand autobiographical poem *Another Life* (1973), Walcott blasts Caribbean artists for their "masochistic veneration of / chains," for revering "the festering roses made from their fathers' manacles.[8] He casts into the volcanic pit of his Antillean hell "the syntactical apologists of the Third World":

> Those who peel, from their own leprous flesh, their names,
> who chafe and nurture the scars of rusted chains,
> like primates favouring scabs, those who charge tickets
> for another free ride on the middle passage. . . .
> . . . .
> they measure each other's sores
> to boast who has suffered most,
> and their artists keep dying,
> they are the saints of self-torture,
> their stars are pimples of pus
> on the night of our grandfathers,
> they are hired like dogs to lick the sores of their people....[9]

Pitching his voice in a willfully intemperate tone, Walcott attributes the scars, scabs, and sores of his damned not only to slavery but to recent masochistic indulgences. Grimly yet gleefully analogizing, Walcott maps onto Africanist returns to the trauma of slavery the Dantean figuration of hell as compulsive repetition of the past.

But in writing an epic poem of his native Saint Lucia, Walcott takes up the postcolonial poetics of affliction he once condemned, anatomizing the wounded body of Caribbean history through Philoctete,[10] injured by a rusted anchor:

> He believed the swelling came from the chained ankles
> of his grandfathers. Or else why was there no cure?
> That the cross he carried was not only the anchor's
>
> but that of his race, for a village black and poor
> as the pigs that rooted in its burning garbage,
> then were hooked on the anchors of the abattoir.
>   (19)

Walcott makes an oblique reference to colonialism, comparing the wound to the "puffed blister of Portuguese man-o'-war" (19); and he also evokes "a wounded race" (299) and "the tribal / sorrow that Philoctete could not drown in alcohol" (129). Even after he is supposedly healed, Philoctete joins Achille in a Boxing Day rite that, like the Caribbean limbo dance, recapitulates the trauma of the Middle Passage, including the primordial deracination that Philoctete reenacts when he slaughters the yams:

> All the pain
>
> re-entered Philoctete, of the hacked yams, the hold
> closing over their heads, the bolt-closing iron....
>   (277)

In using the wound motif to signify slavery and colonialism, *Omeros* resembles countless other texts of African diaspora literature, and the reason for this prominence and pervasiveness is far from obscure. As C. L. R. James recalls in his discussion of the vicious treatment of Caribbean slaves, wounds were inflicted in many gruesome ways, and even "salt, pepper, citron, cinders, aloes, and hot ashes were poured on the bleeding wounds."[11] Early on in *Omeros*, Walcott uses one of Philoctete's seizures to suggest that the inexpressible physical suffering of enslaved Africans is retained in the bodies of their descendants and that the pain still presses urgently for an impossible verbal release:

> His knee was radiant iron,
> his chest was a sack of ice, and behind the bars
>
> of his rusted teeth, like a mongoose in a cage,
> a scream was mad to come out; his tongue tickled its claws
> on the roof of his mouth, rattling its bars in rage.
>   (21)

Naming conditions of black enslavement with the words "iron," "bars," "rusted," and "cage," Walcott portrays the pain of the wound as colonizing Philoctete's entire body. More than any of Walcott's previous works, *Omeros* memorializes the institutionalized atrocity of New World African slavery. Though as late as the 1980s Walcott continued to castigate West Indian literature for sulking—"Look what the slave-owner did"[12]—at the beginning of *Omeros*, Philoctete rolls up his trouser leg and "shows" his punctured shin to paying tourists, figuring, by extension, the poem's large-scale exhibition of Afro-Caribbean pain to the touristic reader (4). And whereas Walcott once locked in hell "those who peel, from their own leprous flesh, their names,"

Philoctete refers to the colonially imposed name as one source of the ancestral wound:

> What did it mean,
>
> this name that felt like a fever? Well, one good heft
> of his garden-cutlass would slice the damned name clean
> from its rotting yam.
>   (20)

Nursed and inspected, magnified and proliferated, the metaphor of the wound forms the vivid nucleus of Walcott's magnum opus. In an interview, Walcott indicates that the figure was the germ of *Omeros*: "A very good friend of mine had died," he recounts, "an actor, and I was thinking about that. And where this poem started was with the figure of Philoctetes, the man with the wound, alone on the beach: Philoctetes from the Greek legend and Timon of Athens as well."[13] How can we reconcile Walcott's earlier and later positions? Part of the answer is that they are less antithetical than my juxtapositions make them appear to be. In spite of his pronouncements, Walcott was already mourning early on what he memorably called the "wound," the "deep, amnesiac blow" of slavery and colonialism.[14] He was deeply aware of the central trauma of Afro-Caribbean history and drawn to bodily figurations of it. Even so, he remained hesitant about fully sounding this theme before *Omeros*, so what made it possible for him to shift from one self-defined stance on the literature of Third World suffering to its apparent opposite? The classical figure of Philoctetes is an important part of the answer, the bridge by which Walcott crosses his own divide. His Afro-Greek Philoctete is a compromise formation, the venerable vehicle legitimizing the tenor of black rage and suffering. While still granting cultural authority to Europe, Walcott also reclaims it for Caribbean blacks more vigorously than before, tropicalizing and twisting an ancient Greek hero into a vibrant new figure for Afro-Caribbean pain. One of the oldest dead white European males is reborn in a wounded black body; a member of the colonizing tribe resigns his part to limp among the colonized.

Walcott's appropriation of the wounded Philoctete broadly resembles other well-known indigenizations of canonical Western characters. To dramatize Caribbean suffering and anticolonialism, Aimé Césaire remakes the doltish Caliban in his play *Une tempête*, Kamau Brathwaite the submissive Uncle Tom in *The Arrivants*, and Jean Rhys the raving Bertha Rochester in *Wide Sargasso Sea*. Racked by an unhealing wound, Philoctete's body literalizes the anguish and anger of his celebrated West Indian counterparts. Like these writers, Walcott poetically inverts the material transfers of colonization, abducting a major character from the Western canon to dramatize the legacy of the West's atrocities. Just as "empires are smart enough to steal from the people they conquer," Walcott has remarked, "the people who have been conquered should have enough sense to steal back."[15]

But whereas Césaire, Brathwaite, and Rhys appropriate characters already oppressed by virtue of their gender, class, or race, Walcott strangely blacks up the classical white male war hero responsible for victory in the Trojan War. Like Walcott's seemingly perverse use of Crusoe instead of Friday to personify the Caribbean condition, the metamorphosis of this wounded Greek castaway is more violent and tangled than that of Caliban, Tom, or Bertha—white to black, colonizer to colonized, classic to contemporary.[16] These dislocations are not merely subversive or "exotic" but emphatically defamiliarizing.[17] Keeping the ironies acute, Walcott presents his Philoctete as even less a self-standing character, even more a signifier of the work of postcolonial reinscription—a Mona Lisa with a distinctively Caribbean mustache.[18] With only minimal credibility as a naturalistic Caribbean fisherman, Walcott's Philoctete seems to have wandered out of Greek literature and stumbled into a textual universe where he suddenly embodies the colonial horrors perpetrated by the West. To highlight his reliance on a culture of slavery to indict the practice of slavery, Walcott pointedly refers to the institution as "Greek" (177) and ironically adduces "the Attic ideal of the first slave-settlement" (63), even as he turns a Greek hero into his synecdoche for all the damage wrought by slavery and colonialism. He repeatedly signals the seeming oddity of Philoctete's name in the Saint Lucian context (greater than that of the simpler Achille or Hector or Helen), as if to make of the name a foreign-language sign hung around his neck. "Pheeloh! Pheelosophee!" scream boys on their way to school (19), and sheep bleat "Beeeeeh, Philoctete!" (20); only at the moment of his apparent cure, "The yoke of the wrong name lifted from his shoulders" (247). Instead of naturalizing the name, Walcott turns it into a trope for violent colonial imposition, a partial cause of the wound to which it is metonymically linked.

Most familiar from Sophocles' eponymous play but also portrayed in countless other retellings from Homer to Seamus Heaney and in the visual arts from Attic vase painting to neoclassical sculpture, Philoctetes, with his exquisitely elaborated pain, has long served as the classical alternative to Christ in the Western iconography of pathos and innocent victimhood. Bitten by a venomous snake and abandoned on the isle of Lemnos by his

Greek compatriots, the groaning, shrieking Philoctetes languishes for nine years, his wound stinking, his body convulsed with pain, his flesh covered only with rags.[19] If Philoctetes enabled Lessing to affirm his neoclassical faith in the "moral greatness" of heroic endurance and helped Edmund Wilson to advance a psychological conception of artistic genius as "inextricably bound up" with "disability" and "disease," he becomes for Walcott, as for Heaney in *The Cure at Troy* (1991), an allegorical figure for the postcolonial condition.[20] As agent of Troy's defeat, Philoctetes might seem a dubious choice to represent the colonial victim, yet it is also true that the Greeks exploit him to conquer Troy, that he is transported to an island and abandoned there, and that he lives in poverty, hunger, and pain. Unintelligible stammerings—literally the discourse of the barbaric—interrupt his Greek when he suffers spasms of pain. And his wound suggests not only affliction but also colonial penetration, evacuation, and forgetting. Faithful to the classical Philoctetes in remembering his stinking wound, island fate, physical misery, and eventual cure, Walcott nevertheless transports him to a different archipelago, darkens his skin, trades his bow for a fisherman's net, transcribes his pained ejaculations in creole, and effects his cure through an obeah woman. While it might be a tempting, if pedantic, exercise to dissect each of these modifications, the risk would lie in trapping Walcott's Philoctete in an exclusive relation to his Greek namesake; but his affinities are more culturally polyphonous than such a narrowly typological analysis could allow.

Despite the apparently obvious line of descent signaled by his name, from Philoctetes to Philoctete, Walcott has spliced a variety of literary genes and even antithetical cultures to create a surprisingly motley character. Like a composite character in one of Freud's dreams, the wound-bearing Philoctete encompasses a strange array of penumbral literary figures. Rei Terada discerns the "variegated" and even "confusingly overdetermined" models behind characters in *Omeros*, but critics have tended to see Philoctete as a character with a simple pedigree.[21] If even the character in *Omeros* who appears to be simplest in his cultural inheritance turns out to have a multiple and contradictory parentage, then perhaps the postcolonial poet's seeming capitulation to or seeming subversion of Western influences needs to be rethought as a more ambiguous and ambivalent synthesis than is usually acknowledged.

Philoctete represents Walcott's absorption and refiguration not only of Philoctetes but also, strangely enough, of Caliban. Caliban? Doesn't Walcott scorn the postcolonial transvaluation of Caliban as West Indian hero? Doesn't this poet, who saw himself in youth as "legitimately prolonging the mighty line of Marlowe, of Milton," belong, unlike George Lamming, Aimé Césaire, and Kamau Brathwaite, among the adherents of Prospero, whose Caribbean makeover as "white imperialist" he debunks as "fashionable, Marxist-evolved" revisionism?[22] Walcott's seemingly shameless mimicry of a character out of the classical tradition distracts us, I believe, from his covert refashioning of the Caribbean paradigm of anticolonial defiance. Philoctete, when we first meet him, describes the cutting down of trees, though for making canoes rather than firewood. Closely associated with the land, he mirrors, as if by magical sympathy, his natural island environment in the Caribbean. He personifies his entire race's grievance against the colonizers. He launches an abortive revolution by demolishing the garden that sustains him. He "curse[s]" because never *"black people go get rest / from God,"* much as Caliban curses and rues his compulsory hard labor (21). At the moment of Philoctete's cursing, "a fierce cluster of arrows / targeted the sore, and he screamed"; similarly, Caliban's curses prompt his master to promise, "I'll rack thee with old cramps, / Fill all thy bones with aches, make thee roar."[23] Seized by the unpredictable onset of physical torment, Walcott's Philoctete fuses a classical paradigm with the Third World's transvaluation of Shakespeare's wretch. But whereas the new Caliban was already becoming a West Indian cliché a couple of decades earlier, Walcott paradoxically refreshes the symbol of postcolonial agony and anger by reaching for a still more wizened prototype. His career-long resistance to Caliban, as to the wound trope, helps him to flush these literary inheritances with new power and complexity.

As figures of Caribbean oppression, Philoctetes and Caliban complement each other: one of them, tormented on an island that is rightly his, is especially well-suited to allegorizing colonization, while the other, transported to an alien island, easily figures the displacement and deracination of West Indian slavery. But whereas Philoctetes has remained the cultural property of the West, Caliban's postcolonial indigenization has been so vigorous that, at least regionally, he is as much a Caribbean as a Shakespearean figure. Walcott's closet Caliban bears the impress of postcolonial revisionism or what he concedes are the often "brilliant re-creations" by fellow Caribbean authors.[24] Unlike Shakespeare's but like Césaire's Caliban, for example, Walcott's Philoctete is suspicious of his cumbersome name and even wants, as we have seen, to slice it from his body. In Césaire's *Une tempête*, Caliban decides he doesn't "want to be called Caliban any longer" because Caliban "isn't [his] name" and his real "name has been stolen."[25] To perpetuate Caliban, Walcott paradoxically de-indigenizes him, reroutes the figure back through colonial culture, and thus makes him new. Exemplifying the twists and turns of intercultural inheritance, this literary maneuver belies the narrative of postcolonial literary development as progression from alien metropolitan influence to complete incorporation within the native cultural body. The culturally alien and native, outside and inside can, it seems, stage a polyrhythmic dance.

Nevertheless, to see Walcott's wounded character as a combination of the classical Philoctetes and the Caribbean Caliban still oversimplifies his genesis. When Walcott yanked Philoctetes out of antiquity to recast him, still other figures from other cultures stuck to the prototype. Philoctete, as Walcott remarks of Crusoe, "changes shape ... with Protean cunning."[26] Drawing on Western classicism for his character's base, veering homeward for a Caribbean admixture, Walcott spins the globe again and picks up other traces from Western modernism. Caliban may seem fishlike, but a Euromodernist text that also interpolates *The Tempest* provides a closer antecedent for Walcott's wounded fisherman, who, with his "unhealed" wound, "limp[s]" and languishes at the waterside, feeling his "sore twitch / its wires up to his groin"—a mysteriously unhealed wound that reflects the wounded condition of the land and indeed the entire region (9, 10). Like the Fisher King in Eliot's *Waste Land*, Philoctete is a synecdochic figure for a general loss, injury, and impotence that must be healed for the (is)lands to be set in order. If Philoctete is a kind of Caribbean Fisher King, Achille plays the role of questing knight who must journey to the Chapel Perilous—in *Omeros*, Africa, site of ancestral enslavement—to rejuvenate the wounded fisherman, the land, and its people.

Remembering the modernist metamyth of the wounded vegetation god, Walcott places *Omeros* in a line that stems not only from Eliot but from a throng of Western artists and anthropologists as well. The animistic opening scene of *Omeros* recalls, for example, Sir James Frazer and Robert Graves in its description of the sacrificial felling of godlike trees for the making of canoes. Philoctete narrates how he and his companions steeled themselves "to turn into murderers," "to wound" the trees they depend on for their livelihood (3). As a tree fell, the sun rose, "blood splashed on the cedars, // and the grove flooded with the light of sacrifice" (5). Achille "hacked the limbs from the dead god, knot after knot, / wrenching the severed veins from the trunk" (6), but once the tree is reborn on the water as a canoe, it and Hector's canoe "agreed with the waves to forget their lives as trees" (8). Alluding to the annihilation of the Arawaks, Walcott adapts the vegetation myths of the aboriginal inhabitants of the island, as mediated through archetypalist modernism: "The first god was a gommier." He metaphorically reenacts a sacrificial rite to open the way for his own tale:

much as the fishermen must kill trees to remake them as canoes, so the poet must hew the linguistic timber of his forebears to remake it as his own vehicle. Introducing the character Philoctete before anyone else, the poem insists on the analogy between his representative wound and what it repeatedly calls the "wound" suffered by the trees. Thus it makes of him the poem's spirit of life, of nature, and of the island, and his wounded body the synecdoche for all the wounds suffered by the island's natives, slaves, and natural beings, possibly even its epic poet.

Like Osiris and other vegetation deities in the modernist metamyth, Philoctete requires the ministrations of a female counterpart to be healed, in his case the obeah woman or sibyl Ma Kilman. Paralleling Achille's magical return to Africa, Ma Kilman discovers an herbal antidote of African origins, transplanted by a sea swift, and she brews the remedy in an old sugar cauldron, allegorized as "the basin of the rusted Caribbean" (247). His "knuckled spine like islands," Philoctete emerges from his healing bath "like a boy ... with the first clay's / innocent prick"—the new Caribbean "Adam" (248). But whereas the concept of the New World Adam resonates throughout Walcott's earlier work, he is now an aspiration, a potential achievement in the New World; the wounded, impotent Adonis, Parsifal, Fisher King, or Philoctetes more nearly represents the New World condition, overcome provisionally and strenuously. Philoctete becomes Adamic because an African flower rejoins him to the African past, not, as in the earlier Walcott, because of his "amnesia." Indeed, at the risk of crowding the field of prototypes still further, we can gauge Walcott's change in the difference between his earlier tendency to imagine the West Indian as healthy castaway and Crusoe's replacement in *Omeros* by another sort of castaway—this one harboring a stinking, ulcerous wound, his body tormented by the persistence of the past, ameliorated only by the retrieval of a precolonial inheritance.[27]

For all Philoctete's links with the Euromodernist figure of the vegetation god, we must spin the globe again to appreciate why the wound-healing quest in *Omeros* turns to Africa. Responsible not only for the postcolonial reappraisal of Caliban but also, of course, for the Caribbean recuperation of African aesthetics and values, negritude might seem an unlikely influence on Walcott, given his testy assessment of it in essays like the grudgingly titled "Necessity of Negritude" (1964).[28] While granting that negritude helped to restore "a purpose and dignity to the descendants of slaves," Walcott suggests that "nostalgia" and uniquely French pressures of "assimilation" produced the movement's "artificial" reconstruction of a black identity rooted in Africa. "Return," Walcott later writes, is "impossible, for we cannot return to what we have never been."[29] Yet in *Omeros* the return to Africa is key to healing the torn black body and racial memory of the Caribbean, as personified by Philoctete. Walcott describes in loving detail how "centuries ago" an African swift managed, in bringing a special seed across the ocean, "to carry the cure / that precedes every wound" (238, 239). This curative plot of return to a precolonial Africa would have been unimaginable without negritude, however long past its heyday and however often resisted by Walcott. Moreover, Ma Kilman commits what would seem to be another cardinal Walcottian sin in reviving the African gods "Erzulie, // Shango, and Ogun" to find the African flower that will cure Philoctete (242). For "the new magnifiers of Africa," Walcott had tartly stated, the "deepest loss is of the old gods," and poets who look "to a catalogue of forgotten gods ... engage in masochistic recollection."[30] True, the narrator of *Omeros* emphasizes that the gods, "their features obscured" and "thinned," "had lost their names and, therefore, considerable presence" (242). Nevertheless, he assures us, "They were there" (243). In one of the most memorable scenes of *Omeros*, the gods, having earlier "rushed / across an ocean" in "loud migration," swarm like bats in Ma Kilman's grove, their wings forming "crisscrossing stitches" that presage the closing of Philoctete's wound (242). Walcott even flirts momentarily with the concept of race-based blood inheritance of African belief: the old gods sprout through Ma Kilman's body, "as if her veins were their roots" and her arms their branches (242).[31]

While negritude overcomes Walcott's resistances in his mythologizing of Africa as site of wholeness and cure, it also plays a part in engendering the wound figure itself. Since Walcott is seldom thought to owe much to negritude poetry, it might be worth pausing on this seemingly improbable point of connection, for all the obvious differences. In *Cahier d'un retour au pays natal* (1947), called by Walcott "the most powerful expression of Negritude," Césaire repeatedly personifies his West Indian homeland as a wounded body.[32] The speaker reconciles himself to returning to and even embracing a land disfigured by its forgotten wounds ("je reviens vers la hideur désertée de vos plaies"; "je dénombre les plaies avec une sorte d'allégresse").[33] Even as he celebrates and idealizes the black body, he also remembers its wounds cut by the slavemaster's whip and brand, wounds that still sound like tom-toms ("tam-tams manes de plaies sonores").[34] One year after the first French edition of the *Cahier* was published, another crucial text of negritude followed hard on its heels in 1948, an anthology of francophone African and West Indian poets, prefaced by Jean-Paul Sartre's influential essay "Orphée Noir." The black poet, according to Sartre, writes great collective poetry when, in part, "exhibiting his wounds."[35] The black poet's capacity for articulation is so fused with a historical condition of pain and injury that, in one of the poems Sartre cites, the Haitian writer Jacques Roumain pleads in an apostrophe to Africa, "make ... / of my mouth the lips of your wound [*plaie*]."[36] The collective memory that unites black poets of different languages and regions, according to Sartre, is one of untold, massive suffering. Slavery, despite its abolition half a century before the negritude poets were born, "lingers on as a very real memory," a point that he supports by quoting first Léon Damas of French Guyana:

> Still real is my stunned condition of the past
> of
> blows from knotted cords of bodies calcinated
> from toe to calcinated back
> of dead flesh of red iron firebrands of arms
> broken under the whip which is breaking loose ...

and, second, the Haitian poet Jean-François Brierre:

> ... Often like me you feel stiffnesses
> Awaken after murderous centuries
> And old wounds bleed in your flesh ...
> [Et saigner dans ta chair les anciennes blessures ...][37]

The vividness of the trope of the wounded black body in these influential negritude texts should prompt us to reconsider the assumption that in *Omeros* Walcott has simply transported the classical Philoctetes among other Homeric types to the Caribbean, reincarnating him in a black body, encasing him in African skin. It may be equally plausible to argue that Walcott places a Greek mask on the wounded black body of negritude.

Yet neither of these paradigms offers the definitive solution to the implicit question I have sought to complicate by oscillating between North and South, West and East, Europe, Africa, and the Caribbean: simply put, where does Philoctete's wound come from? Literally, from a rusty anchor, and allegorically, from slavery; but once the question is shifted from the mimetic to the literary historical register, the puzzle of origins multiplies. Does it come from the wounded black body of Afro-Caribbean negritude or the Euromodernist fertility god? From the Caribbean Caliban or the Greek Philoctetes? Yet even these regional designations are reductive: the

Caribbean Caliban evolved from a Western canonical figure; many vegetation gods appropriated by Western modernists were originally Eastern; and negritude developed in part as a dialectical reversal of Western colonialist stereotypes. In intermingling Caribbean and European literary paradigms, Walcott thickens the cultural hybridity of each. Rather than purify what might be called the "dialectic" of the tribe, Walcott accelerates, complicates, and widens it.

One of Walcott's recurrent metaphors for cultural hybridity may seem, at this point, unsurprising: the scar. Comparing the cultural heterogeneity of the Antilles to a shattered but reassembled vase, Walcott said in his Nobel address that the "restoration shows its white scars" and that "if the pieces are disparate, ill-fitting, they contain more pain than their original sculpture."[38] More somber than Walcott's tropes of webbing and weaving, let alone popular metaphors like melting pot, salad bowl, or callaloo, the scar signifies cultural convergence in the Americas without effacing its violent genesis. At the end of "The Muse of History," Walcott movingly recalls the violent past deposited in his body, apostrophizing a white forefather, "slave seller and slave buyer," and a black forefather "in the filth-ridden gut of the slave ship." But the scars left by the slavemaster's "whip" are metamorphosed in Walcott's magnificent image for his and the Caribbean's fusion of black and white skins, of Northern and Southern Hemispheres: "the monumental groaning and soldering of two great worlds, like the halves of a fruit seamed by its own bitter juice."[39] Even though the wound has scarified in these descriptions, Walcott never reduces the bitterness or pain to a condition that can be repaired completely; rather, it is constitutive of the new synthesis. Walcott returns to this figure near the end of *Omeros*, when he represents the intercultural labor of his poem as having

> followed a sea-swift to both sides of this text;
> her hyphen stitched its seam, like the interlocking
> basins of a globe in which one half fits the next....
>   (319)

In Yeats's words, Walcott suggests that "nothing can be sole or whole / That has not been rent."[40]

Seaming black skin and white masks, white skin and black masks, Walcott's Philoctete stands in a long line of Walcottian personifications of cultural and racial hybridity. His name taken from the culture of colonizer and slaver, yet his wounded black body allegorizing their cruelty, Philoctete recalls the "divided" speaker of "A Far Cry from Africa," cursing the brutality of the colonizers yet cursing them in the language they have given him. Greco-Caribbean, Euro-African, Anglo-Hebraic, Philoctete is a boldly intercultural amalgamation, like the self-defined Shabine of "The Schooner *Flight*":

> I have Dutch, nigger, and English in me,
> and either I'm nobody, or I'm a nation.[41]

Although Philoctete seems at first to represent but one cultural and racial pole of the Caribbean and thus to differ from Shabine and from Walcott's other early hybrids, Walcott suggests that even in constructing a seemingly monocultural character, in this case to allegorize black pain, the Caribbean poet builds into his aesthetic construct inevitably mixed cultural inheritances. Even Philoctete's cure, like his wound, turns out to be transcultural. Ma Kilman relies, as we have seen, on a specifically African plant and on African gods to heal Philoctete's wound. But she attends five o'clock Mass on the day she delivers Philoctete of gangrene. When she finds the curative African flower, she still wears her Sunday clothes. Vacillating between Greece and the Caribbean, the poem calls Ma Kilman "the sibyl, the obeah-woman." This apposition reverses the presumably literal and metaphoric, and succeeding lines perpetuate the whirligig in naming her "the spidery sibyl // hanging in a sack from the cave at Cumae, the obeah / ... possessed" woman (245).

Decades before the academic dissemination of such concepts as hybridity, creolization, cross-culturality, postethnicity, postnationalism, *métissage*, and *mestizaje*, Walcott argued vehemently for an intercultural model of postcolonial literature.[42] Against a "separatist" black literature that "belligerently asserts its isolation, its difference," he counterposes; a vision of the Caribbean writer as inevitably "mixed": New World blacks must use what Walcott ironically calls "the white man's words" as well as "his God, his dress, his machinery, his food. And, of course, his literature."[43] But Walcott also attacks pervasive assumptions about so-called white American literature—a more powerful if less visible identitarian counterpart to negritude and nativism: "To talk about the contribution of the black man to American culture or civilization is absurd, because it is the black who energized that culture, who styles it, just as it is the black who preserved and energized its faith."[44] For Walcott, as for other Caribbean writers such as Wilson Harris and Edouard Glissant, tribalist views from either extreme disfigure the mixed reality of New World culture, repressing it in favor of simplistic narratives of cultural origin.

The twisted skein of intercultural influences in Philoctete reveals the distortion involved in conceiving of postcolonial literature as a progression from colonial dominance to indigeneity, European subordination to nativist freedom.[45] According to this standard narrative, Walcott's use of the Philoctetes type would seem to be a regression to an earlier phase of Eurocentric indebtedness; yet the same linear narrative would also have to note in the figure a progressive step toward indigenous articulation of West Indian suffering. Is Walcott recolonizing Caribbean literature for Europeans by using this and other Greek types? Or is he decolonizing it by representing Caribbean agony? Does the poet reenslave the descendant of slaves by shackling him with a European name and prototype? Or does he liberate the Afro-Caribbean by stealing a literary type from former slavers and making it signify their brutality? Too simplistic for the cultural entanglements of a poem like *Omeros*, the evolutionary model of postcolonial literature is rooted in a discredited model of national development. We need a more flexible language to describe how a poet like Walcott can put into dialectical interrelation literary and cultural influences that may seem incompatible. Critics have seen an evolution in Walcott's work from literary Eurocentrism to Afrocentrism, from denying to embracing African influences on his and others' Caribbean art. Yet Philoctete's wound and cure show Walcott not shedding but deepening his European interests as he explores his African commitments, becoming neither a Eurocentric nor an Afrocentric poet but an ever more multicentric poet of the contemporary world.

Having traced the cross-cultural literary genealogies of the wound and its bearer in *Omeros*, I would like to turn from the vertical axis and questions of literary sedimentation to the horizontal and the wound's intratextual resonances, and here too the profoundly intercultural character of Walcott's trope emerges. Once again this hybridity may be surprising, since the wound in *Omeros* at first seems to encode unambiguously the painful Afro-Caribbean legacy of slavery and colonialism. While using the wound motif to honor the uniqueness of this black experience, Walcott nevertheless cross-fertilizes the trope, extending it to other peoples as well. Hybrid in its intertextual ancestry, the wound is also a trope of polymorphous diversity within the text. No sooner has Walcott identified the wound motif with the black experience than he introduces his principal white character, who also happens to be wounded. "He has to be wounded," because of the poem's cross-racial thematics: "affliction is one theme / of this work" (28). What caused Plunkett's wound, other than Walcott's desire to create a cross-cultural echo? Like Philoctete's wound, Plunkett's has only the bare outlines of a literal pathogenesis. Major Plunkett, wounded in the head by an explosion during the North African campaign of World War II (27), also seems to bear the inherited wound of European colonialism. He even discovers that a midshipman with his name suffered a "fatal wound" in the Battle of the Saints, the famed eighteenth-century battle for Saint Lucia (86). Certainly, Plunkett's wound differs suggestively from Philoctete's: it is to his head, not his body, and it never induces spasms of uncontrollable physical pain. These and other differences point up the more cerebral nature of white suffering in the aftermath of colonialism. Even so, Walcott insists by emblem and analogy that both colonizer and colonized inherit a legacy of affliction in the Caribbean.

As if repeated application of the word "wound" to a Euro-Caribbean and an Afro-Caribbean were not enough to reveal their commonality, Walcott rhymes Plunkett and Philoctete in a variety of ways. Their names may not literally rhyme, except perhaps for the final syllable, but they share an initial *p*, an *l*, and the nearly anagrammatic final letters –*kett* and –*ctete*. Though the men differ predictably in appearance, Plunkett, with "a cloud wrapped around his head" during convalescence, recalls the "foam-haired Philoctete" (28, 9). The stoic Philoctete resolves to "endure" his affliction with the patience of an "old horse" (22), even as Plunkett, true to his own stiff-lipped heritage, rejects the "easy excuse" of blaming his temper on his injury (22, 56). Philoctete's wound apparently renders him impotent, and the great sorrow of Plunkett's life is his inability to father a son (29). Like Ma Kilman, the female anointer of Philoctete's wound, Plunkett's wife, Maud, his nurse in the war, looks after his head injury.[46] After Maud dies, Ma Kilman acts as a medium in Plunkett's effort to contact her. Whether these links are instances of "Homeric repetition," "coincidence," or Joycean counterpoint (96), they make inescapable the connections between one affliction and the other. As early as "Ruins of a Great House" (1962), Walcott tries to hold in a single work the bitter knowledge that "some slave is rotting in this manorial lake" and "that Albion too was once / A colony like ours," that both slave and master inherit histories of excruciating pain, cruelty, and abuse.[47] As Walcott says of "doubt," the wound "isn't the privilege of one complexion" (182).

Walcott's use of the wound at first seems to satisfy Fredric Jameson's well-known generalization: "All third-world texts are necessarily ... allegorical, and in a very specific way: they are to be read as what I will call *national allegories*."[48] Read thus, the Walcottian wound would be a trope of unproblematic referentiality and stand for the particular historical experience of a particular race in a particular part of the world. Long codified as a dominant trope for black enslavement and mimetic of real wounds perpetrated on real black bodies for hundreds of years, the wound would seem to be the perfect, unambiguous allegory of Afro-Caribbean history. But Walcott plays energetically on the instabilities of the trope. For the wound also has, as Elaine Scarry observes, "a nonreferentiality that rather than eliminating all referential activity instead gives it a frightening freedom of referential activity."[49] Discourses of realist fiction and of nationalist politics might seek to control and even defeat the "referential instability" of the wound, affixing it to a particular people, motive, or cause. But by attaching the wound trope to the name Philoctete and to a black body, Walcott already contaminates and disrupts the specificities demanded by "national allegory." Moreover, the lancet wound that Philoctete suffers from confounds inside and outside; it is the point at which racially unmarked interiority erupts as exteriority and the world within breaks through the epidermal surface. While much contemporary criticism views postcolonial texts, more than their metropolitan counterparts, as preeminent examples of the literature of national and ethnographic specificity, Walcott devises a transnational allegory about both the wound of black Saint Lucian history and a larger subject—what he calls "the incurable // wound of time" (319).

To write about pain and mortality as transcultural experiences may seem to risk an easy humanism or discredited universalism. Walcott keeps this tendency in check by reserving for the wound an interpretive opacity. Philoctete's wound is a piece of body language that, like many literary wounds, signifies its status as polyvalent sign by resembling a "mouth" (18). But it is a dumb mouth, a sign that also signifies its inarticulateness. Although it is an external mark that tourists, associated elsewhere in the poem with neocolonialism, pay "extra silver" to see, it remains mysterious, turned inward, folded and guarded. Walcott describes it as "puckered like the corolla / of a sea-urchin," in contrast to "a garrulous waterfall" that tourists hear "pour out its secret." Philoctete "does not explain [the wound's] cure. / 'It have some things'—he smiles—'worth more than a dollar'" (4). Hovering between dumbness and communication, the wound offers touristic readers an entryway into Afro-Caribbean experience even as it reminds them that they can never fully comprehend the local burden of historical pain, that they must remain voyeurs peering from without. Philoctete's wound elicits from him a scream that is "mad to come out" but that is held back "behind the bars // of his rusted teeth" (21). Inducing yet disabling speech, the wound figures both the promise and the limits of language as vehicle of interpersonal and intercultural understanding.

Walcott can thematize Philoctete's wound as language without betraying the Afro-Caribbean experience because Caribbean blacks also suffered the wound of colonially imposed languages, such as French and English, which are interwoven (sometimes in creole) throughout the poem. Just as Philoctete experiences his alien and inscrutable name as a festering wound he wishes he could cut from his body, Achille realizes that he does not share his forebears' belief in an essential connection between names and things, that he does "not know" what his name means: "Trees, men, we yearn for a sound that is missing" (137). If Philoctete's wound is a language—partly readable, partly opaque—his language is also a kind of painful wound haunted by the memory of an Adamic language it has displaced. But this woundlike language is also potentially its own cure: as the narrator remarks near the end of *Omeros*, "Like Philoctete's wound, this language carries its cure, / Its radiant affliction" (323). The line break, in a pregnant syntactic ambiguity, hovers between an elided conjunction (which would make the cure and affliction opposites) and a relation of apposition (in which the cure would be the affliction). The metaphor of light, repeated from earlier descriptions of the wound as "radiant" (9, 21), tips the seeming antithesis toward identity, much as the poet has done earlier in punningly mistranslating Philoctete's complaint in French creole that he is wounded, "*Moin blessé*," as "I am blest" (18). The poet's discovery of likeness between the words *blessé* and "blest," like his monolingual play on "affliction" and "fiction" (28), demonstrates how the European languages inflicted on West Indians can be turned from curses into blessings. Like Yeats, who could never give up his "love," in spite of his "hatred," for the English language, the poet of *Omeros* refers to "the wound of a language I'd no wish to remove," even after the poet character and Plunkett mimic upper-class accents in a linguistic charade (270).

　　Philoctete's wound, no less than the colonial language it partly figures, carries its cure dialectically within itself. Indeed, wound, weapon, and cure belong to a metonymic family that Walcott strengthens by metaphoric substitutions throughout the poem. When Walcott compares a "running wound" to "the rusty anchor / that scabbed Philoctete's shin," for example, he identifies the shape and color of the wound with the weapon, and the word "scabbed" suggests both the injury and its cure (178). As if to close the gap between a punctured leg and the healing agent, Walcott chants their prepositional coalescence: "the flower on his shin," "the flower on his shin-blade," "the foul flower / on his shin" (235, 244, 247). The tropological binding up of seeming antitheses also works in the opposite direction. In writing that the "pronged flower // sprang like a buried anchor," Walcott identifies the curative African plant with the weapon whose injury it reverses, as later with the wound it heals: "The wound of the flower, its gangrene, its rage / festering for centuries, reeked with corrupted blood, // seeped the pustular drops instead of sunlit dew" (237, 244). Using metaphor to leap the gap between destruction and healing, Walcott's language performatively converts injury into remedy. The only flower that can heal Philoctete's wound must match, perhaps even exceed, the wound's "bitterness," "reek," and "stench" (237); thus Walcott suggests that the poem cannot contribute to healing the wounds of Afro-Caribbean history without reproducing their pain. Like the Boxing Day rite in which "all the pain // reentered Philoctete," the poet's language carries a cure that must continually reopen and expose the wound (277). In fashioning a mirror relation between injury and remedy, Walcott represents within *Omeros* the poem's homeopathic relation to the traumatic history of the West Indies. Joining black and white, Old World and New, the wound's cross-cultural metaphoricity exhibits the structural doubleness that is fundamental to the poem's logic.

The wound motif exemplifies the slipperiness and polyvalence of poetic discourse that circulates between races, crossing lines of class and community, bridging differences between West Indian fisherman and Greek warrior. With its resonance and punning, imagistic doubling and metaphoric webbing, Walcott's poetry demonstrates the kinds of imaginative connections and transgressions that have ironically made poetry a minor field in postcolonial literary studies. For poetry, at least in Walcott's hands, is less respectful than prose fiction of racial, regional, national, and gender loyalties.[50]

The lancet wound migrates from Philoctete to a white American woman, when Walcott attributes to Catherine Weldon "the wound of her son's // death from a rusty nail" (176). By means of the wound trope and others, Walcott crosses and recrosses lines of race, nation, and gender. Moreover, Walcott rides the trope across the line between narrative and lyric poetry as he compares his personal loss in a failed marriage to Philoctete's historical and communal injury: "There was no difference / between me and Philoctete" (245), he says, later coupling himself and Philoctete in a mirror image when they wave in greeting: "We shared the one wound, the same cure" (295). Although postuniversalist sensibilities might bridle at such assertions of identity, Walcott signals the distances he traverses by trope. The poet stays at a hotel; the fisherman lives in a poor village. The estranged poet looks "down" from a "height" at his island, "not like Philoctete // limping among his yams and the yam flowers" (250). Philoctete is a contemporary black man; Catherine Weldon is a nineteenth-century white woman. But Walcott refuses to accept the identitarian fear that shuttling across these enormous differences erases them; he shoots the gulf (in Emerson's phrase), suggesting that the greater danger lies in becoming captivated by the narcissism of differences. As the poem's primary wound-bearer, Philoctete embodies the principle of metaphorical coupling, mediating not only between Greece and Africa, white and black, wound and cure but also between Achille and Hector ("Philoctete tried to make peace between them" [47]), between capitalist and Marxist parties (he campaigns for "United Love" [107]), and between the living and the dead (he names drowned fishermen [128]), as well as between male and female (he and Achille become "androgynous / warriors" during their Boxing Day dance [276]).

The wound joins the major characters of *Omeros* in a large metaphorical company. The pervasive love wound is one example of this effect: Hector's transport or minivan is like a "flaming wound" because he fears Helen still loves Achille (118); Achille "believed he smelt as badly as Philoctete / from the rotting loneliness" (116); Helen so misses Achille that it seems the nightingale's "monodic moan // came from the hole in her heart" (152); Plunkett is afflicted with another wound on the death of his wife (309); and Saint Lucia's fishermen suffer "that obvious wound / made from loving the sea over their own country" (302). Promiscuously linking various characters in amorous anguish, the wound trope also comes to signify the love that poets like Shelley have long associated with metaphor. A metaphor for metaphor, the wound even circulates through various parts of the nonhuman world, from the volcano whose "wound closed in smoke" (59) to the French colonial ship *Ville de Paris* "wallowing in her wounded pride" (85), and from a field (170), a bay (238), a cauldron (246), and a hut (272), to shacks (178), coves (249), the entire island (249), the sky (313), even the whole Caribbean basin (247). Unleashing the pathetic fallacy, Walcott sees the region's brutal history reflected throughout its natural and human landscape. While a prodigious passion for likeness is characteristic of Walcott's poetry, this passion also typifies a much older and larger propensity of poetry, harnessing the metaphorical play of resemblance within language to amplify and free it. Acknowledging this legacy, he presents the phantasmagoria of the poet, *Omeros*, as the ideal embodiment of metaphorical conjuncture. *Omeros*'s language is a "Greek calypso," and his images flicker between black and white, the living and the dead, the real and the fantastic (286).

From the perspective of the identity politics that sometimes underwrites the study of Third World literatures, metaphor and postcoloniality might seem to be strange bedfellows, but they should be regarded as reciprocal, interwoven, and mutually enlarging. The movement of metaphor across ethnic, regional, and gender boundaries is well suited to

the openly hybrid and intercultural character of postcolonial literature and
finds perhaps its fullest articulation in poetry, from Walcott to Ramanujan,
Soyinka, and Agha Shahid Ali. Forced and voluntary migration, crossings of
one people with another, linguistic creolization, and racial miscegenation—
these are the sorts of displacements, wanderings, and interminglings that
poetic metaphor can powerfully encode in the fabric of a postcolonial text.
To trace the spiralings of the wound motif in *Omeros* is to begin to
understand how a poetic imagination as fecund as Walcott's can, in its restless
work of discovering and creating resemblance, confound tribal, ethnic, or
national limits.

"Trauma" is, of course, Greek for wound, and Walcott's *Omeros* could
be said—extending a psychological analogy of Glissant's—to remember,
repeat, and work through the trauma of Afro-Caribbean history.[51] But this
ameliorative work should not be confused with a definitive healing. Although
both the character Philoctete and the "phantom narrator" are represented as
being cured, Walcott so proliferates and disperses the trope that, even after
the climactic scene of healing, the wounds of history and language are shown
to persist. As early as the opening of *Omeros*, to which I return by way of
conclusion, we can already see that Walcott turns the trope with such vigor
that no fictive cure will ever put a stop to its motion. Even in this first canto,
the wound bounces from trees to earth to blacks to native people. In the
poem's scene of origination, Walcott wants to show victimizer and victimized
to be ambiguous, shifting positions.[52] Philoctete starts out as neocolonial
victim: he "smiles for the tourists, who try taking / his soul with their
cameras." Walcott suggests that the neocolonial tourist and, by implication,
the touristic reader perpetuate the colonial trauma in trying to penetrate the
interior of the Caribbean descendant of slaves ("trauma" derives from a word
for "to pierce" [*tetrainein*]). But soon enough Philoctete is telling how he and
the other fishermen had "axes" in their "eyes," as the tourists have piercing
gazes. Indeed, he and his comrades, like latter-day colonizers, become
"murderers": "'I lift up the axe and pray for strength in my hands / to wound
the first cedar'" (3). Suddenly reader, tourist, and colonizer become
vulnerable to the wounding they at first seemed accused of committing. If
metaphor turns Philoctete's wounds into weapons, it also inverts his black
victimization as soon as that status is established. But neither is the
alternative role stable, for Philoctete now reveals his own painful scar, which
identifies him with the wounds that he will perpetrate on the trees. And as
Walcott alludes to the annihilation of the Arawaks and their language, he
recalls a still-earlier trauma from which there can be no question of recovery.
Sharing a fate of island suffering yet surviving it to replace the native

population, Philoctete and the other black fishermen soon resume the role of inflicting, not receiving, wounds: they turn off the chain saw and then, ripping "the wound clear" of vines, "examine the wound it / had made," as the blood of a Saint Lucian sunrise "trickled" and "splashed" on the trees (5).

Is Walcott, as poet of cross-cultural affliction, a "fortunate traveller" of transnational trope? Because he sets this most politically loaded of metaphors spinning, does he irresponsibly confound distinctions between colonizer and colonized, oppressor and oppressed? How can this cross-racializing of the wound be reconciled with the asymmetrical suffering that marks colonialism and postcoloniality, let alone slavery? These are the undeniable risks of Walcott's free riding of the wound trope across moral and historical divisions, but his wager is that they are risks worth taking.

If exclusive fidelity to a single history of affliction is required of the Third World poet, then Walcott certainly fails this test. But Walcott conceives the Antilles as a site of multiple and inextricable histories of victimization and cruelty, histories deposited not only in its landscape and its languages but even in his body. From an identitarian perspective, poets like Walcott who metaphorically enact interethnic connections falsify the historical specificity of their people's experience. But for Walcott, the greater falsification would lie in an aesthetic separatism blind to the culturally webbed history of the Caribbean, of his ancestors, and of his imagination, in a viewpoint hostile to the cross-racial and cross-historical identifications the New World offers.

As graphic emblem of convulsive, bodily pain, the wound in *Omeros* memorializes the untold suffering of Afro-Caribbeans, yet as trope, it inevitably poeticizes pain, compares this particular experience with others, and thus must either mar or deconstruct experiential uniqueness by plunging it into the whirlpool of metaphorical resemblance and difference. Anchor-like in shape and origins, the wound trope in *Omeros* drifts from the ground of a particular people's experience to the afflictions of native peoples, Greeks, Jews, colonial Americans, even the English. Because Walcott's intermappings of suffering never occlude Philoctete's primacy and never sugarcoat the trauma of slavery, they keep in view differences between oppressor and oppressed, even as they open up and reveal the connections between the experiences of Afro-Caribbeans and others. Appropriating a Western icon of suffering and refashioning a polysemous and multiparented trope, Walcott's *Omeros* champions a postcolonial poetics of affliction that unravels the distinction between "victim's literature" and its supposed opposite.

NOTES

1. Derek Walcott, *Conversations with Derek Walcott*, ed. William Baer (Jackson: University Press of Mississippi, 1996), 59.

2. Derek Walcott, "Leaving School" (1965), in *Critical Perspectives on Derek Walcott*, ed. Robert D. Hamner (Washington, D.C.: Three Continents Press, 1993), 32.

3. Recalling Yeats's description of the Black and Tans as "drunken soldiery" ("drunken officer of British rule"). Walcott also transmutes Yeats's lines, "All men are dancers and their tread / Goes to the barbarous clangour of a gong," into a similarly bleak description of the compulsive brutality of "man": "Delirious as these worried beasts, his wars / Dance to the tightened carcass of a drum." See W. B. Yeats, *The Poems*, rev. ed, ed. Richard J. Finneran (New York: Macmillan, 1989), 207, 208; Derek Walcott, *Collected Poems, 1948–1984* (New York: Noonday–Farrar, Straus & Giroux, 1986), 17–18. Laurence A. Bremer dates the first publication of "A Far Cry from Africa" in *An Introduction to West Indian Poetry* (Cambridge: Cambridge University Press, 1998), 159; 247, n. 20.

4. Derek Walcott, *Omeros* (New York: Farrar, Straus & Giroux, 1990), 199. All further references to *Omeros* appear parenthetically in the text. Although Joyce is the more direct influence on *Omeros*, Yeats's presence is evident from the introduction of the two major female characters in the story: an Irishwoman notably named Maud and a local woman named Helen, who caribbeanizes a Greek paradigm as Yeats had earlier "irished" her.

Walcott has often been fruitfully discussed as a poet of "mixed" culture, "divided" inheritance, and "schizophrenic" allegiance; see Paul Breslin, "'I Met History Once, But He Ain't Recognize Me': The Poetry of Derek Walcott," *Triquarterly* 68 (1987): 168–83; Joseph Brodsky, "On Derek Walcott," *New York Review of Books*, 10 November 1983, 39–41; James Dickey, review of *Collected Poems, 1948–1984*, by Derek Walcott, *New York Times Book Review*, 2 February 1986, 8; Rita Dove, "'Either I'm Nobody, or I'm a Nation,'" review of *Collected Poems, 1948–1984*, by Derek Walcott, *Parnassus* 14, no. 1 (1987): 49–76; J. D. McClatchy, review of *Collected Poems, 1948–1984*, by Derek Walcott, New Republic, 24 March 1986, 36–38; James McCorkle, "'The Sigh of History': The Poetry of Derek Walcott," *Verse* ("Derek Walcott Feature Issue," ed. Susan M. Schultz) 11, no, 2 (1994): 104–12; J. A. Ramsaran, "Derek Walcott: New World Mediterranean Poet," *World Literature Written in English* 21, no. 1 (1982): 133–47; Red Terada, *Walcott's Poetry: American Mimicry* (Boston: Northeastern University Press, 1992); Helen Vendler, "Poet of Two Worlds," review of *The Fortunate*

Traveller, by Derek Walcott, *New York Review of Books*, 4 March 1982, 23+; Clement H. Wyke, "'Divided to the Vein': Patterns of Tormented Ambivalence in Walcott's *The Fortunate Traveller*," *Ariel* 20, no. 3 (1989): 55–71; and John Thieme, Derek Walcott (New York: Manchester University Press, 1999).

A biographical synopsis may be helpful for readers new to Walcott. He was born in Castries, Saint Lucia, on January 23, 1930. His father, a civil servant and amateur painter, died before he was a year old. His mother was the head teacher at a Methodist infant school on the predominantly Catholic island. His background was racially and culturally mixed. His grandmothers were of African descent, his white grandfathers a Dutchman and an Englishman. Speaking the Standard English that is the official language of the island, Walcott also grew up speaking the predominant French creole (or patois) that is the primary language of the street. At the age of fifteen, Walcott published a poem in the local newspaper, drawing a sharp rebuke in rhyme from a Catholic priest for his heretical pantheism and animism. A few years later, he borrowed money from his mother to print a booklet of twenty-five poems, hawking it on the streets to earn the money back. This book and his first major play, *Henri Christophe*, also met with disapprobation from the Catholic church.

In 1950 he left Saint Lucia to enter the University of the West Indies in Mona, Jamaica, where he was a vibrant literary entrepreneur among the university's first graduating class in liberal arts. Staying on in Jamaica, he made his living through teaching and journalism. He moved to Trinidad in 1958, still working as a reviewer and art critic but also pouring energy into directing and writing plays for the Trinidad Theater Workshop until 1976. His poetry began to receive international attention with *In a Green Night* (1962).

Since 1981, he has been teaching regularly at Boston University. He recently built a home on the northwest coast of Saint Lucia where he paints and writes. Among his major plays are *Ti-Jean and His Brothers* (1958), Dream on Monkey Mountain (1961), and *The Odyssey* (1993). He received the Nobel Prize for literature in 1992. See Bruce King, *Derek Walcott: A Caribbean Life* (New York: Oxford University Press, 2000); and Paul Breslin, *Nobody's Nation: Reading Derek Walcott* (Chicago: University of Chicago Press, in press).

5. In *Omeros* the name is spelled "Philoctete" and pronounced "Fee-lock-TET," in accordance with the French creole of Saint Lucia.

6. Edward [Kamau] Brathwaite, *The Arrivants: A New World Trilogy* (Oxford: Oxford University Press, 1973), 210, 249, 265; Walcott, "The Muse

of History: An Essay," in *Is Massa Day Dead? Black Moods in the Caribbean*, ed. Orde Coombs (Garden City, N.Y.: Anchor-Doubleday, 1974), 3.

7. Walcott, "Tribal Flutes" (1967), in *Critical Perspectives*, ed. Hamner, 43, and "The Muse of History," 8, 2–3. Brathwaite and Walcott have often been compared; see, e.g., Patricia Ismond, "Walcott versus Brathwaite," in *Critical Perspectives*, ed. Hamner, 220–36; and J. Edward Chamberlin, *Come Back to Me My Language: Poetry and the West Indies* (Urbana: University of Illinois Press, 1993), 154–55.

8. Walcott, *Collected Poems*, 269, 286.

9. Ibid., 269, 270.

10. Walcott uses the Philoctetes type in his unpublished play *The Isle Is Full of Noises* (1982), but there the wound signifies indigenous political corruption, not inherited colonial injury. I am grateful to Paul Breslin for sharing with me the play's typescript.

11. C. L. R. James, *The Black Jacobins: Toussaint L'Ouverture and the San Domingo Revolution*, 2d ed. (New York: Vintage-Random House, 1989), 12.

12. Walcott complains bitterly that such "historical sullenness" results in "morose poems and novels" of "one mood, which is in too much of Caribbean writing: that sort of chafing and rubbing of an old sore." See Edward Hirsch, "The Art of Poetry" (1986 interview), in *Critical Perspectives*, ed. Hamner, 79.

13. D. J. Bruckner, "A Poem in Homage to an Unwanted Man" (1990 interview), in *Critical Perspectives*, ed. Hamner, 397.

14. Walcott, "Laventille," in *Collected Poems*, 88.

15. Anthony Milne, "Derek Walcott" (1982 interview), in *Critical Perspectives*, ed. Hamner, 62.

16. On Walcott's use of Crusoe instead of Friday, see his "The Figure of Crusoe" (1965 lecture), in *Critical Perspectives*, ed. Hamner, 33–40.

17. Walcott earlier belittles "exotic," cross-racial recasting of characters like Hamlet; see "Meanings" (1970), in *Critical Perspectives*, ed. Hamner, 47.

18. Other Greek-named characters in *Omeros* share a similar genealogy, but their looser affinities with their namesakes make them more independent characters than the allegorical Philoctete. On the relationships between Walcott's characters and their Homeric counterparts, see Robert Hamner, Epic of the Dispossessed: Derek Walcott's "Omeros" (Columbia: University of Missouri Press, 1997); Terada, *Walcott's Poetry*, 183-212; Geert Lernout, "Derek Walcott's *Omeros*: The Isle Is Full of Voices," *Kunapipi* 14, no 2 (1992): 95–97; and Oliver Taplin, "Derek Walcott's *Omeros* and Derek Walcott's Homer," *Arion*, 3d ser., 1, no. 2 (1991): 213–26.

19. On the traditional fascination with Philoctetes' pain, see Oscar Mandel, *Philoctetes and the Fall of Troy* (Lincoln: University of Nebraska Press, 1981), 35–36. Mandel surveys Philoctetes' iconography (123–49).

20. Gotthold Ephraim Lessing, *Laocoön*, trans. Edward Allen McCormick (Baltimore: Johns Hopkins University Press, 1984), 29; Edmund Wilson, *The Wound and the Bow* (London: W. H. Allen, 1952), 257, 259; Seamus Heaney, *The Cure at Troy: A Version of Sophocles' "Philoctetes"* (New York: Noonday-Farrar, Straus & Giroux, 1991).

21. Terada, *Walcott's Poetry*, 188, 187.

22. Derek Walcott, "What the Twilight Says: An Overture," in "Dream on Monkey Mountain" and Other Plays (New York: Farrar, Straus & Giroux, 1970), 31, "The Figure of Crusoe," 36, and see also "The Muse of History," 4; Rob Nixon, "Caribbean and African Appropriations of *The Tempest*," *Critical Inquiry* 13 (1987): 557–78; and A. James Arnold, "Caliban, Culture, and Nation-Building in the Caribbean," in *Constellation Caliban: Figurations of a Character*, ed. Nadia Lie and Theo D'haen (Amsterdam and Atlanta, Ga.: Rodopi, 1997), 231–44, and other essays in the latter collection.

23. Shakespeare, *The Tempest*, 1.2.369–70. Walcott's remark about Timon of Athens and his script for *The Isle Is Full of Noises* indicate an additional Shakespearean prototype for the cursing Philoctete.

24. Walcott, "The Figure of Crusoe," 36.

25. Aimé Césaire, *A Tempest*, trans. Richard Miller (Paris: Editions du Seuil, 1986), 17, 18.

26. Walcott, "The Figure of Crusoe," 37, 35.

27. As an indication that Walcott closely associates Philoctetes and Crusoe, he gives the nickname "Crusoe" to the Philoctetes character in *The Isle Is Full of Noises*. Carol Dougherty argues for yet another Western prototype: Walcott introduces the scar-bearing Philoctete "as an Odysseus of sorts" ("Homer after *Omeros*: Reading a Homeric Text," *South Atlantic Quarterly* 96 [1997]: 339–47).

28. Walcott, "Necessity of Negritude," in Critical Perspectives, ed. Hamner, 20–23. On negritude and various conceptions of Africa in West Indian poetry, see Bremer, *An Introduction to West Indian Poetry*, 156–64.

29. Walcott, "The Caribbean: Culture or Mimicry?" (1974), in *Critical Perspectives*, ed. Hamner, 53.

30. Walcott, "The Muse of History," 7, 8.

31. At a more general level, Walcott follows the lead of negritude writers insofar as he, like them, dialectically inverts colonial stereotypes. Fanon, who worried about negritude's tendency to duplicate colonial views through such inversion, mentions as one of colonialism's dehumanizing

terms the "stink" of the native. When Walcott stresses the foul "smell" of Philoctete's wound, he not only remembers the Greek prototype but also flouts a repressive stereotype (10). See Frantz Fanon, *The Wretched of the Earth*, trans. Constance Farrington (New York: Grove Press-Présence Africaine, 1963), 212–13, 42.

32. Walcott, "Necessity of Negritude," 21.

33. Aimé Césaire, *Cahier d'un retour au pays natal*, 2d ed. (bilingual), English trans. Emile Snyders (Paris: Présence Africaine, 1968), 40, 126.

34. Ibid.: "whip" (130), "brand" (114), "tom-toms" (94).

35. Jean-Paul Sartre, "Black Orpheus" (1948), trans. John MacCombie, reprinted in *The Black American Writer*, ed. C. W. E. Bigsby (Deland, Fla.: Everett/Edward, 1969), 2:13. The anthology in which Sartre's "Orphée Noir" was originally published is *Anthologie de la nouvelle poésie negre et malgache de langue française*, ed. Léopold Sédar Senghor (Paris: Presses Universitaires de France, 1948).

36. Sartre, "Black Orpheus," 36; "Orphée Noir," 41.

37. Sartre, "Black Orpheus," 31–32; "Orphée Noir," 36.

38. Walcott, "The Antilles: Fragments of Epic Memory," reprinted in *Dictionary of Literary Biography Yearbook* (Detroit: Gale Research Co., 1992), 14.

39. Walcott, "The Muse of History," 27.

40. Yeats, "Crazy Jane Talks with the Bishop," in *Poems*, 260.

41. Walcott, *Collected Poems*, 346.

42. See Edward Kamau Brathwaite, *The Development of Creole Society in Jamaica, 1770–1820* (Oxford: Oxford University Press, 1971), and *Roots* (Ann Arbor: University of Michigan Press, 1993); Homi K. Bhabha, *The Location of Culture* (New York: Routledge, 1994); Edouard Glissant, *Caribbean Discourse: Selected Essays*, trans. J. Michael Dash (Charlottesville: University Press of Virginia, 1989); Roberto Fernández Retamar, *Caliban and Other Essays* (Minneapolis: University of Minnesota Press, 1989); and David A. Hollinger, *Postethnic America: Beyond Multiculturalism* (New York: Basic, 1995). The mixture in some models is primarily cultural, in others racial, and Walcott often conflates; the two. Regarding the West Indies, "almost all contemporary approaches to Afro-Caribbean culture(s)," according to Richard D. E. Burton, "stress its (their) syncretistic or mosaic character," with significant differences in emphasis (*Afro-Creole: Power, Opposition, and Play in the Caribbean* [Ithaca, N.Y.: Cornell University Press, 19971, 3). On the hybridity of Caribbean literature, see Antonio Benitez-Rojo, *The Repeating Island: The Caribbean and the Postmodern Perspective*, trans. James Maraniss (Durham, N.C.: Duke University Press, 1992); Silvio Torres-

Saillant, *Caribbean Poetics: Toward an Aesthetics of West Indian Literature* (Cambridge: Cambridge University Press, 1997); and J. Michael Dash, *The Other America: Caribbean Literature in a New World Context*, New World Studies (Charlottesville: University Press of Virginia, 1998).

43. Walcott, "Necessity of Negritude," 20.

44. Walcott, "The Caribbean," 52.

45. See Frantz Fanon's classic formulation of the three-stage "evolution" of native writing, from "unqualified assimilation" to nativist "exoticism" to "revolutionary," truly "national literature" (*The Wretched of the Earth*, trans. Constance Farrington [New York: Grove, 1963], 222–23). For a more recent example, see Bill Ashcroft, Gareth Griffiths, and Helen Tiffin, *The Empire Writes Back: Theory and Practice in Post-colonial Literatures* (New York: Routledge, 1989), 4–5: "Post-colonial literatures developed through several stages which can be seen to correspond to stages both of national or regional consciousness and of the project of asserting difference from the imperial centre." For Ashcroft, Griffiths, and Tiffin, as for many other critics, this literary historical narrative remains fundamental, despite a growing interest in "models of hybridity and syncreticity" (33–37).

46. According to John Bartell, the traditional image of Philoctetes, "with his wounded and unsupported foot, ... express[es] the fear of castration," which "derives from the belief that the woman is castrated" and thus "produces the need for the companion representation" of a female figure (*The Birth of Pandora and the Division of Knowledge* [Philadelphia: University of Pennsylvania Press, 19921, 213).

47. Walcott, *Collected Poems*, 20. Joseph Farrell comments on the "unending succession whereby formerly enslaved and colonized peoples become oppressors in their own right" ("Walcott's *Omeros*: The Classical Epic in a Postmodern World," *South Atlantic Quarterly* 96 [1997]: 265).

48. *Fredric Jameson*, "Third-World Literature in the Era of Multinational Capitalism," *Social Text* 15 (1986): 69.

49. Elaine Scarry, *The Body in Pain: The Making and Unmaking of the World* (New York: Oxford University Press, 1985), 119; and see 121 for the ensuing quotation.

50. Arguably, even postcolonial novels such as Michelle Cliffs *No Telephone to Heaven* and J. M. Coetzee's *Waiting for the Barbarians*, which like *Omeros* allegorize the wound and scar, more readily satisfy the imperatives of much postcolonial criticism than poetry does.

51. Glissant, *Caribbean Discourse*, 65–66.

52. On the ambiguous historicity and positionality of trauma, see Cathy Caruth, introduction to *Trauma: Explorations in Memory*, ed. Cathy

Caruth (Baltimore: Johns Hopkins University Press, 1995), 3–11; and Dori
Laub, "Bearing Witness; or, the Vicissitudes of Listening," in *Testimony:
Crises of Witnessing in Literature, Psychoanalysis, and History*, ed. Shoshana
Felman and Dori Laub (New York: Routledge, 1992), 57–74.

PAUL BRESLIN

Another Life: *West Indian Experience and the Problems of Narration*

CONTEXTS

From very early in his career, amid the Federalist hope that the West Indian archipelago would emerge as a New World counterpart of ancient Greece, Walcott has been fascinated with analogies between ancient Greece and the West Indies. And out of these analogies came, very early, his aspiration to write a West Indian counterpart of Homeric epic. But his first epic-length poem, *Another Life* (1973), is not so much an epic as an autobiography, albeit of an atypical kind. His second, *Omeros* (1990), certainly looks like an epic, but he has denied that it is, insisting that the poem ultimately disowns its extensive parallels to Homeric counterparts.

Undertaking a long poem for the first time in *Another Life*, Walcott confronted the problems of narration posed by what Glissant would call a "non-history." Yet at first glance, the poem seems more straightforward than its Anglo-American modernist counterparts. In its unhurried pace, it recalls nineteenth-century examples such as *The Prelude*, *In Memoriam*, or *The Ring and The Book*. it is almost Victorian in its expansiveness and unapologetic delight in elevated rhetoric, extended painterly description, and digressive metaphors.

From *Nobody's Nation: Reading Derek Walcott*. © 2001 by the University of Chicago.

The unusual qualities of Walcott's autobiographical long poem may partly derive from his interest in prose models. Walcott claims that Pasternak's *Safe Conduct* was the strongest influence on the style of *Another Life*. His friend Robert Lowell, who had urged him to "put more of [himself] into his poems,"[1] had been working since the late 1950s toward a style that could recover some of the prose virtues—especially flexibility, capacious registration of experience, and immediacy of communication—for poetry. In 1961 Lowell had suggested that "[t]he ideal modern form seems to be the novel and certain short stories. Maybe Tolstoy would be the perfect example—his work is imagistic, it deals with all experience, and there seems to be no conflict of the form and content."[2] In the prose memoir embedded in *Life Studies* (1959), Lowell uses objects as a sort of Perseus' shield in which to contemplate otherwise unbearable or confused memories: "[E]ach [object] has its function, its history, its drama.... The things and their owners come back urgent with life and meaning—because finished, they are endurable and perfect."[3] Writing to Walcott about *Another Life*, he thought that the poem's "core is the French novel of recollection, the time caught and lost between childhood and middle age. The must [sic] brilliant writing is in the innumerable St. Lucia descriptions, most of them recaptured moments, and so, though not necessarily narrative, [they] are autobiography."[4] He recognized the debt to prose models, having sought them out himself in the period when he was writing *Life Studies*, and also the displacement of "narrative" into "descriptions."

Both *Another Life* and *Omeros* grow out of explorations begun in Walcott's early years. He has referred to *Epitaph for the Young* as something of an "Ur-text" for both of them—which would suggest that both, albeit in different ways, continue the questing "toward" some emerging West Indian identity begun in that effort of 1949. The early stages of composition are more fully documented for *Another Life* than for most of Walcott's poetry, for in 1965 and 1966 he filled two exercise books with notes and drafts, and these have been placed in the archives of UWL Jamaica. In draft, the poem began as a prose memoir; only toward the end of the first notebook does Walcott shift to verse. Edward Baugh's deeply researched and in many ways excellent monograph has made use of these notebooks, but my interest in Walcott's conception of narrative leads me to different parts of them. Baugh treats *Another Life* almost as if it were an outsized lyric, organized by patterns of imagery and symbolism. The poem's tendency to replace narration with emblematic landscapes or objects partly justifies his approach. But its motifs function metonymically as well as symbolically, acquiring shifting implications as the poem repeats them in different contexts. Like such novelists as Joyce, Woolf, and Faulkner, Walcott finds the meanings of events primarily in a slow accretion of emotional resonances.

Walcott's verse autobiography has drawn comparisons, not least from Baugh, to Wordsworth's *Prelude*. But Walcott told me: "I felt much closer to the prose of Pasternak than I did to any poetry at all at that time. I'd never read *The Prelude*; I'd read bits of it. But because thematically it is the same sort of subject, I imagine, the comparisons are made about 'attempting' a *Prelude*; I had no such intention."[5] And in a 1966 essay for the *Trinidad Guardian*, he wrote: "I cherish at least one minor masterpiece of Pasternak's prose, his autobiography 'Safe Conduct.'" He praises the way, in Pasternak's work, "everything, churches, trains ... snow, insects are returned with a dulled but fixed sheen," so that "the naming of things, the simplest things, like buckets, sofas, the sound of rain, are [sic] merely, by the act of his naming them, reverberations," conveying "the sadness of common things, common occurrences."[6] Walcott begins the first notebook under the aegis of Pasternak by transcribing the last two stanzas of his poem, "The Wedding Party," which already hint at the difficulties of autobiography:

> And life itself is only an instant,
> Only the dissolving
> Of ourselves in all others
> As though in gift to them;
>
> Only a wedding, bursting
> [I]n through the windows from the street,
> Only a song a dream
> Of grey-blue pigeon[.][7]

These stanzas set the problem of the nascent poem: how to narrate an identity that is constantly "dissolving," becoming self-present only in flashes of intense experience.

Safe Conduct appears to have been useful to Walcott in three ways: for its style, which renders the inward experience of events through a painterly description of landscape, setting, and objects; for its digressive musings on the nature of biographical narrative and the vocation of the poet; and also, it may be, for certain parallels between Pasternak's experience and his own. Both works depict a fragile, innocent first love (though that is a standard feature of *Bildung* narratives) and formative artistic influences; more significantly, the suicide of Mayakovsky darkens the ending of Pasternak's memoir as the suicide of Harold Simmons shadows the closing chapters of

Walcott's. With both deaths comes an elegiac closure, a suggestion that both men were forerunners, embodying the collective aspirations of a people. Of Mayakovsky, Pasternak writes: "And it occurred to me then ... that this man was perhaps this State's unique citizen. The novelty of the age flowed climatically through his blood. His strangeness was the strangeness of our times of which half is as yet to be fulfilled."[8] Walcott offers a similar apotheosis of Simmons: "he is a man no more / but the fervour and intelligence / of a whole country" (*CP*, 277).

The kinship of style and of narrative form between the two works is deeper and harder to illustrate concisely. Some of Pasternak's critique of the limits of literal description and linear narration resembles Walcott's. "I think," writes Pasternak, "that only heroes deserve a real biography, but that the history of a poet is not to be presented in such a form. One would have to collect such a biography from [i]nessentials.... The poet gives his whole life such a voluntary steep incline that it is impossible for it to exist in the vertical line of biography where we expect to meet it."[9] Walcott, in a long entry for October 11, 1965, expresses a similar impatience: "I can't give facts. I do not know where to find them, how to arrange them. The blonde hair on a young girl's forearm, I should call it 'down,' is more important to me than the precise rearrangement of her features, or the date that I did something. Of course it is merely affectation, building a monument to the self." Later in the entry, he suggests that

> [a]ll biographies should be in the third person. The pretext
> of confession, whose real purpose is not exploring but
> ennobling life, is the supreme fiction; there is no style tha[t]
> can record the diurnal boredom, the fact, interminably
> longer than any fact, shock or revelation, that we spend life
> in a state of nothing. I do not mean enervation or lassitude;
> but any 'life' that told the truth would be too boring, too
> true.

Pasternak similarly asks: "What does an honest man do when he speaks the truth only? Time passes in the telling of truth, and in this time life passes onward. His truth lags behind and is deceptive. Should a man speak in this manner everywhere and always?"[10]

If the literal record of events, one after another in time, cannot narrate the development of an artist, the emphasis must turn away from what happened toward the imaginatively transformed experience of what happened. The artist, and the artist as autobiographer, must be "[f]ocussed on a reality which feeling has displaced," and "art is a record of this displacement." In that record, "[d]etails attain clarity, losing independence of meaning. Each detail can be replaced by another. Any one is precious. Any one chosen at random serves as evidence of the state which envelops the whole of transposed reality."[11] This method is both more and less subjective than conventional narrative. If it concentrates on the inward registration of experience on the artist's consciousness, it emphasizes that inwardness only insofar as it is part of the artistic process. "The more self-contained the individuality from which the life derives, the more collective, without any figurative speaking, is its story."[12] Both Walcott and Pasternak tell their stories largely as their response to encounters with other artists, and with works of art. We see Pasternak as the composition student of Alexander Scriabin and the admiring friend of the brilliant, enigmatic Mayakovsky. Just as Pasternak tried music and philosophy with some success before turning to literature, Walcott pursued his painting as keenly as his writing. *Another Life*, like *Safe Conduct*, is painterly in its depiction of places and things; it is also full of allusions to European art, which Walcott had discovered as a boy through reproductions in books.

One can trace Walcott's unease about narrative not only to his encounter with Pasternak's autobiography, but to the reflections of such West Indian writers as Wilson Harris, whom he had admiringly reviewed in the early 1960s for *Trinidad Guardian*. Harris's masterpiece, the *Guyana Quartet*, emphasizes the subjectivity of its characters and treats time as repeatable or reversible,[13] so that its first novella, "The Palace of the Peacock," can open with the death of its central character. In "Tradition and the West Indian Novel," Harris argued that "the depth of inarticulate feeling and unrealized wells of emotion belonging to the whole West Indies" challenged writers to develop a "*native* tradition of depth" in place of the "ruling and popular convention" of fiction. "The native and phenomenal environment of the West Indies, as I see it, is broken into many stages in the way in which one surveys an existing river in its present bed while plotting at the same time ancient and abandoned, indeterminate courses the river once followed." Instead of following clock time, fiction must offer a simultaneity of present and past, giving form to indeterminate alternatives, in order to be true to the fragmented, repeatedly interrupted development of West Indian cultures. It required an intensive rather than extensive method, bearing in on "the smallest area one envisages, island or village, prominent ridge or buried valley, flatland or heartland" until it became "charged immediately with the openness of imagination."[14] He speaks of fiction, but what he says could be applied to Walcott's poem.

Another Life "progresses not by narration but by a sequence of tableaux."[15] But the tableaux are informed with the traces of past movement, just as for Pasternak, "[i]nanimate objects ... were the living models of still-life, a medium particularly endearing to artists. Piling up in the furthest reaches of the living universe and appearing in immobility, they gave a most complete understanding of its moving whole, like any boundary which strikes us as a contrast."[16] Consider, for instance, Walcott's description of the house he grew up in. "Why," he asks, "should we weep for dumb things?" Perhaps because "a house ... / ... bears the depth of forest, of ocean and mother," and there is "a radiance of sharing" that "extends to the simplest objects" (*CP*, 155). People and things have a "true alignment," as if composed in a painting, from which they cannot be moved (*CP*, 157). The concentration on objects, landscape, and allusions to painting also gives form to feelings otherwise too inchoate for literary representation.

Not only does *Another Life* render experience as place or artifact, a still life instinct with the lingering traces of violent and contradictory movement; it follows Harris's directive to charge each small thing with "the openness of imagination." One might find its language excessive, seething with an intensity in excess of any apparent motive. And yet, the disproportion between extravagant description and uneventful narrative may register something important in Walcott's early experience. One need only compare the young Pasternak's social mobility and privilege (financially unburdened, wandering freely from Russia to Germany to Italy, encountering great artists such as Rilke, Scriabin, and Mayakovsky) with Walcott's islanded boyhood. In a revealing passage from the first notebook, Walcott meditates on the struggles of the young St. Omer, which he sees as representative of the West Indian artist's predicament:

> This rage, although I couldn't recognise it that early, was the demon that possessed Dunstan ["Gregorias" added in margin]. Its chart is a schizophrenic's: manic depressive with or without the aid of liquor. Then our native drink is more destructive than wine. He would move from a frightening exhilaration in life, whatever surrounded him[,] to an unshakeably silent despair.... [h]e see-sawed madly between dreams of fame, money, power and immortality to an acceptance of his calling as a lie, a lay-about's self-deceit. The deterioration set in early because he was the victim of what we had been taught: the rewards of art, of inevitable immortality, of a society—so rapt in his own vision of it that it would change. He loved it and thought as love makes a

woman radiant, that his country would become beautiful. Platonist victim.... So Gregorias virtually attacked each blank canvas as if it were his last chance for immortality. He assaulted its surface, singing loudly to the landscape all the while.[17]

One might say that in *Another Life*, Walcott similarly attacks the blank page as if seeking a last chance for immortality, singing loudly to the landscape all the while.

ART AND DIVIDED CONSCIOUSNESS

Painting, in addition to encouraging frozen tableaux as an alternative to narrative, provides the young poet with a cultural mirror in which to recognize himself. When Walcott portrays his childhood persona as "The Divided Child," he means not only the racial divisions of black and white, or the cultural divisions of English and West Indian; he means also the dualism of art and life, as his epigraph from Malraux's *Psychology of Art* suggests. According to Malraux, a young artist is "more deeply moved by the sight of works of art than by that of the things which they portray." However moved the young Walcott may have been by his experience, his deepest motive for writing and painting was the love of poems and paintings themselves.

The opening chapter of Malraux's book, "The Museum without Walls," suggests that with the aid of reproductions, a modern student of art anywhere in the world may make a wider comparison of artworks than even the best-traveled European of earlier days. Walcott, though he did not leave the West Indies until he was twenty-seven, had Thomas Craven's *Treasury of Art Masterpieces* (1939), which Baugh calls "a profound influence on his youth."[18] He could, with Malraux's endorsement, claim an equal footing with any European in his study of painting. But if art was to some extent its own world, it also kept referring back to "life." Whether Walcott's ambition was to confer the universality of art on St. Lucian experience, or to discover a universality, already latent within that experience, remains uneasily ambiguous throughout the poem. In Chapter 1, we meet the young Walcott as "the student" of art, sketching a landscape on Vigie promontory. He has "magnified the harbour," as if to confer a heightened significance on it. He waits at sunset for "the tidal amber glare to glaze / the last shacks of the Morne till they became / transfigured sheerly by the student's will, / a cinquecento fragment in gilt frame" (*CP*, 146). The shacks must be "transfigured," but the resulting image remains a "fragment" in a gilded (and guilty) frame. As Baugh points out, the ensuing lines undercut the student's efforts: "The vision died, / the black hills simplified / to hunks of coal," returning us from Renaissance Italy to the coal-carriers and *charbonniers* of St. Lucia.[19]

To a large extent, the racial split and the split between art and life are connected. The art that the young Walcott ardently admired was European, with depictions of white flesh by white artists, in a landscape remote from his own. When he attempts to see himself in the art of Giotto and Cimabue (referred to in the Malraux epigraph), disparities of race and culture exacerbate the inherent split between body and representation. The first clear allusion to a particular artwork occurs on the first page of the poem, when Walcott, describing himself, writes: "The dream / of reason had produced its monster: / a prodigy of the wrong age and colour" (*CP*, 145). He refers to Goya's *El sueño de la razón produce monstruos*, which depicts an Enlightenment gentleman asleep at his desk, his pen lying where it had fallen. Nearby lies a large cat-like creature, about the size of an ocelot. Owls crowd at his back, staring down at him, while indistinct bats hover behind him in the shadows. By allying himself with the cat, the bats, and the owls, rather than with the dreamer, Walcott depicts himself as the feared, repressed other of European civilization. The ambiguity of Goya's title (*sueño* can mean either "sleep" or "dream") is very much to the point: from the Enlightenment point of view, when reason falls asleep, the monstrosity it had subdued breaks free. But to translate *sueño* as "dream" implies that reason produces the very monstrosity it suppresses.[20] Walcott suggests that he is an inevitable product of the very civilization that would reject him. But at the outset of the poem, the monstrous prodigy is still trying to take up reason's work where the sleeper left it, willing a St. Lucian landscape into the conventions of European painting. No wonder that "with slow strokes, the master [Simmons] changed the sketch," or that he would counter his student's yearning "for whiteness, for candour,"[21] by reading from the Jamaican poet George Campbell: "Holy be / the white head of a Negro, / sacred be / the black flax of a black child" (*CP*, 147, 146, 148–49).

That "new book" seemed to inaugurate "another life" (*CP*, 149), but this beginning has to be constantly reenacted. In the very next section, describing the funeral of a light-skinned St. Lucian girl who had been nicknamed "Pinkie," Walcott superimposes upon her image Thomas Lawrence's portrait, "Pinkie," which depicts "Miss Barrett" in a bonnet and ethereally flowing gown. The portrait, from 1795, predates Goya's *El sueño de la razón* by just four years but belongs to a different world, still clinging to a decorum in which reason is very much awake and in control. Simmons, too, had confronted the struggle for a synthesis of European art with his own heritage, as evidenced by the presence in his studio of both a "plaster-of-Paris Venus" and his own "kerchiefed, ear-ringed portrait: Albertina" (*CP*, 147).[22]

The opening chapter concludes with a reminder that in one sense, at least, "everything whitens": everything dies. Death immediately becomes associated with photography: its arrest of movement in a "still," the whiteness of bones in X-rays, of a flashbulb, of the moon (still abroad to trouble some dreaming Makak). The starkness of the photograph contrasts with the rich amber glaze of the old masters. The contrast may be the old dichotomy between photography that (supposedly) records and painting that "transfigures," but there is also a parallelism: if the legacy of "Europe" includes the painting and poetry that the young Walcott admires, it also includes the objectifications of modern technology, the human body subjected to the unsparing gaze of camera (especially when used by tourists), X-ray, and electric light.

As Baugh remarks,[23] the first six chapters of *Another Life* set forth the social and personal circumstances from which Walcott emerged. After locating the first chapter on Vigie promontory, significant as the site of Simmons's studio, Anna's home, and the emergency housing where all classes mingled after the Castries fire of 1948,[24] Walcott narrows the focus to the house in which he grew up. Taken together, the opening chapters insist on grounding identity not on any principle or abstraction, but on the most immediate and local attachments, a particular house in a particular part of a small island. In this way, the poem declares at once its faith in the power of minute particulars to generate larger, more universal insights, as they are "magnified" in the medium of art. The poem moves outward from this center, which remains somewhat cloistered, keeping the fascinating but frightening peasant lore of the supernatural at a safe distance: "One step beyond the city was the bush. / One step behind the church door stood the devil" (*CP*, 167).

Chapter 3 turns outward toward the streets of Castries, gathering material for the "pseudo-epic" (*CP*, 183) under construction. "The candle's yellow leaf next to his bed / re-letters *Tanglewood Tales* and Kingsley's *Heroes*," just as Walcott will "re-letter" those accounts of the Greek myths in a St. Lucian alphabet, so that "[t]he black lamplighter" of Castries holds "Demeter's torch." In a manner reminiscent of the "Wandering Rocks" section of Joyce's *Ulysses*,[25] Walcott gives a catalogue of persons, places, and things. A few of these ("Helen," "Midas," "Nessus," "Troy town") continue the classical motif, but most are locally named as well as locally observed.

The transformation of Helen into "Jamie, the town's one clear-complexioned whore, / with two tow-headed children in her tow" (*CP*, 161) may seem ironically deflating.[26] But as with Joyce's parallelism of the *Odyssey* and modern Dublin, the cumulative effect is less to place the modern analogues in a belittling shadow than to discover a latent mythical potential in unpromising material. And some of these characters harbor a protest against the conditions that have produced them. Weekes, a grocer and solid citizen, is also a Garveyite awaiting Exodus to Africa; even the filthy "Nessus" "rises in sackcloth, prophesying / fire and brimstone on the gift wooden towers of / offices, odures, on / Peter & Co. to burn like Pompeii, on J. / Q. Charles's stores" (*CP*, 163, 162). The catalogue concludes with a valediction on them all: "These dead, these derelicts, / that alphabet of the emaciated, / they were the stars of my mythology" (*CP*, 164). Here mythology functions as painting has in the first two chapters: it is a mirror in which to see, imagine, and redefine one's world, even if the extreme distance of the mirror from the imaged world turns self-recognition into a leap of faith.

The young Walcott's access to folk tales of obeah and *gens gajés*[27] came through his aunt Sidone, in whose voice, as he put it in *Midsummer*, "shadows stood up and walked.[28] Despite the influence of Catholic or Methodist church, the "atavism" of folk tradition runs deep, for its "tubers gripped the rooted middle class, / beginning where Africa began: / in the body's memory" (*CP*, 167). These lines illuminate Walcott's frequent use of the word "amnesia," which comes into this poem early in Chapter 1 ("Darkness, soft as amnesia, furred the slope"—*CP*, 146). The middle class may have chosen to forget such "atavism," but the body's memory is not the same as the mind's. As we have seen, amnesia for Walcott is the body's form of memory, because the mind's inability to remember is the somatic trace of an old wound.

The tale of the supernatural that follows resembles the story of Le Brun in "Tales of the Islands," though the possessed man is here named Manoir. "He was the first black merchant baron" (*CP*, 170), and precisely because a black man's success in business seemed so implausible in those colonial times, the rumor sprang up that Manoir was one of the *gens gajés* pledged to the devil. As Manoir dies, struck down while prowling in canine form, a priest attempts to exorcise the spirit that has possessed him. The priest calls, in Latin, upon the maker of the world to cast the spirit into Gehenna (*CP*, 170), but a fly, speaking as a representative of Beelzebub his lord, is also praying "at [Manoir's] ear well," and this prayer is in French. The clash between French and Latin parallels the clash between folk religion and religious orthodoxy, and both parallel the clash between the artificial paradise of European art and St. Lucian experience. But Walcott also connects European art to St. Lucian experience when he likens the fly to a detail of a painting reproduced in the *Treasury*: "Some jewelled insect in a corner of Crivelli" (*CP*, 165). He alludes to a Virgin and Child in which mother and child look down at an exquisitely painted fly in the lower left foreground. Even in a religious painting from Europe, the devil's insect appears. The infernal powers are not confined to the islands.

If the young poet's imagination kindles to folk tales of the supernatural, he is also drawn to "the Jacobean English" he heard in church, "the speech of simple men, / evangelists, reformers, abolitionists," whose "text was cold brook water" (*CP*, 166). He associates the eloquence of the chapel with the figure of Matthew Arnold. "I know those rigorous teachers of your youth," he says, recalling the Victorian poet's "Stanzas from the Grand Chartreuse." Arnold, like the "divided" child of Walcott's poem, felt trapped "between two worlds, one dead, / The other powerless to be born." Arnold's lost paradise is the Catholic faith of the monks, whereas Walcott's is the folk culture. Nonetheless, because of "the passionate, pragmatic / Methodism of [his] infancy," he fears what he longs for as "traumatic, tribal" (*CP*, 166), and malign.

By Chapter 5, Walcott has begun to recapitulate material from the opening sections; he opens with a recollection of Manoir's commercial empire, then evokes the "black hills" that were "simplified / to hunks of coal" (*CP*, 146) in a description of coal carriers at work "on black hills of imported anthracite" (*CP*, 171). Yet returns of this kind are not flashbacks, since no narrative timeline has been established, but rather a network of simultaneous association, the metamorphic convertibility of images into each other. That is why it is possible for Baugh, with considerable success, to read *Another Life* as a giant lyric poem, held together by patterns of imagery. But this circling back also allows a slow, metonymic accretion of context. For instance, Chapter 5's epigraph is the colonial motto of St. Lucia, the Virgilian phrase *Statio haud malefida carinis*. Against this motif of safety stands Manoir's sign, "LICENSED TO SELL / INTOXICATING LIQUOR" (*CP*, 171): his ambition is associated with forbidden intoxications of drink and magic. His anomalous wealth also contrasts starkly with the poverty of the coal-carrying women. The Latin motto sounds increasingly ironic as the stifling poverty and colonized psychology of the island becomes apparent. A schoolboy, translating the motto in his strongly accented speech, renders it, more aptly than he knows, as "a safe anchorage for sheeps" (*CP*, 172).

In Chapter 7, which closes the first of the poem's four parts, the relation of art and life returns to central importance. "Provincialism loves the

pseudo-epic," Walcott begins, "so if these heroes have been given a stature /
disproportionate to their cramped lives, / remember I beheld them at knee-
height" (*CP*, 183). He apologizes for his unprepossessing characters, yet
claims that the perspective of childhood justifies their magnification as a
subjective truth.

Walcott's adoration of European art awakens an apparently opposite
quest. Schooled by European masterpieces, his aspiring painter's "hand"
sought "in the deep country" for

> the natural man,
> generous, rooted.
> And now I yearned to suffer for that life,
> I looked for some ancestral, tribal country....
>
> (*CP*, 184)

As yet, the yearning to suffer remains a willed primitivism, as the increasingly
self-mocking continuation of the passage recognizes: "I looked from the bus
window / and multiplied the bush with savages" (*CP*, 184). Walcott's heroes
among the artists were Gauguin, who went off to Tahiti and the Marquesas
to find (and become) the unspoiled natural man, and van Gogh, who believed
that rural scenes, caught in the open air, brought authenticity to his art.

Only when an experience of deep identification with the island's poor
comes over him unbidden does the self-conscious yearning to suffer for the
folk become spontaneous compassion. "About the August of my fourteenth
year / I lost my self somewhere above a valley / owned by a spinster-farmer,
my dead father's friend." The place links the experience to the legacy of the
poet's father, but, as the separation of "my self" into two words emphasizes,
it entails not some passage into identity but rather a complete forgetfulness
of self. "I dissolved into a trance" (*CP*, 184), the poem tells us, and one might
read the pronoun as in implied quotation marks. This experience is
completely involuntary: "I was seized by a pity more profound / than my
young body could bear"; "uncontrollably I began to weep"; "I felt compelled
to kneel" (*CP*, 185). And yet it is still empathy at a distance: "the poor still
move behind their tinted scrim" (*CP*, 185), as if veiled for a mysterious ritual.
The passage ends, however, with a stronger sense of identification: "in that
ship of night, locked in together, / through which, like chains, a little light
might leak, / something fastens us forever to the poor" (*CP*, 185). The
implied metaphor is the hold of a slave ship, as all of the island's people are
connected by the trauma of the Middle Passage. But the slave ship is the
vehicle, not the tenor, of a metaphor about the night: it is also as if, in the

solitude of night, sleep, and dreams, class differences dissolve in a common uncertainty and fear of death. But there is still a distinction between "us" and "the poor."

Returning from the account of his "trance," Walcott asks himself, "But which was the true light? / Blare noon or twilight?" The question abruptly poses yet another dichotomy. The opposition of twilight and noon remains incompletely defined until Part Two, in which Walcott and "Gregorias" embrace an art of "blare noon," acolytes of "Vincent [van Gogh], saint / of all sunstroke" and "Paul [Gauguin], their heads plated with fire" (*CP*, 198–99). In Part One, art is suffused with vague yearning, a twilight activity. That transitional light is appropriate for the half-awakened vocation of the young artist. But Chapter 7 brings a moment of conversion, in which, "like Saul, unhorsed," he was changed completely. He "fell in love" and at the same time "fell in love with art, / and life began" (*AL*, 186). The conversion occurs, to be sure, under the auspices of Michelangelo, Raphael, and Uccello, but it sends him back to the common life of the island.

Walcott's epigraph for Part Two, "Homage to Gregorias," contrasts with the Malraux quotation of Part One, in which a European writer describes the apprenticeship of famous European painters. Instead, a Caribbean writer, Alejo Carpentier, describes Caribbean people of various races—whites, blacks, and Amerindians—trapped in futile pursuit of a European ideal, "more and forgetful of the sun they had left behind, trying desperately to imitate what came naturally to those whose rightful place was in the net." Having wasted their youth in "unlighted studios," they eventually come home exhausted, having lost the "heart to set themselves the only task appropriate to the milieu that was slowly revealing to me the nature of its values: Adam's task of giving things their names"[29] (*CP*, 189). The European art of Cimabue and Giotto, who according to Malraux loved paintings even more than they loved the natural world, has led to an Adamic poetics, in which the artifice so strenuously acquired must forget itself in a return to primal beginnings. At some times Walcott sees himself as a sophisticate in search of the natural man; at others, he claims citizenship in the Edenic place that Carpentier's protagonist must seek from afar.

The poem quickly establishes the "sun-struck" intensity of open-air painting in its tropical setting: "Days welded by the sun's torch into days!" (*CP*, 193). Gregorias brings a martial resolve to his encounter with heat and the elements, "the easel rifled on his shoulder, marching / towards an Atlantic flashing tinfoil." As he advances, he sings "'O Paradiso'" (*CP*, 194), finding his heaven on the same coast the French priest of Chapter 6 had

experienced as hell. The pact between the poet and Gregorias, to pay full
homage to the island in their art, follows:

> But drunkenly, or secretly, we swore,
> disciples of that astigmatic saint,
> that we would never leave the island
> until we had put down, in paint, in words,
> as palmists learn the network of a hand,
> all of its sunken, leaf-choked ravines,
> every neglected, self-pitying inlet muttering
> in brackish dialect, the ropes of mangroves
> from which old soldier crabs slipped
> surrendering to slush,
> each ochre track seeking some hilltop and
> losing itself in an unfinished phrase,
> under sand shipyards where the burnt-out palms
> inverted the design of unrigged schooners,
> entering forests, boiling with life;
> *goyave, corrosol, bois-canot, sapotille.*
>
> (*CP*, 194)

The island may be "Paradiso," but an enjambment qualifies the promise not
to leave it with "until." Once every feature of the island has been "put down"
in their paintings and poems, the young artists will be free to go. Their art is
a labor of love, but it also discharges a debt. The language suggests an almost
magical faith in the power of art to embody the experienced world: not to
depict but to "put down" intact ravines, mangroves, palms, and forests. The
artist is like a "palmist" (a pun, linking the fate written in the hand with the
fronds of the trees he attempts to capture in paint); he interprets signs that
are already given, to be studied rather than transformed. But much of the
description implies an incompleteness in the landscape as found: the "ochre
track" up the hillside trails off in "an unfinished phrase," the ravines are
"sunken" and "leaf-choked," their breath and power of speech stifled. The
inlets are "muttering in brackish dialect," quietly and indistinctly. Much of
the landscape suggests exhaustion (the aged soldier crabs "surrendering to
slush," the "burnt-out palms"), yet the forests of the interior are "boiling
with life." To the initiated, this landscape discloses a primal fecundity,
suggested by the catalogue of creole plant-names at the end of the passage.
The vitality of the landscape reveals itself through the creole speech of those
who truly inhabit it. The young Walcott and St. Omer do not fully inhabit it

until, through their art, they arrive as "conquerers who had discovered home" (*CP*, 195).

The chapter closes with a reflection on the paradox it has raised: that the landscape is already eloquent in a language that waits to be heard and written down, but in the meantime remains mute, "choked," inarticulate. "For no one had written of this landscape / that it was possible," the last section begins, and the enjambment insists that merely to write of it is not enough; one must write "that it was possible" for art and literature. The place has an oral language, creole, but not yet a written one. Things have names, but the names conceal, or are concealed; the weeds proliferate, "hiding in their names," and "whole generations died, unchristened, / growths hidden in green darkness, forests / of history thickening with amnesia" (*CP*, 195). Weather and geography conspire with cultural trauma to sustain this "amnesia," as "the lost Arawak hieroglyphs and signs / were razed from slates by sponges of the rain," and "the archipelago like a broken root / [was] divided among tribes." The young artists aspire to recover this "life older than geography," deep sources of identity threatened with erasure.

Walcott depicts the painter's work as furious struggle, recalling van Gogh's letters from Arles, where "from seven o'clock in the morning till six in the evening" he often "worked without stirring except to eat a bite a step or two away," painting "landscapes done more rapidly than ever before." For van Gogh as for his St. Lucian disciples, painting was "headlong work."[30] As Baugh says, Chapter 9 of *Another Life* "is a remarkable poetic re-creation of the act of painting,"[31] but it also includes, in its second section, a critique of language as the medium of that re-creation, since the very metaphors used to evoke the act of painting signal the difference between the crablike ambiguity of metaphor and the "linear elation" of Gregorias's brushstrokes.

Walcott's language at once insists on the complete fusion of the energies of art with those of nature and on a stubborn, mocking resistance within nature itself. The painting is latently present before the first brushstroke: "There are already, invisible on canvas, / lines locking into outlines. The visible dissolves / in a benign acid." This auspicious beginning, which grants to art the power to dissolve the given and reshape it, soon generates its own countermovement: "[o]ver your shoulder the landscape / frowns at its image" (*CP*, 197). Nature becomes a disapproving critic of the emerging painting. The energies of art and natural fecundity interpenetrate each other, but the resulting profusion of forms can intimidate as well as inspire:

April ignites the immortelle,
the leaf of a kneeling sapling
is the yellow flame of Lippi's "Annunciation."
Like the scrape of a struck match, cadmium orange,
evened to the wick of a lantern.
Like a crowd, surrounding the frame,
the muttering variegations of green.

(*CP*, 197)

The yellow of nature and the yellow of Fra Lippo Lippi's palette coincide. But the "variegations of green" crowd around the easel-frame, "muttering" like the inlets (*CP*, 194). What tints will represent the indistinct variegation, what artistic language will translate its muttering? The censorious landscape has now multiplied into a "crowd" of natural presences, under whose inspection the painter must continue his work. As the artist struggles, he sees his strain mirrored in nature: "The mountain's crouching back begins to ache" (*CP*, 197).

The imagery evokes a scene of medieval combat, as "a bird's cry tries to pierce / the thick silence of the canvas" (*CP*, 198). The artist's canvas, initially offered as a field receptive to natural energies, has become impervious, silent, and resistant, like a shield held up in defense. The landscape grows more threatening: "At your feet / the dead cricket grows into a dragon, / the razor grass bristles resentment ... // and a crab, the brush in its pincer, / scrapes the white sand of canvas." The crab becomes the artist's *Doppelgänger*, painting the natural "canvas" of the beach. The artist too acquires armor as "the sun plates [his] back" (*CP*, 198). He resembles a knight in combat against his carapaced adversaries, the cricket-dragon in its exoskeleton, the crab in its shell. His work grows increasingly violent, as "the sun explodes into irises, / the shadows are crossing like crows, / they settle, clawing the hair, / yellow is screaming" (*CP*, 199). These crows first appear in a metaphor: "From the reeds of your lashes, the wild commas / of crows are beginning to rise" (*CP*, 198). Though subjectively generated, the "crows" are at that point understood as part of the landscape. Now they become a figure for "shadows" and settle in the painter's hair, returning to the head that first conjured them. Subject and object, painter and landscape, like the "Days welded by the sun's torch into days" (*CP*, 193), disappear into the fire that consumes them both: "Nature is a fire, / through the door of this landscape / I have entered a furnace. // I rise, ringing with sunstroke!" (*CP*, 199). The fire consumes the appearances that feed it so completely that only the fire itself remains visible. This moment might seem an apotheosis, but only five lines later, "the mouth is sour with failure" (*CP*, 199).

The artist's labor fails because the subjective experience of fusion with the energies of nature itself has not been transferred to the canvas. The moment of intensity has left no lasting trace: "Nothing will show after this, nothing / except the frame which you carry in your sealed, surrendering eyes" (*CP*, 200). Looking back on the reasons for his failure, Walcott concludes that although he could depict "the visible world that [he] saw / exactly," he was too much given to second thoughts. In contrast to the "circuitous instinct" of his own "poor crab" of a hand, Gregorias "would draw / with the linear elation of an eel / one muscle in one thought" (*CP*, 201).

The crab-painter, casually introduced in the first section, turns out to be an emblem of the young Walcott. The indirection of metaphor and paradox, and the historical self-consciousness of "that style, / this epoch, that school" (*CP*, 201), constrain his efforts. Gregorias, in contrast, "abandoned apprenticeship / to the errors of his own soul." As a result, "[h]is work was grotesque, but whole, / and however bad it became / it was his, he possessed / aboriginal force" (*CP*, 201). Through Gregorias's unswerving "linear elation," the initial dream of a landscape "set down" in paint has come true: "Now, every landscape we entered / was already signed with his name" (*CP*, 201). Walcott's divided, complex temperament will require verbal rather than painted images as its artistic medium.

The energies of painting are self-delighting, as we find in Chapter 10, which describes Gregorias's "first commission" from the young French priest at the church in Gros Îlet, a village just north of Rodney Bay on the leeward coast. In this pre-Vatican II work, St. Omer could not depict the holy family or saints as black, though he did sneak a few black faces into the background;[32] yet his delight in his work shines through the borrowed European styles:

> Above the altar lace
> he mounted a triptych of the Assumption
> with coarse, purpureal clouds, a prescient Madonna
> drawn from Leonardo's "Our Lady of the Rocks."
> He soared on his trestles,[33] the curled days shorn
> by the adze of St. Joseph the Worker,
> till dusk, the tree of heaven, broke in gold leaf.
>
> (*CP*, 205)

When he comes down from his trestles, however, Gregorias faces the same dilemma as the young Walcott: how shall he make a career as an artist in a place that cannot sustain an artistic career? Gregorias faces a difficult future, as a "darkness" gathers within him. Somehow, he will have to negotiate the gap between the "black nudes gleaming sweat / in the tiger shade of the fronds" (CP, 203) that he produces in the privacy of his studio and the evocations of Leonardo required for the Gros Îlet commission. And he will be unable to earn a living from his painting. He affects an indifference to the public response to his work: "Man I ent care if they misunderstand me, / I drink my rum, I praise my God, I mind my business!" and he claims that in contrast to Walcott, whose "poetry too full of spiders, / bones, worms, ants, things eating up each other," he "love[s] life" (CP, 206). He exclaims of himself, "Ah, Gregorias, you are a genius, yes! / Yes, God and me, we understand each other" (CP, 207). There is a compensatory bravado in his gestures, as he portrays Europe as suppliant rather than conqueror:

> As if the thunderous Atlantic
> were a record he had just put on.
> "Listen! Vasco da Gama kneels to the New World."
>
> (CP, 207)

But he is aware of his own exaggerations, at once defiant and self-mocking.

The sight of "the insane asylum" (CP, 207) across the harbor triggers a consideration of madness. Walcott draws a distinction between Gregorias's "madness" and his own obsession with "our history" (CP, 208). As Baugh remarks, the manuscript draft includes an account of Walcott's "experience in boyhood of living through the breakdown of an uncle, his mother's brother, who had lived in their house and died in a mental asylum."[34] Walcott writes:

> Up to now I do not remember where my uncle was buried. Probably in the asylum itself, although I doubt that ignorance could have been vicious and frightened enough to separate the graves of the mad from the graves of the sane, as the Church distinctly separated suicides from the blessed dead.[35]

This passage, though it has no counterpart in the poem, tellingly foreshadows *Another Life*'s association of madness with suicide and both with the figure of the artist. Shadowing the poem is the awareness that the story of the artist's life may be a narrative with a (literally) dead end. In retrospect, the ecstasies of artistic awakening that Walcott shared with Gregorias are at once sacred and premature. "[I]n the beginning, all / Drunkenness is Dionysiac, divine" (CP, 219), and it remains forever an article of faith that "Gregorias, lit, / we were the light of the world!" (CP, 220). But the time was coming when "we too would resemble / those nervous, inflamed men, / fisherman and joiner, / with their quivering addiction / to alcohol and failure" (CP, 220–21). Lit with inspiration, the artist borrows divine energies and may without blasphemy appropriate the words of Christ. But to be "lit" can also simply mean to be drunk. Gregorias had sung "O paradiso," and Walcott had felt himself to be Adam in paradise, but the future will reveal them to be "damned poet and damned painter" (CP, 220), akin on the one hand to their tormented heroes, Gauguin, van Gogh, and Baudelaire, and on the other to the common people—this time not in their latent glory but in their frustration and failure. If the artist longs to be one with the fisherman and joiner, in many a fisherman and joiner there is a balked artist: "We saw, within their eyes, / we thought, an artist's ghost" (CP, 221).

Despite his quest for the St. Lucian "natural man," the young Walcott had tried to make the history he learned at school into a usable past. In his fantasies, he "butchered fellaheen, thuggees, Mamelukes, wogs" (CP, 211) as enthusiastically as any white colonist. At such moments, he remembers, "my head roared with gold. I bled for all. I thought it full of glory" (CP, 211). Gold has been the color of awakening artistic vocation, sexual desire, and love for Anna, all of which occurred in the same "golden year" (CP, 192). But the same color has also evoked the "golden, bugled epoch" (CP, 180) of colonialism at its zenith. The convergence of all of these motifs on the word "gold" suggests the seductive danger of identifying artistic achievement, sexual desire, and even love itself with European ideals of beauty and power. In Drums and Colours, we recall, gold was the European "God."

Even within a fantasy of himself as a white eighteenth-century soldier stunned by the heat and hardship of his tropical post, Walcott holds to his own sense of experience as a series of self-erasing gestures followed by new beginnings: "This forest keeps no wounds, this nature heals / the newest scar, each cloud wraps like a bandage / whatever we enact" (CP, 212). In this poem, one is always beginning "another life" rather than continuing a course of action. But self-erasure resists narrative: whatever happens is soon rubbed out, and we return to an open beginning.

Ideas of the divine, too, are always being destroyed and remade: "I am pounding the faces of gods back into the red clay they / leapt from the mattock of heel after heel, as if heel / after heel were my thumbs that once gouged out as sacred / vessels for women the sockets of eyes" (CP, 213). The run-on syntax and breathless enjambment enacts the furious smashing of forms, unmaking the gods and tracing their manufacture back to its primal origins. God-making is bloodthirsty work from the outset, and it remains so despite the apparent progress from "primitive" worship of clay figures to Christian monotheism, which has sanctioned the butchery of "fellaheen, thuggees, Mamelukes, wogs" (*CP*, 211), not to mention Caribs and Africans. Better to pound all gods "back into what they never should have sprung from, / staying un-named and un-praised where I found them— / in the god-breeding, god-devouring earth!" (*CP*, 213). In the end, the earth survives its gods. With "history" discredited and the gods deposed, the ground of origin recedes in infinite regress: "Where else to row, but backward? / Beyond origins, to the whale's wash, / to the epicanthic Arawak's Hewanora,[36] / back to the impeachable pastoral" (*CP*, 217). Once again, this resolution resists narrative form. Pastoral does not move.

AFTER THE "IMPEACHABLE PASTORAL": LOVE, DEPARTURE, AND "HISTORY"

The transition to the third part of the poem comes with one of those random events that assume such prominence in a Glissantian "non-history" and resist the writer's desire for plot to unfold from what has already happened. And yet, this event, which sweeps the inert social order of the town away, inaugurates something the poet will call "history." With the Castries fire of 1948, the "impeachable pastoral" is over:

> And then, one night, somewhere,
> A single outcry rocketed in air,
> the thick tongue of a fallen, drunken lamp
> licked at its alcohol ringing the floor,
> and with the fierce rush of a furnace door
> suddenly opened, history was here.
>
> (*CP*, 221)

Here is one more permutation of the word "lit," connecting the energies of creation to those of destruction. The lamp, like the two young painters, runs on alcohol. The kindling of the fire is figuratively likened to drunkenness, and the "thick tongue" of the lamp recalls the "tongue of the carpenter's plane" and the "tongues of shavings" that "coil from the moving pen" (*CP*, 216) of the poet. Earlier, "through the door of this landscape" Walcott had "entered a furnace" (*CP*, 199) as he vainly struggled to wrestle a resistant nature onto his canvas. "History," too, is an ungovernable fire, and it leaps through a breach opened by mere chance.

The title of the third part of the poem, "A Simple Flame," emerges from the fiery arrival of "history," diverting fire again from destruction to ardor. The epigraph from César Vallejo braces the poem for change: "All have actually parted from the house, but all truly have remained. And it's not the memory of them that remains, but they themselves. Nor is it that they remain in the house, but that they continue because of the house" (*CP*, 223). Chapter 2 had grounded the future poet's career in the experience of growing up in his mother's house, that "sang softly of balance, / of the rightness of placed things" (*CP*, 157) and preserved the memory of his late father. Now the "house" expands, becoming a figure for the island itself as the nurturing environment of its people. St. Lucians who seek a name in the world must eventually leave the house, but everything they do remains grounded within it. As Vallejo puts it, "[t]he functions and the acts go from the house by train, or by plane or on horseback," but "[w]hat continues in the house is the subject of the act" (*CP*, 223).

The first "flame" that we encounter in Part Three is that of the Castries fire itself, described in a language reminiscent of Pasternak's description of a fire in *Safe Conduct*.[37] It shatters the order of time ("They heard the century breaking in half") and space ("the telephone wires sang from pole to pole / parodying perspective"; "the sea was level with the street"), so that the cosmos itself seems no longer upheld by "the broken axle tree" (*CP*, 225). And yet the fire unifies, as "those who thought their lives strange to their neighbours" (*CP*, 225) find their "lives casualty tangled like unsorted laundry." Divisions of class dissolve in "some pact / of common desolation" (*CP*, 226) among the displaced families on the Vigie promontory. Despite the insistent repetition of "burnt" and "broken," images of regeneration begin to appear as "the grid of stars budded with lights" and the stunned refugees began another life" (*CP*, 226).

Despite the violent eruption of history into Walcott's life, the motions of nature—the moon's rising and setting, or the wind's continuous rippling of the waves—go on as before. To the extent that he aspires to escape from history into primal relation with the natural world, Walcott is tempted to collapse the linearity of narrative into the circling back of natural process, or into a profusion of appositive description that keeps adding and adding, like the lapping of waves on the shore. Actions, as well as words, can appropriate these natural rhythms. In the third section, as Walcott watches the approach of the boat that will take him across the harbor to Anna, he admires the oarsman's stroke, "unstudied, pentametrical, / one action, and one thought" (*CP*, 227). The passage recalls the single-minded purity of Gregorias's painting, "one muscle in one thought" (*CP*, 201). In such approximations of natural force art finds its greatest power as well as its connection to the life of the body.

The fourth section brings the encounter with Anna, portrayed throughout in imagery of sunlight and gold: "The sixteen-year-old sun / plates her with light" (*CP*, 229), just as sun had "plate[d]" Walcott's "back" as he painted with Gregorias, and had once "plated with fire" the heads of van Gogh and Gauguin (*CP*, 198–99). At the moment when he "asked her, 'Choose'" and "she nodded," history seems magically repealed: "that nod / married earth with lightning. / And now we were the first guests of the earth, / and everything stood still for us to name" (*CP*, 230–31). But within a few lines, Eve mutates to "that flax-bright harvester / Judith, with Holofernes' lantern in her hand" (*CP*, 231), foreshadowing the trouble ahead—and foreshadowing, too, its connection with Walcott's artistic vocation, for the image is again out of a painting, Carlo Sarcani's "Judith and Holofernes," which appears in full-page reproduction in Malraux's *Psychology of Art*.[38]

The division of Anna into, a vision of angelic innocence and a potentially dangerous Judith becomes more intelligible as Walcott describes a split in his own desire. From the "divided child" has come a divided youth. He portrays Anna, singing with the choir at Christmas, as a "profile of hammered gold, / head by Angelico, / stars choiring in gold leaf" (*CP*, 231). In the sixth section, he undercuts the idealized portrait: "But this as well; some nights, after he left her, / his lechery like a mongrel nosed the ruins, / past Manoir's warehouse" (*CP*, 232). He loves an innocent girl out of Fra Angelico but also seeks an earthier satisfaction on the seamier side of town. The reference to "Manoir's warehouse" recalls the story of Manoir's pact with the devil, lending a sulphurous undertone to Walcott's own lust. It also connects lust with the poorer, blacker side of St. Lucian life, while Anna remains associated with whiteness and European art. Gregorias warns him, "You are creating this, and it will end. / The world is not like this, / nor is she, friend" (*CP*, 232).

The long first section of Chapter 14, "Anna awaking," is written from Anna's point of view, the only sustained excursion into another voice that occurs within the poem. It reminds me of Randall Jarrell's remark about Lowell's "The Mills of the Kavanaughs": that the heroine seems less a real person than a "symbiotic state of the poet," so that "[y]ou feel, 'Yes, Robert Lowell would act like this if he were a girl'; but whoever saw a girl like Robert Lowell?"[39] Even Baugh, more attuned than I to this part of the poem, concedes that Anna is "a metaphor of certain states of feeling which Walcott is temperamentally inclined to cultivate."[40] In her monologue, his ventriloquism is readily apparent. Walcott blames youthful artistic self-consciousness for separating him from Anna, but the wall still appears to be there when the mature poet attempts to speak from her perspective. Perhaps the interiority of other people is intractable within his method of displaced narration through landscape and objects as images of his own subjectivity.

As if aware that Anna has begun to vanish as he tries to depict her, Walcott asks, "Who were you, then?" (*CP*, 239). He is compelled to "wake / to the knowledge that things / sunder from themselves, like peeling bark," leaving no core of identity but only "the emptiness / of a bright silence shining after thunder" (*CP*, 240). This is the closest thing to an underlying vision of experience the poem has offered so far: the one stable truth is that things change, and change entails a painful rupture with a previous self. Hence the perpetual experience of being on the threshold of "another life" that gives the poem its title; hence the suspicion of linear narration, since all stories tell only that "things sunder / from themselves." All narratives are narratives of loss and mutability. In a sense the plot of *Another Life* is the fall from innocence into experience, but its insistence on an Adamic poetics looks not toward an accommodation with that fallen state but toward a paradise regained through defiance of time's narrative, just as the straining after universality (Anna as "all Annas") seeks an abiding wholeness behind the particular loss.

Chapters 16 and 17 conclude the third part of the poem with meditations on the young poet's impending departure from the island. As Castries, the "cement Phoenix," recovered from the fire, "things found the memory of their former places" (*CP*, 245). But things, being sundered from themselves, cannot return to their prior innocence. The war "had infected language," leaving behind its horrifying images of "[t]he shoes / of cherubs piled in pyramids / outside the Aryan ovens," so that the very smell of Castries in sunlight brings to mind "[b]urnt flesh" (*CP*, 246). History has come to Castries, and the young Walcott prepares to go out to meet it.

The young poet begins to attract notice in the wider world, attending "Tea with the British Council Representative," who encourages him, perhaps a bit backhandedly, in his work ("of course you will soon shed your influences" [*CP*, 248]). The talk is of Eliot, Elgar, and Britten, and of future travel ("England then. When?"). At last, the island prodigy is to move among the giants of the metropolis. The prospects of fame and achievement are closely linked with sexual desire, as the young man's attention strays from the conversation of "Mr. Winters" to Mrs. Winters's sexual allure (*CP*, 248).

When the next section evokes Anna practicing the piano, supervised by "Sister Annunziata" next to "the convent balcony" (*CP*, 248), the disparity between the two scenes suggests that Walcott will soon part from his virginal first love.

The section closes with Walcott's prayer that when he leaves, "what I have sworn to love [may] not feel betrayed." "Make of my heart an ark, / let my ribs bear / all, doubled by memory" (*CP*, 250). The ark fits suggestively with the metaphors of artistic representation that dominate the poem: a single pair of each species was rescued within it. Here, the pairing is the doubling of memory, each creature accompanied not by a flesh-and-blood mate but by a mental trace, and even the Noah of this ark will survive as "the image of a young man on a pier," not the young man incarnate. Ultimately, the ark-heart is

> a ship within a
> ship within a ship, a bottle
> where this wharf, these
> rotting roofs, this sea,
> sail, sealed in glass.

(CP, 250)

The nesting of ships within ships suggests an infinite regression. And yet, somewhere within the concentric ships, everything to be left behind must be sealed in an inviolable core, safe from change, so that even the "rotting roofs" will remain as they are instead of crumbling away.

With thoughts of departure come temptations to disloyalty. "How often didn't you hesitate / between rose-flesh and sepia, / your blood like a serpent whispering / of a race incapable of subtler shadow, / of music, architecture, and a complex thought" (*CP*, 251). Leaving the island could be a first step toward a cultural "whiteness," a rejection of West Indian traditions for a Europeanized identity. To leave is also to leap into the unknown, and the only way to prepare for it is to "be happy / in every uncertainty" (*CP*, 251). In this restless mood, the young poet finds his friends "too preoccupied / with balance" (*CP*, 251), the very quality that his mother's house had sung so softly (*CP*, 157). It is time to leave the house, and the extended household that is the island. The surf's "monotonous scrawl" now seems to have been "for years trying to reach" him, with its message, "[g]o" (*CP*, 252).

Chapter 17 closes with the departure, incorporating lightly revised versions of a sonnet from the 1958 *Bim* version of "Tales of the islands," dropped in the revision for *In a Green Night*, and the final sonnet of the sequence, embedded within a longer verse paragraph. As Walcott turns from the island, it turns away from him. Suddenly, "things ... would not say what they once meant" (*CP*, 255). The materials of his art abandon him: "No metaphor, no metamorphosis, / as the charcoal-burner turns / into his door of smoke" (*CP*, 257). Once, "through the door of this landscape" (*CP*, 199), he had entered the fire of artistic inspiration. Now, the charcoal-burner, archetypal figure of St. Lucian folk culture, disappears behind a door not of fire, but of smoke, and along with him, "three lives dissolve in the imagination, / three loves, art, love and death, / fade from a mirror clouding with this breath" (*CP*, 257). The flesh-and-blood figures are gone, replaced by their immortal but incorporeal counterparts in imagination. The last line of Part Three, as if longing to return from art to life, calls the fictionalized characters "Gregorias" and "Anna" by their literal names: "Harry, Dunstan, Andreuille" (*CP*, 257).

Walcott titles the fourth part of his poem "The Estranging Sea," a phrase in its epigraph from Matthew Arnold's "To Marguerite." For Walcott, Arnold's phrase, "longing's fire," becomes not just his love for Anna, but everything else evoked by "fire" in his context: the blazing days spent painting with Gregorias, the first awakenings of artistic vocation and erotic desire. The poem, returning to Harry Simmons, shows us the grim result when longing's fire burns itself out.

Harry, like the young Walcott and Gregorias, had followed Gauguin's example, painting the unsophisticated beauty of "black lissome limbs" (*CP*, 261), while withdrawing on his houseboat to secluded parts of the coast. Despite his squalid housekeeping, Simmons persuades himself "that although it stank / this was the vegetable excrement of natural life," and

> that there on the ocean with his saints,
> Vincent and Paul, his yellowing *Letters to Theo*
> and *Noa Noa*, though the worms bored their gospel,
> he no longer wanted what he could become,
> his flame, made through their suffering, their flame,
> nightly by the brass-haloed lamp, he prayed
> whatever would come, come.
>
> (*CP*, 261–62)

In his very attempt to follow the uncompromising path of van Gogh and Gauguin, Simmons renounces "what he could become." The underlying motive appears to be loss of confidence in his own powers, a growing self-conscious "thought and the shadow of that thought" lying "across coarse canvas or the staring paper" (*CP*, 262). He is "a man used / to giving orders," but now "the surface would acquire its own ambition," fighting the artist much as it had resisted the young Walcott in Chapter 9. In a poignant twist on the imagery of Walcott's "golden year" of artistic and erotic flowering, Simmons discovers himself in "the legend of Midas and the golden touch"; his hand brings ruin instead of fulfillment, and "everything he touches breaks."

Walcott resists any suggestion that *Another Life* attributes Simmons's suicide to social causes.[41] But I am inclined to trust the tale and not the teller:

> And perhaps, master, you saw early
> what brotherhood means among the spawn of slaves
> hassling for return trips on the middle passage,
> spitting on their own poets,
> preferring their painters drunkards,
> for their solemn catalogue of suicides....
>
> (*CP*, 265)

The idea that Simmons took his life because St. Lucian society could not or would not appreciate its artists runs strongly through Chapter 21, and some such notion seems implicit when Walcott follows his account of Simmons's breakdown with an angry chapter of invective against betrayers of the West Indian people.

Chapter 19 bears the subtitle "Frescoes of the New World II" (*CP*, 269). Gregorias's "heaven" of Chapter 10 ("Frescoes of the New World I") has become a Dantesque hell, with Anna as Beatrice (filling in for Virgil) guiding the tour, while the sulphur volcano of Soufrière is the final abode of Caribbean political hucksters, inflicting "their own sulphur of self-hatred" upon

> all o' dem big boys, so, dem ministers,
> ministers of culture, ministers of development,
> the green blacks, and their old toms,
> and all the syntactical apologists of the Third World
> explaining why their artists die
> by their own hands, magicians of the New Vision.
>
> (*CP*, 269)

The "green blacks" (i.e., inexperienced in government, but also newly reinvented as "blacks") are as reprehensible as the accommodating "old toms." Those who promise a New Vision nonetheless excuse the status quo as inevitable. Like "the academics crouched like rats" (CP, 269), the politicians worship the god of "history" (CP, 270), who justifies unacceptable actions in the present as the inevitable result of the past. "They are the dividers, / they encompass our history, / in their hands is the body / of my friend and the future, / they measure the skulls with calipers" (CP, 270). Instead of seeing all human beings as fundamentally alike, they divide according to races and ideologies. "Encompass," as the image of the measuring "calipers" confirms, evokes the image of Blake's famous plate of Urizen with his drawing compass, marking a boundary to the possible. The vulnerable body is not safe in these hands that worship an abstract god. Nonetheless, Gregorias will survive: "their vision blurs, their future is clouded with cataract, / but out of its mist, one man, / whom they will not recognize, emerges / and staggers towards his lineaments" (CP, 270). With the Blakean overtones of "lineaments," Gregorias becomes a sort of St. Lucian giant Albion struggling to free himself of his specters.

Despite Chapter 19's affirmative close, Chapter 20 strikes an elegiac tone. It combines Walcott's mourning for Harry Simmons with his celebration of Gregorias's narrow escape from a similar fate. Walcott has heard ominous reports of Gregorias "driven deep in debt, / unable to hold down a job, painting so badly / that those who swore his genius vindicated / everything once, now saw it as a promise never kept" (CP, 272). When they are reunited, at Piarco Airport in Trinidad, Gregorias tells of his own near-suicide. Moved by his story, Walcott "saw him brutally as Mayakovsky" (CP, 273) in Pasternak's Safe Conduct. The comparison again reinforces the suggestion that West Indian social conditions drive artists to despair, for Mayakovsky appears in Pasternak's account as a great poet tormented by Soviet culture's incomprehension of his art.

Gregorias has "entered life" (CP, 272), but Harry Simmons is not so resilient. News of Simmons's death comes during a long spell of rain, figured as a suicidal protest in its own right: "All day, on the tin roofs / the rain berates the poverty of life, / all day the sunset bleeds like a cut wrist" (CP, 275). The death of Simmons confirms premonitions hinted at even in the midst of the idyll with Anna. In Chapter 9, that youthful love "came / out of the Book of Hours," which included a pastoral "reaper with his scythe" (CP, 202); now the harvest's "autumnal fall of bodies" has been gathered, for "in the Book of Hours, that seemed so far, / the light and amber of another life, / there is a Reaper busy about his wheat" (CP, 275), as the picturesque reaper of Chapter 9 becomes the familiar personification of death.

In the elegy that ends the chapter, Simmons appears as the kind of artist he and Gregorias had aspired to be, one who has absorbed St. Lucian life and landscape completely and embodied them in all of his actions: "People entered his understanding / like a wayside church, / they had built him themselves" (*CP*, 276). Just as Pasternak eulogizes Mayakovsky as the personification of the emergent spirit of the new Russia, Walcott writes that although Simmons "is a man no more," he survives as "the fervour and intelligence / of a whole country" (*CP*, 277). As in a traditional elegy, Walcott summons the people of the countryside to join in the mourning. He evokes not stylized shepherds, but ordinary St. Lucians, whom Simmons knew, engaged in their everyday labors:

> Leonce, Placide, Alcindor,
> Dominic, from whose plane vowels were shorn
> odorous as forest,
> ask the charcoal-burner to look up
> with his singed eyes,
> ask the lip-cracked fisherman three miles at sea
> with nothing between him and Dahomey's coast
> to dip rainwater over his parched boards
> for Monsieur Simmons, *pour* Msieu Harry Simmons,
> let the husker on his pyramid of cocoanuts
> rest on his tree.
>
> (*CP*, 277)

The vowel-producing carpenter's plane, linking poetry to physical labor, recalls also Gregorias's depiction of the carpenter Joseph in the church at Gros Îlet (*CP*, 205), as well as the "tongues of shavings" that "coil from the moving pen" (*CP*, 216). The charcoal-burner, his eyes "singed" by his fire, and the fisherman, "lip-cracked" on the "parched boards" of his boat, are counterparts of Simmons's spirit, parched and singed by despair. The fisherman's clear path to "Dahomey" reminds us that Simmons, despite his worship of European art, was one of the first St. Lucians to value and study the African and Amerindian contributions to the island's culture. His example to Walcott and Gregorias was not only the discipline of European artistic tradition, but also the fusion of that tradition with the materials of West Indian common life. But his work remains incomplete: "Blow out the eyes in the unfinished portraits" (*CP*, 277), Walcott continues. The "simple flame" of the idyll with Anna, the "light of the world" kindled by artistic awakening, is extinguished in mourning. The lament closes with the wish that "His island forest, open and enclose him / like a rare butterfly between its leaves"[42] (*CP*, 277), completing the fusion of Simmons with the "whole country."

Chapter 21 poses the question "Why?" (*CP*, 278), and despite Walcott's objection to sociological explanations of Simmons's death, the poem takes such speculations quite seriously. We are instructed to "Go down to the shacks," or to "follow the path / of the caked piglet through / the sea-village's midden," to "smell the late, ineradicable reek / of stale rags like rivers / at daybreak, or the dark corner of the salt-caked shop where the cod / barrel smells of old women" (*CP*, 278). The answer has something to do with the constricting poverty of the island. After experiencing these sights and smells, "you can start then // to know how the vise / of horizon tightens / around the throat" (*CP*, 279). We recall Walcott's description of his own restlessness, just before his departure for Jamaica: "The horizon tightened round his throat" (*CP*, 253). He can guess how Simmons felt. But finally, he abandons the search for an answer and must settle for an "assent founded on ignorance" (*CP*, 280). Against the harsh fact of this death, and "the young deaths of others," there is still "something which balances" in the valedictory image of Simmons "bent under the weight of the morning, / against its shafts, / devout, angelical, / the easel rifling his shoulder, / the master of Gregorias and myself" (*CP*, 280).

As he looks back on the losses of Anna and Harry, Walcott recalls the self-forgetfulness of the hillside vision of his fourteenth year (*CP*, 184–85). In that moment, the depth of his pain and gratitude had erased the boundaries of identity, and the distinctions of man and woman, parent and child, even statement and its logical contradiction: "I knelt because I was my mother, / I was the well of the world, / I wore the stars on my skin, / I endured no reflections." His "sign was water," or "Janus,"[43] since he "saw with twin heads, / and everything I say is contradicted" (*CP*, 281). In this condition, he felt released from his egotism and indecisiveness: "I shared, I shared, / I was struck like rock, and I opened / to His gift!" (*CP*, 282). Now, in that spirit of generosity, he begs Simmons's pardon for using him as a character in the poem, which now seems an exploitation: "Forgive me, if this sketch should ever thrive, / or profit from your gentle, generous spirit" (*CP*, 282). Even in death the master changes the sketch, as he did so long ago in life (*CP*, 147): "When I began this work, you were alive, / and with one stroke, you have completed it!" (*CP*, 282). This closure, however painful, frees Walcott, who can now say, with Villon, that he has "swallowed all [his] hates." The chapter closes with a celebration of his marriage to "one whose darkness is a tree.... // Who holds my fears at dusk like birds." Her treelike stability gives an organic continuity to the rhythms of everyday life and the advance of generations; in her "leaves," their "children / and the children of friends settle / simply, like rhymes" (*CP*, 282). But this metaphor does not entirely convince as a resolution. The next chapter returns to the language of perpetual starting over that permeates the rest of the poem.

Chapter 22, set at Rampanalgas, on Trinidad's northwest coast, affirms the triumph of West Indian nature, over "the Muse of history" (*CP*, 284). The landscape will refuse interpretation; beside its "water-coloured water, / let the historians go mad, ... / from thirst" (*CP*, 283).[44] The tautology of "water-coloured water" mocks the powers of language itself. Even the "astigmatic geologist" finds "not a sign" (*CP*, 284). Poets too may have nothing to add, for "[a]ll of the epics are blown away with the leaves" (*CP*, 284).

In this historyless landscape where time moves at the glacial pace of evolution itself, "while the lizards are taking a million years to change" (*CP*, 284), Walcott watches his son and two daughters at play. Each is "a child without history, without knowledge of its pre-world," and in this is "like his father." The children have a vague sense of their past as a fusion of diverse races and origins (Margaret Walcott is part East Indian, part Afro-Caribbean, while Derek Walcott, as his poetry often reminds us, has African, English, and Dutch ancestry): "That child who puts the shell's howl to his ear, / hears nothing, hears everything / that the historian cannot hear, the howls / of all the races that crossed the water" (*CP*, 285). This heritage is too tangled and extensive to be made articulate, unless through poetry; the shell is an "intricately swivelled Babel" (*CP*, 285) that speaks in a confusion of all languages. The past survives only as a primal knowledge beneath the level of language and memory, for "the crossing of water has erased their memories / and the sea, which is always the same, accepts them. / And the shore, which is always the same, / accepts them" (*CP*, 285–86). The ambiguous pronoun reference allows us to read that sea and shore have accepted the memories, or accepted the children. Both possibilities seem relevant. The earth we live on and by does not care what we remember but accepts us among its creatures. But the memories have been transferred to the sea and shore, which are the abode of an eternal present: "In the shallop of the shell, / in the round prayer, / in the palate of the conch, / in the dead sail of the almond leaf / are all of the voyages" (*CP*, 286). With such an understanding of the past's life in the present, the historian's temptation to "gild cruelty," to "see a golden, cruel, hawk-bright glory / in the conquistador's malarial eye, / crying, at least here / something happened" (*CP*, 286), becomes inadequate. It forgets that all possibilities of human nature are latent in all settings. We "begin again, / from what we have always known, nothing" (*CP*, 286). The alternative to such a new beginning is determination by the past, which for art means "penitential histories passing / for poems" (*CP*, 287). The passage culminates in the outburst "*Pour la dernière fois, nommez! Nommez!*" (*CP*, 288), recalling the priest's attempt, in Chapter 4, to exorcise the demon that possessed Auguste Manoir (*CP*, 170). The modern demon is history-worship, which turns the living into *gens gajés* in thrall to the dead. Walcott affirms to his son the inviolable sacredness of the present, despite the "tortured" look of the almond trees (*CP*, 289). Not only "holy" but "holiest" of all is "the break of the blue sea below the trees, / and the rock that takes blows on its back / and is more rock" (*CP*, 289). He singles the rock out for praise because instead of capitulating to the blows it endures, it becomes even more itself. in praising the sea that strikes the blows along with the rock that endures them, Walcott figuratively confirms his ideal of the Caribbean present as a reconciliation of former oppressors and oppressed. He imagines himself merged, in old age, with both:

> I wanted to grow white-haired
> as the wave, with a wrinkled
>
> brown rock's face, salted,
> seamed, an old poet,
> facing the wind
>
> and nothing, which is,
> the loud world in his mind.
>
> (*CP*, 290)

The closing lines, which recall the radical emptying of self in Wallace Stevens's "The Snow Man," leave the poet as a historyless consciousness among elemental presences.

Chapter 23 closes the poem in St. Lucia. Looking at the surf, Walcott sees an accelerated likeness of the passing of human generations, in the midst of which the island, like the sea-beaten rock, goes on being itself. But the landscape no longer resonates with his own subjectivity. The mimosa, instead of greeting him like an old friend, says "You mightn't remember me" (*CP*, 292). The poet cannot reenter the past: "I would not call up Anna. / I would not visit his [Harry's] grave." As he watches tourists on horseback galloping down the beach, he sees the scene as if it were a painting, a tarted-up version of the lonely, heroic art he had emulated with Gregorias. It is a canvas "out of Gauguin by the Tourist board." Things have changed more than he had noticed at first. He repeats the imagery of the opening lines, in which the "divided child" tries to read "the pages of the sea" (*CP*, 145). It is still the same "eternal summer sea" (*CP*, 292), but the human artifacts are mutable:

> And what if it's all gone,
> the hill's cut away for more tarmac,
> the groves all sawn,
> and bungalows proliferate on the scarred, hacked hillside,
> the magical lagoon[45] drained
> for the Higher Purchase plan,
> and they've bulldozed and bowdlerized our Vigie,
> our *ocelle insularum*, our Sirmio
> for a pink and pastel NewTown where the shacks and huts stood
> teetering and tough in unabashed unhope....
>
> (*CP*, 292–93)

In contrast, "the untroubled ocean" continues as before. "[T]he moon will always swing its lantern / and evening fold the pages of the sea" (*CP*, 293).

The passage brings out a tension between the desire to keep the island's cultural integrity intact and the recognition that, after all, much of that culture is rooted in poverty, and that to resist development for aesthetic reasons is dangerously close to wanting the "folk" as a romantic backdrop. Walcott follows his elegy for the lost landscape by asking the "folk" to "forgive our desertions" (*CP*, 293). The plural suggests that his departure is only one desertion among others.

The last section of the poem is reserved for praise, not penitence, and its closing benediction alights on Gregorias. He is the hero of the poem because he sustains an art (and by his example, a poetry as well) grounded in St. Lucia: "you painted our first, primitive frescoes" (*CP*, 294). Returning to the imagery of fire and gold, Walcott calls his friend "A sun that stands back / from the fire of itself, not shamed, prizing / its shadow, watching it blaze!" Gregorias has both the intensity and the detachment of the artist, and he has exorcised the racial self-contempt instilled by colonialism: he is not ashamed of the fire's dark "shadow." Gregorias's energy, and Walcott's own, may have been a "destructive frenzy / that made our years one fire," but it was also a sacred fire. Walcott echoes his words from Chapter 12 (*CP*, 220):

Gregorias, listen, lit
we were the light of the world!
We were blest with a virginal, unpainted world
with Adam's task of giving things their names,
with the smooth white walls of clouds and villages
where you devised your inexhaustible,
impossible Renaissance,
brown cherubs of Giotto and Masaccio....

(*CP*, 294)

The Adamic moment, though shadowed by Harry's suicide, Walcott's "desertions," and St. Omer's struggles with despair, remains a source of possible renewal. In that "lit" state of inspiration, there was "nothing so old / that it could not be invented," and the fusion of St. Lucian culture and European art was "inexhaustible," producing "brown cherubs" that are also progeny of the European masters. The poem ends with a reaffirmation of the promise of Part Two, that the light of the world, once lit, never goes out entirely. For as the Master of "the master of Gregorias and [himself]" has said, "Just as long as I am in this world, I am the light of the world."

NOTES

1. Edward Hirsch, "The Art of Poetry XXXVII: Derek Walcott," *Paris Review* 101 (1986); reprinted in *Critical Perspectives on Derek Walcott*, ed. Robert D. Hamner (Boulder, Colo.: Rienner, 1997), 81.

2. "An Interview with Frederick Seidel," reprinted in *Robert Lowell: Collected Prose*, ed. Robert Giroux (New York: Farrar, Straus & Giroux, 1987), 241.

3. Robert Lowell, "91 Revere Street," in *Life Studies* [1959] and *For the Union Dead* (New York: Farrar, Straus & Giroux, 1964), 13.

4. Robert Lowell to Derek Walcott, February 19, 1973. Walcott Archive, Box #1, UWI, St. Augustine.

5. Conversation with the author, April 10, 1989, Milwaukee.

6. Walcott, "Contemplative Is Word for His Genius," *Trinidad Guardian*, 15 October 1966, 5.

7. First notebook for *Another Life*, 1 (March 28, 1966). I have not found the translation Walcott used.

8. Boris Pasternak, *Safe Conduct, an Autobiography and Other Writings*, trans. Beatrice Scott (New York: New Directions, 1958), 146.

9. Pasternak, *Safe Conduct*, 28.

10. Pasternak *Safe Conduct*, 60.

11. Pasternak, *Safe Conduct*, 72.

12. Pasternak, *Safe Conduct*, 28.

13. Rei Terada argues that the concept of "reversibility" emerges fully in Walcott's essay of 1974, "The Caribbean: Culture or Mimicry": "All of Walcott's poetry after 1974 builds upon its conclusions, and Walcott never lets go of the 'reversible' map of the world he defines there." *Derek Walcott's Poetry: American Mimicry* (Boston: Northeastern University Press, 1992), 25. Cf. also Wilson Harris, "Tradition and the West Indian Novel" [1964]: "one relives and reverses the given "conditions of the past." Reprinted in *Tradition the Writer & Society* (London: New Beacon Books, 1967), 36.

14. "Tradition and the West Indian Novel," 28, 30, 31.

15. Paul Breslin, "'I Met History Once, but He Ain't Recognize Me': The Poetry of Derek Walcott," *TriQuarterly* 68 (1987): 178.

16. Pasternak, *Safe Conduct*, 31.

17. First notebook for *Another Life*, 13.

18. Edward Baugh, *Derek Walcott: Memory as Vision: Another Life* (London: Longman, 1978), 36 n. 10.

19. Baugh, *Derek Walcott*, 21.

20. Goya's accompanying gloss, it is only scrupulous to point out, continues in good Enlightenment fashion: "La fantasia abandonada de la razón, produce monstruos imposibles: unida con ella, es madre de las artes y origen de sus mirabillas." ["Imagination abandoned by reason produces impossible monsters: united with her, she is the mother of the arts and the source of their wonders."] But Philip Hofer remarks in the introduction to his Dover edition of *Los Caprichos* on the "elusive nature of the captions beneath each plate," regarding this one in particular as "deliberately deceptive," disguising Goya's debt to a pictorial frontispiece in Rousseau's *Philosophie*. That allusion could have got him in trouble in the reactionary Spain of 1799. Francisco Goya y Lucentes, *Los Caprichos*, with an introduction by Philip Hofer (New York: Dover, 1969), 3, 2.

21. This phrase, too, is an allusion, to Pound's "what whiteness? what candor" (Canto 74); as with Graves's "white goddess," Walcott's appropriation adds a racial irony not suggested in the source.

22. Baugh comments on this juxtaposition; *Derek Walcott*, 22.

23. Baugh, *Derek Walcott*, 33.

24. Baugh, *Derek Walcott*, 19.

25. According to Baugh, Walcott was also thinking of Dylan Thomas's *Under Milkwood* and Galway Kinnell's "The Avenue Bearing the Initial of Christ into the New World." *Derek Walcott*, 28.

26. In West Indian usage, "clear-complexioned" means light-skinned, white or nearly white.

27. *Gens gajés* are persons who serve the devil in exchange for power or wealth.

28. Walcott, *Midsummer* (New York: Farrar, Straus & Giroux, 1984), xiv.

29. *The Lost Steps* [1953], trans. Harriet de Onís (New York: Farrar, Straus & Giroux, 1989), 72–73.

30. *Dear Theo: The Autobiography of Vincent van Gogh* [through an arrangement of the letters] [1937], ed. Irving Stone, with Jean Stone (New York: Penguin/Plume, 1995), 391, 361, 362. Harry Simmons's "yellowing *Letters to Theo*" (*CP*, 262) was probably this book; my net searches of library catalogues turned up nothing for the title *Letters to Theo*.

31. Baugh, *Derek Walcott*, 39.

32. Dunstan St. Omer, conversation with the author, July 1989.

33. St. Joseph the Worker is a very large church; local tradition has it that the priest responsible for its construction misread the plans, doubling both height and width. Dunstan St. Omer, conversation with the author, July 1989.

34. Baugh, *Derek Walcott*, 27.

35. Second notebook for *Another Life*, 87. [The entry is typed and pasted into the exercise book; the typed insert is number "91," but it is the eighty-seventh page of the manuscript.]

36. This name, which has been bestowed on the airport at Vieux Fort, derives from the Arawak name for the island, which Walcott renders in *Omeros* as "Iounalo," meaning "where the iguana is found."

37. See Pasternak, *Safe Conduct*, 16.

38. Malraux, *The Psychology of Art*, 1.109.

39. Randall Jarrell, *Poetry and the Age* [1953] (New York: Vintage, 1959), 234–35.

40. Baugh, *Derek Walcott*, 53.

41. Walcott, conversation with the author, March 23, 1995. Cap, St. Lucia.

42. In addition to his many other pursuits, Simmons also collected butterflies.

43. Walcott's birthday, January 23, makes him an Aquarian, and the month of January is named for Janus.

44. Perhaps a glance at Villon again (his "Ballade du concours de Blois," which begins with Charles D'Orléans's line, "Je meurs du soif auprès de la fontaine").

45. Cf. Chapter 13, section iv (*CP*, 228): "Magical lagoon, stunned by its own reflection!"

WES DAVIS

Derek Walcott: The Sigh of History

During an interview after his public reading of "A Tribute to C.L.R. James" in 1991 Derek Walcott was asked about his apparent preoccupation with words like *epoch*. His first response was a parry that appeared to dismiss the question. "I use it," he said, "because it rhymes with rock."[1] As a joke this works not only because it pretends to elevate sound over sense, but also because it crosses one of the battle lines of contemporary poetry. Walcott is blurring the line between a discursive poetry that dwells in ideas and a meditative poetry that lets the mind linger in the vicinity of things. Walcott himself comes so readily to that available rhyme, perhaps, because landscape is for him the tablet on which history in the Caribbean is written. But a shift like that from *epoch* to *rock* is, at the same time, readable as just what it appears to be, a turning away from the question of history and toward a world of things at their most concrete.

Those two possibilities implied in the joke closely mirror the polar division in criticism of Walcott. One or the other position informs most treatments of his poetry, producing partial readings that elide the tensions that actually inhabit the poems. Seamus Heaney, though, drawing on what he has learned in his own poetic practice, takes a broader and more accurate view of Walcott's poetry. In *The Government of the Tongue* he writes of Walcott's "The Star-Apple Kingdom" that "the pitch of the writing could

Printed for the first time in this volume. © 2002 by Wes Davis.

hardly be described as meditative or discursive....as if the years of analysis and commitment to thinking justly had resolved themselves for the poem into a sound half-way between sobbing and sighing."[2] Walcott has never been as sure as the critics about the separation of the two temperaments. Even his explication of a serious answer to that night's question moves between the two available interpretations of his joke. "No, no!! This is the subject of every Caribbean writer. This is history," he began. But pursuing that theme, Walcott showed his version of history to be, as much as the rhyme is, an effect of language.

> The word "epoch" is a historical word, an aspect of time, and it has an archaic sound that is deliberated because any definition of time, any aspect of the definition of time is archaic and contains its finish.[3]

Finally the word *epoch* as he apprehends it doesn't signify time by its semantic content at all, but rather sounds the passage of time associated with its own history. Its sound, archaic to Walcott's ear, signals change that is poetically palpable though it may not be sequential or narratable.

In his best poems Walcott never quite separates his historical impulse from his desire to linger in the words that describe the landscape of history. A sufficient reading has to make an account of both. Walcott's imagination is novelistic, dialogic, to use Bhaktin's expression, and it is only in the dialogue between those two temperaments that he justifies, for example, his obsession with metaphors that turn lived experience into landscape and landscape into text—or justifies his sense that history resides somewhere inside the language that can produce a relationship between epoch and rock, and can make a joke of it.

The results of ignoring that dialogue are heard in complaints like the one registered in a recent review of *The Bounty* in the *New York Times Book Review* : "what you remember in Walcott is the texture, never the text."[4] Although the remark positions itself as an aesthetic critique, its complaint lines up with criticism of Walcott's later poetry as, to use terms already invoked, all rock and no epoch. Lodging that complaint as an aesthetic critique deepens the damage it does by naturalizing a myth of Walcott's disengagement as somehow evident in the widespread critical preference for the formal excellence of his early lyric poetry. The rhyme of rock and epoch taken seriously, though, implies that the texture of the poems, particularly what critics have dismissed as mere atmosphere or gratuitous landscape, is partly the look of a historical mode peculiar to the West Indies. At the risk of echoing a McLuhanesqe poetics, it may be right to say that for Walcott the texture is the text. Texture is the text of the poem and the text of history.

The timing of the *epoch* question was not merely fortuitous. The lecture that preceded it opened up the issues of poetic engagement and political activism. Speaking before a group convened at Wellesley to honor C.L.R. James, the author of *The Black Jacobins* and other works that have influenced the way New World history is written, Walcott had revealed his anxiety about the poet's responsibilities toward history. Thinking about the relationship between poetry and protest, Walcott pushed himself beyond the realm of poetry to isolate his own unassailable moment of political action. Appropriately, what he remembered that night was his response to the arrest of James by the government of Eric Williams, the Prime Minister of Trinidad and Tobago from 1956 to 1981.

In 1965, more than twenty-five years after he published his history of the Haitian slave revolt, James was known in popular culture mainly for his brilliant writing on cricket. Early that year he traveled back to Trinidad to cover a test series between the West Indian and English cricket teams. When he arrived he was placed under house arrest. Eric Williams, who issued the arrest order, has nothing to say about the incident in *British Historians and the West Indies*, which he published the following year.[5] He does, though, give a clue there to his shifting opinion of James, his former teacher and mentor.

> James, in his *Black Jacobins*, rescued the Haitian slave revolution and the rise of Toussaint L'Ouverture from historical oblivion, and his analysis is of profound and enduring significance, if only as one of the first challenges to the British interpretation of the abolition of the slave system. But his incursion into West Indian history was only a temporary deviation from the author's preoccupation with Marxism and the world revolution that was so confidently expected in the Bloomsbury set of the thirties.[6]

Williams is careful to protect the revolutionary line inaugurated by James's most important book, but finally indicts the man on charges of trading with the British literary establishment. Those charges foreshadow accusations that would eventually be made against Walcott, in Trinidad and elsewhere, calling him a "New Yorker Poet" and suggesting that he had sold out to America. In any case the irony of James's absence from the match, not because of English law but because of Williams, struck Walcott, who was present at the cricket grounds that day, as a call to action.

> As I looked across the street, I saw a limousine or town car coming out of the oval with, I think, a police escort, and I knew it was the Prime Minister, Eric Williams. I remember walking across the street and shouting at the closed window, "Release C.L.R. James!!!" That's the only heroic act I've ever done ... physically.[7]

That ellipsis is Walcott's. It is the pause, I imagine, in which various versions of heroism and protest reside; and the gap in which Walcott lodges the idea that poetry itself might constitute engagement in other forms.

Still, the option of resisting injustice physically is seductive for someone who spends his life in words. In an interview in 1977 Walcott suggested that the artist's responsibility during a time of political strife may be to put down the pen and take overt action: "If the struggle is intense, the role of an artist is to pick up a gun like everyone else..... One can write poems *and* carry guns, you know."[8] One can, it might be said, but one generally doesn't. Seamus Heaney, in fact, packs this opposition between action and poetry into the paradoxical simile that closes "Digging." "Between my finger and my thumb the squat pen rests, snug as a gun," Heaney's poem concludes, as if to inscribe the fact that a poet, perhaps especially in Northern Ireland, picks up a pen almost specifically instead of a gun.

In a paper called "The Figure of Crusoe"—presented at the University of the West Indies, St. Augustine, Trinidad in October 1965—Walcott conceded that under most circumstances poets, unarmed, have only their work to offer. "But the people do not want poetry. They want its concomitants: explanation, justification, order."[9] The statement feels right to whatever extent Walcott is willing to include poets, at least some of the time, in this image of the people. His language here reveals a version of the longing for action evident in the interviews. Like many poets Walcott wants to believe that what he calls the concomitants of poetry—explanation, justification, order—do have at least that collateral relationship to poetry.

At the same time, he has little tolerance for poetry that sacrifices aesthetic endurance for political expediency. Asked in the 1977 interview to comment on Ted Joans's concept of revolutionary "hand grenade poems," Walcott gave an equivocal affirmation that "one may become convinced of the right in something that may be consciously ephemeral—just as a revolution between one goal and the next is a moment, however long that moment lasts—and it may then become expedient to write that kind of poem."[10] But it was clear in what followed that Walcott doesn't take the expediency itself as justification for indifferent poetry. His revision of Auden's "poetry makes nothing happen," while recalling Yeats's concern about the effects of *Cathleen Ni Houlihan* in 1916, separates form and function:

> Poetry itself may not make anything happen, but it has incited people to make things happen. The danger for the poet—for there is excitement in the passion of what he is believing—is to confuse what he thinks a poem can do with poetry itself.[11]

Poetry can have a function, Walcott is saying, but that function is not poetry's sufficient cause.

The dilemma this creates for Walcott is similar to the one Seamus Heaney would describe in his own Nobel address. Both Heaney and Walcott work in a poetry that discovers itself in the surprises of language, a discovery Walcott conceives as the result of a journey back to the root level of language, the point at which the poet, as Adam or Crusoe, struggles to speak the new names of every new thing. The poem is an act of the language in the process of astonishing itself. But there are times—more or less frequent depending on the social and political forces that condition the writing—when poets want to have that subject act upon the world it discovers. "We want the surprise to be transitive," Heaney says, "like the impatient thump which unexpectedly restores the picture to the television set, or the electric shock which sets the fibrillating heart back to its proper rhythm."[12]

Heaney's ideal of poetic function here is instructive for readers of Walcott's poetry as well. That longing for activity is right at the surface in Heaney's poems, from "Digging" on. From the start he was negotiating with himself an agreement to view poetry as work: both in the sense of earnest labor and political operation. A similar aspiration is present in Walcott, though it is often lost sight of, since his best known lines, like those that close "A Far Cry from Africa," are about turning away, or about turning the world into the word.

For a number of years the theater provided Walcott with at least the sensation of social activism. From 1956 to 1976 he wrote for and directed the Trinidad Theater Workshop producing plays, like *Dream on Monkey Mountain* and *Ti Jean and His Brothers*, that dwelt on the historical situation of the West Indies in a way that must have taken some pressure away from the poetry. There is an Irish model for that too, of course. Accepting the Noble Prize in 1923 W.B. Yeats revealed the connection between drama and his own anxieties about poetic engagement by addressing the Royal Academy of Sweden on the subject of his plays rather than his poetry. "Perhaps the English committees," Yeats suggested, "would never have sent you my name if I had written no plays, no dramatic criticism, if my lyric poetry had not a quality of speech practiced upon the stage, perhaps even—though this could be no portion of their deliberate thought—if it were not in some degree the symbol of a movement."[13] Yeats, even at the pinnacle of poetic achievement, craved a direct connection with the movement, and particular movements, of history. In his poems he questioned the historical effects of literature, yet even then the imagined point of contact is famously theatrical. "Did that play of mine send out / Certain men the English shot?" he would ask in "The Man and the Echo," thinking of the play *Cathleen Ni Houlihan*, and the sixteen men who died in the Easter Rising of 1916.

Walcott in his own Nobel lecture in 1992, nearly twenty years distant from his work with the Trinidad Theatre Workshop, would also speak about drama, or rather about an event he mistook for drama, in a way that both echoes Yeats's attention to speech and clarifies the turn Walcott's poetry took when he left the Theatre Workshop in 1976. What Walcott described in the Nobel lecture, published as *The Antilles: Fragments of Epic Memory*, is his misunderstanding of a performance in Felicity, Trinidad, of *Ramleela*, a dramatization of the Hindu epic *Ramayana*.

> I misread the event through a visual echo of History—the cane fields, indenture, the evocation of vanishing armies, temples and trumpeting elephants—when all around me there was quite the opposite: elation, delight in the boys' screams, in the sweets-stalls, in more and more costumed characters appearing; a delight of conviction, not loss. The name Felicity made sense.[14]

Naming and language come into a sensible relationship with the present landscape. More important, though, may be the relationship Walcott pushes aside: "History—the cane fields." That is the relationship his later poetry relies on, but it begins here in a model of dialect that looks forward to *Omeros*: "The performance was like a dialect, a branch of its original language, an abridgment of it, but not a distortion or even a reduction of its epic scale."[15]

Dialect figures here as signal of history, but Walcott is not willing to privilege the performance as a totem to the larger historical narrative that describes the evolution of the performance from the subcontinent to the plain of Trinidad. He is interested in history not History, the history of lives lived in this landscape, not the History of ruins. He left before the play actually began, to view scarlet ibises in the Caroni Swamp as they returned to their nests at dusk.

> In a performance as natural as those of the actors of the *Ramleela*, we watched the flocks come in as bright as the scarlet of the boy archers, as the red flags, and cover an islet until it turned into a flowering tree, an anchored immortelle. The sigh of History meant nothing here. These two visions, the *Ramleela* and the arrowing flocks of scarlet ibises, blent into a single gasp of gratitude. Visual surprise is natural in the Caribbean; it comes with the landscape, and faced with its beauty, the sigh of History dissolves. We make too much of that long groan which underlines the past. I felt privileged to discover the ibises as well as the scarlet archers of Felicity.[16]

Felicity is the name of the small town in Trinidad where the performance took place. Walcott returns to it throughout the essay because it carries both the irony and truth of the names, and it gives him the link between landscape and language that parallels the line between landscape and text in his poems. In each case landscape becomes a counterweight to history.

Earlier in Walcott's career, poetry was both fueled and limited by dialect and the visual surprise of the Caribbean. In "What the Twilight Says: An Overture," the introduction to a collection of plays published in 1970, five years after the incident with Eric Williams, he explored the relationship between island inspiration and island inaction, starting with an epigraph from *Waiting for Godot*: "But I see what it is, you are not from these parts, you don't know what our twilights can do. Shall I tell you?" Beckett was himself echoing Shaw's suggestion in *John Bull's Other Island*, that there is no Irish race, only an Irish place and climate, which together condition certain behaviors.[17] For Walcott, what the twilight can do is what the landscape can do. It makes theater out of the poverty of life it scripts, and it shapes the language it reflects: "For us the ragged, untutored landscape seems as uncultured as our syntax."[18]

The rest of the title, "An Overture," acknowledges the influence of James's *The Black Jacobins* on Walcott's effort to see the heroic aspect of the West Indian artist. The essay links the subject of James' major work to the central themes of Walcott's own. The challenges facing the West Indian writer all arise in this densely allusive rehearsal of Walcott's evolution toward the theater. It begins in an island landscape at twilight where poetry resides in the tension between poverty and beauty, as when in the slanting light of a tropical sunset "Deprivation is made lyrical, and twilight, with the patience of alchemy, almost transmutes despair into virtue"(3). Tradition is the ground of a similar contradiction: "We knew the literature of Empires, Greek, Roman, British, through their essential classics; and both the patois of the street and the language of the classroom hid the elation of discovery"(6). And, compounded of all that, there was the pull toward revenge. James's history of the slave revolt in Haiti gave Walcott a vision not only of political action, but also a vision of that action as derived from literary truths already close to him. It was a way out of revenge and into the activism of language.

> At nineteen, an elate, exuberant poet madly in love with English, but in the dialect-loud dusk of water-buckets and fish-sellers, conscious of the naked, voluble poverty around me, I felt a fear of that darkness which had swallowed up all fathers. Full of pre-cocious rage, I was drawn, like a child's mind to fire, to the Manichean conflicts of Haiti's history. The parallels were there with my own island, but not the heroes: a black French island somnolent in its Catholicism and black magic, blind faith and blinder over-breeding, a society which triangulated itself mediaevally into land-baron, serf and cleric, with a vapid, high-brown bourgeoisie. The fire's shadows, magnified into myth, were those of the black Jacobins.(11)

James' *The Black Jacobins* had inscribed the myth in 1938, and in 1960, a decade after Walcott's epiphany, George Lamming would further its magnification in *The Pleasures of Exile*. Like Walcott's, Lamming's reading of James would emphasize the literary qualities of James' hero, Toussaint L'Ouverture. In selecting passages for his summary, Lamming solidified the image of Toussaint as a reluctant activist, the literary man brought to action by the extremity of the social situation working on a mind readied for leadership by his reading of the western tradition—from Caesar's Commentaries to the writing of Abbé Raynal.

Those same literary resonances sounded the usefulness of James' narrative for West Indian poets of Walcott's generation. Walcott, characteristically, sealed the relationship he needed in a play on words. The black Jacobins, his essay goes on to imagine, "were Jacobean too because they flared from a mind drenched in Elizabethan literature out of the same darkness as Webster's Flamineo, from a flickering world of mutilation and heresy" (11). In other contexts Walcott associates Jacobean poetry with a clarity missing from contemporary literature. The contrast that idea makes with the world of mutilation and heresy suggests that Walcott, as if extending the model of the Movement poets who drew a specifically English lineage from Hardy as a way of overleaping the oppressive example of international Modernism, goes back beyond Romanticism and Modernism to plant the roots of his tradition in the period marked by the conflicts it imposed on his own culture. In any case "What the Twilight Says" becomes in James's honor Walcott's overture, even his L' Ouverture.

At the close of his tribute to James in 1991, Walcott read a passage from *Omeros* in which he had sought, using landscape as a syntax, to reproduce in poetry the essential action of James' historical project. His selection helps to clarify the role James played in his career. It is a passage that relies on the metaphorical association that is at the core of Walcott's larger poetic project, maybe the sufficient unity across his entire body of work: a shuttling between landscape and text. Walcott has used this conflation—reading the sea or sky as the book's page, palms as parentheses—since his earliest poems. The long autobiographical poem *Another Life* puts the metaphor at the beginning of its narrative, symbolically at the beginning of Walcott's work as a poet. Its opening stanza has this:

> Verandahs, where the pages of the sea
> are a book left open by an absent master
> in the middle of another life—
> I begin here again,
> begin until this ocean's
> a shut book, and, like a bulb
> the white moon's filaments wane.

In *Midsummer* this self-conscious tic of conflating the landscape and text comes to the brink of self-parody.[19] The idea of inscription is everywhere in its poems: in the "ideograms of buzzards / over the Chinese groceries" ("VI"), "patterns of birds / migrating in Aramaic" ("LIII"). The book's opening lines announce its preoccupation in a complicated multiple trope of textuality:

> The jet bores like a silverfish through volumes of cloud—
> clouds that will keep no record of where we have passed,
> nor the sea's mirror, nor the coral busy with its own
> culture; they aren't doors of dissolving stone,
> but pages in a damp culture that come apart.

Even while allowing the metaphor to proliferate this way, Walcott introduces a new ambivalence toward his literalized world. In "XLVIII" his texts are inscribed on an island world closer to Caliban's than Crusoe's, one where writing should be erased to eliminate the trace of an oppressive regime.

> Let us darken like stones that have never frowned or know
> the need for art or medicine, for Prospero's
> snake-knotted staff, or sea-bewildering stick;
> erase these ciphers of birds' prints on the sand.

Read in the light of his discussion of James in the "Overture" and the "Tribute," though, Walcott's typical conflation of text and landscape in the *Omeros* passage looks like an extended objective correlative for James's more direct engagement with history, and even of Toussaint's making of history. The passage comes from the middle of Book Seven, close to the end of the poem. It starts in the clarity Walcott habitually associates with Jacobean literature, but the dominant ancestor here is Homer:

> My light was clear. It defined the fallen schism
> of a starfish, its asterisk printed on sand,
> its homage to Omeros my exorcism.
>
> I was an ant on the forehead of an atlas,
> the stroke of one spidery palm on a cloud's page,
> an asterisk only.[20]

This opening gives a new dimension to Walcott's old trick. Suddenly the usual metaphor that links landscape and text begins to imply a hierarchy. The starfish supplies a form that becomes an asterisk. That much is not new; and Walcott as usual doesn't privilege either image, so it isn't clear which is the tenor and which the vehicle—which is glossed by the other. But in this case the metaphor is extended. The asterisk signals a footnote, and turns the speaker into a footnote to the history of Achille. The explicit question the passage eventually comes to—"Why waste lines on Achille, a shade on the sea floor"—requires an answer that explicates all those relationships. It is an annotation of Walcott's entire poetic project:

> History has simplified
> him. Its elegies had blinded me with the temporal
> lament for a smoky Troy, but where coral died
> it feeds on its death, the bones branch into more coral,

and contradiction begins. I lie in the schism
of the starfish reversing heaven; the mirror of History
has melted and, beneath it a patient, hybrid organism

grows in his cruciform shadow. For a city
it had coral parthenons. No needling steeple
magnetizing pilgrims, but it grew a good people.

"The Figure of Crusoe," a paper presented at the University of the West Indies five years after George Lamming published *The Pleasures of Exile*, shows Walcott searching for a distinctly Caribbean image for the activity of poetry. The image Walcott found defines itself in large part against Lamming's use of Caliban as a figure for West Indian artists trapped in relationship to a language that carries in it the truth and history of their oppression. Lamming didn't share in V.S. Naipaul's controversial opinion that "nothing was created in the British West Indies" but that is the effect, I think, of his appropriation of Caliban. In countering that image with the image of Crusoe, Walcott is both taking up a political position relative to Lamming's Caliban, and adopting a different formal stance. The latter, the formal difference, is in the different poetic modes toward which the two figures direct our interest, Caliban toward the lyric, Crusoe toward narrative. Walcott's revision of Naipaul is similar to the former: "Perhaps it should read that 'Nothing was created *by the British* in the West Indies.'"[21] Crusoe, like the English language is no longer British—neither is the region; Walcott subtly encodes the difference in that shift of *British* from adjective to noun, so that the historical presence is still there, but as a particular, not an effect.

Crusoe, though, is for Walcott more than just a counter to Caliban or an appropriation of the English novel. His interest in the figure begins in its relevance to the condition of poets generally:

I have used that image of the hermit and the bonfire because I have found that it has a parallel for the poet. The metaphor of the bonfire, in the case of the West Indian poet, may be the metaphor of tradition and the colonial talent. More profound than this, however, is that it is the daily ritual action of the poet creating a new poem. He burns what he has made the day before by adding new wood to the flame. All becomes pure flame, all is combustible, and by that light, which is separate from him, he contemplates himself.[22]

That pure flame flickers close to the idea of pure poetry, and from this perspective it looks wrong to say that the image of the poet burning to contemplate himself purely is more profound than the insight Walcott has, briefly, into the relationship between West Indian poetry and the English tradition.

The Crusoe Walcott wants, he keeps saying, is not the Crusoe of the tourist board. His Crusoe is a person equipped, perhaps haphazardly, but effectively, with sufficient remnants of a tradition (however unsuitable to his present condition). The line of his previous life has been, by a strange bias of history, steered to an un-imagined destiny. Because he shares in the condition that, in Lamming's view, defines Caliban, Crusoe's only recourse is to adapt the remnants he has.

> I am claiming, then, that poets and prose writers who are West Indians, despite the contaminations around us, are in the position of Crusoe, the namer. Like him, they have behind them, borne from England, from India, or from Africa, that dead bush, that morphology ... but what is more important is that these utterances, these words, when written are as fresh, as truly textured, as when Crusoe sets them down in the first West Indian novel.[23]

Though Walcott by then claimed to have lost interest in Crusoe, the image re-emerged in the Nobel address. Here again it is clear that he is chiefly interested in the way Crusoe works as a metaphor for the peculiar linguistic situation of Caribbean artists.

> The original language dissolves from the exhaustion of distance like fog trying to cross an ocean, but this process of renaming, of finding new metaphors, is the same process that the poet faces every morning of his working day, making his own tools like Crusoe, assembling nouns from necessity, from Felicity, even renaming himself.[24]

The split between Crusoe and Caliban mirrors the one that separates the two essential ways of viewing the history of the West Indies. British writers have emphasized the isolation of the region, viewed the Caribbean apart from all traditions, except the patient tradition of British observation. When development is at issue, the colonial narrative presents as a sudden extrusion under the accumulated weight of colonial presence. Take this example from Cyril Hamshere's *The British in the Caribbean*:

In 1934 there was not a single bookshop in Kingston, the largest city in the West Indies, although there were books on sale in two department stores. In the late thirties, however the stirring began that has lead to the present flourishing growth of West Indian art and literature.[25]

Hamshere is, in a way, a sympathetic viewer; he does see cultural exuberance as one phase of West Indian history. Still he gives in to the impulse to see colonial regions always as culturally inert right up to the moment—in this case the late 1930s—when undeniable achievement drags the natives into the cultural first world. James, of course, published *The Black Jacobins* in 1938, a fact that wouldn't conflict with Hamshire's narrative except that James's achievement is much more continuous with its varied pasts than has been recognized. Hamshire's kind of colonizing gaze is interested primarily in registering the moment when Prospero's instructive presence finally has its effect, and Caliban against great odds begins to speak.

Antonio Benítez-Rojo, conducting a postmodern reading of the Caribbean as a "meta-archipelago," completely overturns the British narrative of colonial instruction. In *The Repeating Island* Benítez links the region by geographic configuration to a strong history of cultural attainment in Greece and in Indonesia. And, since geographically the Caribbean "has the virtue of having neither a boundary nor a center," its imaginative cultural reach amounts to a kind of carnival, cut loose in time and space, flowing

outward past the limits of its own sea with a vengeance, and its *ultima thule* may be found on the outskirts of Bombay, near the low and murmuring shores of Gambia, in a Cantonese tavern of circa 1850, at a Balinese temple, in an old Bristol pub, in a commercial warehouse in Bordeaux at the time of Colbert, in a windmill beside the Zuider Zee, at a café in a barrio of Manhattan, in the existential *saudade* of an old Portuguese lyric.[26]

Although Benítez's carnival comes to rest in lyric, its orientation is novelistic. It is interested in movement, addition rather than substitution. The way Benítez caresses the names—Bombay, Gambia, Bristol—echoes similar collations that are typical of Walcott, his ringing of Ashanti against Warwickshire, or the pairing of "Egypt, Tobago." Benítez's version of the Caribbean shares with Walcott's an appreciation for its complex association with the English tradition, an appreciation for, as Benítez puts it, "the unforeseen relation between a dance movement and the baroque spiral of a colonial railing."[27]

Walcott's finished lyric forms make a firm peace between tradition and talent, between the traditions of English prosody and Walcott's individual metrical gifts. But, whatever their ostensible subject, those lyrical poems appear always at least vaguely limiting—though not limited—in their reactions to the general conditions of the West Indian artist. They seem more often to allude to what is colonial, or post-colonial, in Walcott's talent, than to include it. In contrast, Walcott's recent loose, and loosely narrative, poems, coming closer to Defoe's novel—Walcott's candidate for first West Indian book—come closer, too, to the chorus of sensations that comprise the colonial experience. Poems in *The Gulf* already expressed Walcott's frustration with the limits of his particular version of lyric. "Resisting poetry I am becoming a poem," he says in "Metamorphosis." The poem he becomes has something in common with Gregor's state in those first moments of his metamorphosis, stunned and unable to act:

> That frozen glare,
> that measured, classic petrifaction.
> Haven't you sworn off such poems for this year,
> and no more on the moon?
>
> Why are you gripped by the demons of inaction?
> Whose silence shrieks so soon?[28]

Read under the interrogation of those lines, Walcott's most frequently anthologized poem, "A Far Cry From Africa," becomes a startling example of this lyrical dilemma. The poem was published in *The Castaway* in 1965,[29] but Walcott left it out of the selection of poems from that volume to be included in an expanded version of *The Gulf* in 1970. Both books play on the Crusoe image. The title of *The Castaway* is obvious. *The Gulf* plays both on *gulf* as the neighbor to the Caribbean and on the word's use in the Defoe passage that served as epigraph to the poem "Crusoe's Journal":

> I looked now upon the world as a thing remote, which I had nothing to do with, no expectation from, and, indeed no desires about. In a word, I had nothing indeed to do with it, nor was I ever like to have; so I thought it looked as we may perhaps look upon it hereafter, viz., as a place I had lived in but was come out of it; and might well say, as Father Abraham to Dives, "Between me and thee is a great gulf fixed."

Walcott's interest in this passage looks forward to his sense of elegy as a place distanced from the ordinary world of poetry. "Far Cry," though, fixes the gulf bounded by Caliban and Crusoe inside the individual poetic consciousness. The poem begins with images of the British suppression of the Mau-Mau revolt, and then compares those with Hitler's move into Spain, insisting that both are motivated by a "brutish necessity" that recalls the "fatal ananke" in Stevens's "Owl's Clover." But it is the close of the poem that I want to look at. It ends with a series of questions:

> Where shall I turn, divided to the vein?
> I who have cursed
> The drunken officer of British rule, how choose
> Between this Africa and the English tongue I love?
> Betray them both, or give back what they give?
> How can I face the slaughter and be cool?
> How can I turn from Africa and live?

What is limiting here has an emblem in the rhythm of that last line. It wants, I think, to be regular, to sound a pentameter as expected and easy as Shakespeare's. That reading of the stress would find a comfortable rule-proving exception in the substitution of a trochee in the first foot. The line takes a little swing of speed from shoving the unstressed second and third syllables together. HOW can I TURN from AFriCA and LIVE. The irony is that an easy regularity like that takes the stress off the *I* that wants to find a place for itself in the English tradition. And Africa doesn't easily accept all of the stress that should go on its last syllable.

The reading that comes closer to what I hear the poem struggling with would have to give some stress to every syllable but *from* and the middle of *Africa*, and takes some, too, off *Africa*'s last. That gives to my ear a particular emphasis to *can* and urges us to hear that question as one in search of an answer. HOW <u>CAN</u> I TURN from AFrica and LIVE.

Walcott builds enough ambiguity into the poem to undercut the rhetorical reading and make this one possible. *A far cry*, to begin with, is both a distant cry and a dissimilarity or a great distance separating places. The syntax helps create an ambiguity about place: *this* sets Africa close at hand, while England isn't quite *that*, but *the*. The definite article marks a kind of neutrality. Referring to English as a "tongue," though, internalizes the English tradition in a way *language* wouldn't. "Give back what they give" suggests both rejecting what they give and repaying what they give. Walcott, in other words, is able to imagine conferring on both traditions contributions that would compensate for what he takes from each.

All this mincing with language holds together, and never quite violates the official drift of the poem, because Walcott maintains at least the possibility of regularity. There is enough conformity here to make the one suspended line—"I who have cursed"—a kind of curse itself, a departure from the norm established by the pentameter. It calls attention to the uncomfortable fit Walcott makes himself in the position of Shakespeare's Caliban pitching his curse at Prospero.[30] Or, a former Caliban—Walcott's cursing is in the perfect tense—faced now with the choice of inscribing or changing that condition. The lyric reading, frozen like that at the moment of choice, doesn't have room for the imagined narrative of change. In this version of things, the questions that the poem puts can only be taken as rhetorical. Where shall I turn when there is no place to turn? How can I choose when choice is impossible?

But, like the close of Yeats's "Among School Children," this poem becomes more richly complicated when its questions are read literally. The figurative reading gives us a condition, as Caliban is a condition recognized by Lamming. It inscribes that condition as a permanence. The duration reminds me of Browning's version, in which Caliban can give grammar to the future—"will sprawl"—but it is a future without subject, and intransitive; the future tense, and the future itself, might just as well be infinitive. "A Far Cry from Africa" is about the effects of the same kind of amputation performed on the past, locking the poet in the "schizophrenic boyhood" of "What the Twilight Says." If its questions are rhetorical then the life Walcott imagined in "Twilight," and lived in his youth, is diminished to a condition of impossibility. The career that follows the poem, though, is a long, more or less conscious, attempt to take those questions grammatically. And seriously.

By the time he published *Sea Grapes* in 1976, the year he ended his affiliation with the Trinidad Theatre Workshop, Walcott would present that divided condition in terms of exile. The turning away of "Far Cry" had now to be conceived as a departure.

> Why do I imagine the death of Mandelstam
> among the yellowing coconuts,
> why does my gift already look over its shoulder
> for a shadow to fill the door
> and pass this very page into eclipse?
> Why does the moon increase into an arc-lamp
> and the inkstain on my hand prepare to press thumb-downward
> before a shrugging sergeant?
> What is this new odor in the air

that was once salt, that smelt like lime at daybreak,
and my cat, I know I imagine it, leap from my path,
and my children's eyes already seem like horizons,
and all my poems, even this one, wish to hide?

I sense in Walcott's evocation of Mandelstam a premonition of what Robert Hass will call the western *longing* for the consequences associated with poetry in Eastern Europe. Walcott is writing from a contested position but in a place where the poet is still rarely viewed as politically dangerous.[31] C.L.R. James was arrested, not Walcott. "I've always told myself that I've got to stop using the word 'exile'," he said in the *Paris Review* interview in 1985. "Real exile means a complete loss of the home. Joseph Brodsky is an exile; I'm not really an exile."[32] Exile in this poem has particular antecedents in the economic and social conditions of the West Indies, but it is also a figurative exile, and one that may be the inevitable exile of the artist, the condition of Heaney's "inner émigré."

The Star-Apple Kingdom was the first book of poems written after Walcott's departure from the workshop. The theme of exile is evident in its opening poem "The Schooner *Flight*," but the source of Walcott's exile may be more visible in the gulf readers have fixed between that poem's language and the language of Walcott's other work. If the theater provided an escape from the impasse registered in "Far Cry" it makes sense that a dramatic element would enter the poems once theater began to play a lesser role in Walcott's creative life.

When Edward Kamau Brathwaite delivered his talk on the voice of Caribbean poetry at Harvard in 1979, he adopted Claude McKay as the ancestral figure for modern Caribbean poetry. But when he published the lecture, Brathwaite added a footnote that argued that McKay wrote "*dialect* as distinct from *nation* because McKay allowed himself to be imprisoned in the pentameter; he didn't let his language find its own parameters....."[33] Brathwaite goes on to ask whether McKay could have broken the spancel of tradition, given his historical and personal situation. Strangely, the lines he cites in the footnote are these from McKay's *Songs of Jamaica*:

I've a longin in me dept's of heart dat I can conquer not,
'Tis a wish dat I've been havin' from since I could form a t'o't ...
Just to view de homeland England, in de streets of London walk,
An' to see de famous sights dem 'bouten which dere's so much talk ... [34]

The meter, which isn't pentameter anyway, is the least of the problem in McKay's failure to establish here a model of post-colonial nationalism. The poem offers, in one sense, evidence that neither meter nor dialect has an inherent relationship to colonial ideology. But when Brathwaite points to what he sees as Walcott's "first major nation language effort"—that is, his first effort to capture the sound of his native place in a way that transcends what Brathwaite sees in McKay as the mere importation of dialect into an alien tradition—it isn't Walcott's focus on the particularity of the Caribbean, but the departure from pentameter that draws his attention:

> In idle August, while the sea soft,
> and leaves of brown islands stick to the rim
> of this Caribbean, I blow out the light
> by the dreamless face of Maria Concepcion
> to ship as a seaman on the schooner *Flight*.[35]

The irony, of course, is that even in those lines where Walcott does break the pentameter, he does it with the chisel blow of Langland's mid-line caesura. For Brathwaite that irony is covered over by the fact that Piers Ploughman— the prelude to which Walcott is echoing: "In a somer seson, whan soft was the sonne, / I shope me into shroudes, as a shepe were"—did not "make it into *Palgrave's Golden Treasury* which we all had to 'do' at school."[36] Seamus Heaney, though, will hear Walcott's poem as a murmur of a distinctly English tradition.[37] Whatever the case, the line dividing nation language from what is not nation language is difficult to see. Brathwaite cites Walcott's "Sainte Lucie" in *Sea Grapes*, as an example of "wonderfull speech effects being achieved in a more formal context."[38] But he doesn't include that poem among Walcott's works listed as "Nation Language Poetry Texts" in his bibliography.[39]

Braithwaite's doctrinaire attempt to make the division, and then the difficulty of setting its criteria, offends the approach to language evident in Walcott's poems. Maybe finding his models in novels gives Walcott a better ear for dialogic play than the one that guides Brathwaite's hearing of nation language. That may account for the fact that while Brathwaite tended to list the nation language works of some writers, including himself, by volume, he lists for Walcott only specific poems. "The Star-Apple Kingdom" is a good example of why that's true. Not only is Shabine's voice in "The Schooner Flight" itself a carnival encompassing elements from dialect and patois to those metapoetic flights, but other poems placed in the volume speak in a variety of voices. Dialect is in there, but is one voice. The consistent thing is that the voices, whatever their position relative to standard English, speak the dialect of the local landscape.

Aimé Césaire has it this way: "Storm, I would say. River, I would command. Hurricane, I would say. I would utter 'leaf.' Tree. I would be drenched in all the rains, soaked in all the dews." The descent into particularity, from storm to hurricane, continues in the dip into the particularity of words as words. Césaire has 'leaf' not leaf; but that is a momentary gesture and, sounding like Yeats extrapolating from leaf to blossom to bole in "Among School Children," he rises back out of the lexical particular. The path up leads through the particularity of the landscape—marked by that syntactically isolated "Tree"—and out into the generality of "of all the rains—all the dews." Walcott turned to this bit of Césaire in "Twilight."

At the close of the first section of the essay, Walcott comes round to the problem that confounded the Irish revival, the issue of hybridity. The Gaelic League, searching for purity through language, couldn't see that the past as well as the future resided in the awkward position occupied by Yeats. His special awareness of the role of language in this problem motivated both the theatrical and poetic phases of Walcott's project; the West Indian artist, he knew, needn't force himself to Africanize his English, since his utterance of every word that could find a home in the Caribbean landscape—storm, hurricane, leaf—is already a matter of dialect.

> Pastoralists of the African revival should know that what is needed is not new names for old things, or old names for old things, but the faith of using old names anew, so that mongrel as I am, something prickles in me when I see the word Ashanti as with the word Warwickshire, both separately intimating my grandfathers' roots, both baptizing this neither proud nor ashamed bastard, this hybrid, this West Indian. The power of the dew still shakes off our dialects, which is what Césaire sings....[40]

"Pastoralists" is a bit of a reproach in this context. Walcott sees as pastoral those images which only enter the West Indian experience through literature, words divorced from the real work of the region. *Wheat* is pastoral, in Walcott's landscape, *sugar* is not. An uncritical African revival, then, is not much different from an uncritical colonial identification. And poetry, in any case, is not about identity. "What you're taking on is really not a renewal of your identity but actually a renewal of your *anonymity*, so that what's in front of you becomes more important than what you are."[41] The poet saying *Ashante* when *storm* or *hurricane* are in front of him is renewing a membership in African identity, while Walcott's anonymity speaks in the dialect of the landscape.

Walcott's more recent work records his effort to discover the rich profusion of bounties that provide the material of that natural dialect. The natural rhythms, like the rhythm of the sea giving rhythm to a country dance, have always spoken through Walcott of continuance, even continuity. In *The Bounty* the rhythm does continue but the message it carries is changing.

> ... I hear a language receding,
> unwritten by you, and the voices of children reading
> your work in one language when you had both.

With respect to language Walcott's response is not, judging by these poems, to try now to write both, but to sing the process of loss.

The volume *The Bounty* opens a poem by the same name, an elegy for Walcott's mother, Alix Walcott.[42] From the outset he signals his discomfort with the idea of honing the large shapeless mass of his grief down to a formal truth. The poem fits awkwardly in a tercet stanza, maybe the stanza least receptive to poetry in English, but one that must feel natural to Walcott after *Omeros*. For some reason the tercet has been the stanza that holds the sea. Auden used it in "The Sea and the Mirror," his version of "The Tempest." Walcott's stanza resonates most with Stevens, who used tercets for nearly all the great later poems. Early on it was for Stevens the formal correlative of the exotic. It is the shape of Tehuantepec in "Sea Surface Full of Clouds," and of that strange alienation in "Tea at the Palace of Hoon," for example. Walcott in "Sea Grapes" associates the tercet with the "ancient war / between obsession and responsibility." That war finds its way into the poetry in various forms: the early conflict between "this Africa and the English tongue," between poetic craftsmanship and the lived experience it wants to carry.

"The Bounty" starts out between cultures, between times, between truths. If autobiography is "Another Life," elegy is between lives.

> Between the vision of the Tourist Board and the true
> Paradise lies the desert where Isaiah's elations
> force a rose from the sand. The thirty-third canto
>
> cores the dawn clouds with concentric radiance,
> the breadfruit opens its palms in praise of the bounty,
> bois-pain, tree of bread, slave food, the bliss of John Clare,

torn, wandering Tom, stoat-stroker in his county
of reeds and stalk-crickets, fiddling the dank air
lacing his boots with vines, steering glazed beetles

with the tenderest of prods, knight of the cockchafer,
wrapped in the mists of shires, their snail-horned steeples
palms opening to the cupped pool—but his soul is safer

than ours, though iron streams fetter his ankles.

Walcott's suspicion of elegy is felt in the tension between the travelogue
vision and the true paradise. *Paradise* is always an equivocal term, and
especially in this instance, questioned by that modifying *true*. A poem in
Arkansas Testament got at the duplicity of the word by interrogating one of its
contemporary substitutes:

Nothing hurts as much as the word "California,"
the wincing light of Los Angeles. In unfinished Venice
a fresco interrupted in its prophecy looks phonier
than what it promised: gondolas, palazzos, its own Bridge of Sighs.
It fades under its graffiti, a transferred paradise.[43]

The poem is "Summer Elegies." Maybe it shouldn't be surprising that
Walcott on two elegiac occasions questions the authenticity of paradise; it is
fascinating, though, that he manages each time to wring an elegy of sorts
from his doubt. The opening of "The Bounty"—sounding like Thomas
Carew on the death of John Donne, forcing from widowed poetry one last
elegy—says something about the difficulty of those efforts.[44]

Walcott's lyrical elegies, the ones for example in *Arkansas Testament*,
dwell on the endpoints of various histories: island histories, as in "The
Lighthouse," domestic histories, in "The Young Wife," literary histories at
the point where they intersect with the personal, as in the "Eulogy to W.H.
Auden." They celebrate the richness of the language the poet is empowered
to apply to such moments. "The Bounty" is another sort of elegy. It differs
in overall effect, and especially in its relationship to the past. The poem
doesn't participate in the same kind of lyric temperament. Lyrical effects
populate the lines but the lines and images form themselves into something
closer to narrative. The poems of the volume are as death-obsessed as those
of *Arkansas Testament*, but obsessed with death as a starting point. What
starts is not just a singular occurrence of poetry, but the poet's journey back

beyond memory and history still, or already, living in the quick resources of language. The journey is one Walcott associated with the theater in "Twilight," where he made heroes of actors "because they have kept the sacred urge of actors everywhere: to record the anguish of the race."[45]

> To do this, they must return through a darkness whose terminus is amnesia. The darkness which yawns before them is terrifying. It is the journey back from man to ape. Every actor should make this journey to articulate his origins, but for these who have been called not men but mimics, the darkness must be total, and the cave should not contain a single man-made, mnemonic object.[46]

Race, like grief, somehow lives in its anguish beyond mnemonic forms like poetry.

The lyric orientation of the Auden eulogy assumes the stability of its position in the English tradition Auden himself carried forward. This other elegy is, as Walcott says of his summoning of Crusoe, "trying to make a heretical reconciliation between the outer world, and the world of the hermit, between, if you wish, the poet and the objects surrounding him that are called society."[47] Or between, to resume his earlier language, "tradition and the colonial talent." Elegy in "The Bounty" exists almost wholly in the poem's own consciousness of itself as a negotiation between individual grief and the traditional forms of its expression.

Walcott locates the poem between the false and the true, or in the falseness of the true and the truth of the false. That is the landscape of the negotiation. As an elegy it wants to move toward the true paradise held in the spring-like Jacobean clarity of the English Bible. "As the hart," the poem keeps remembering like an image of its own thirst for that clarity, "that panteth for the water-brooks." The whole volume is in one way or another about the truth of fictions, and the artificial nature of truth. And our need for both. There may be more here of Stevens than his stanza, but if there is Walcott lets some of the grandiose air out of the notion of the supreme fiction.

The "thirty-third canto" here points to the close of Dante's *Paradiso*, giving Walcott an end from which to begin.

> Oh grace abounding, wherein I presumed to fix my look on the eternal light so long that I wearied my sight thereon!
> Within its depths I saw ingathered, bound by love in one volume, the scattered leaves of the universe;

Substance and accidents and their relations, as though together fused,
after such fashion that what I tell of is one simple flame.

With that passage in mind Walcott may be himself looking for something
very close to what he called the concomitants of poetry: explanation,
justification, order. Those are varieties of what Dante's poem grasps after,
and they are close to what Walcott found in this passage when he quoted it
in the same essay in which he laid out his concomitants. "The supreme vision
of Dante is not frenzied," he said in 1965, "but one of calm, order, and of a
serene, steady unearthly light."[48]

What Walcott needs to explain and justify is first of all his mother's
death. What has to be given order is grief. The poem begins with that
sentence which wonders across five stanzas and gives way to this one before
it can come around to its burden:

> Frost whitening his stubble, he stands in the ford
> of a brook like the Baptist lifting his branches to bless
>
> cathedrals and snails, the breaking of this new day,
> and the shadows of the beach road near which my mother lies,
> with the traffic of insects going to work anyway.

The poem is worried about the inherent falseness of place, something the
language holds, or holds at bay, in the ambiguity of the verb *to lie*. What
resides or rests between the vision of the Tourist board and the true paradise
is, both because it falls short of the true and because of the testimony of
language, a kind of lie or lying. His mother, in the shadows, is somehow a lie
about what she was in the light, while the poet's work in the light of each
breaking day is bound to falsify, at its two extremes, the depth or the limits
of his grief.

But there is another worry inherent in the invocation of an elegiac
muse. Elegy is a form Walcott has carried off beautifully, whether on private
occasions as in "The Young Wife," or public ones, as in the "Eulogy for W.
H. Auden." But both of those poems appear in the section labeled
"Elsewhere" in that curiously divided volume *Arkansas Testament*, as if
Walcott already thought of elegy as a place apart from the ordinary
experience of language. An elegiac mood applied to the Caribbean
particularly troubles him. "By writers even as refreshing as Graham Green,
the Caribbean is looked at with elegiac pathos," he said in the Nobel address,
"a prolonged sadness to which Lévi-Straus has supplied an epigraph: *Tristes*

Tropiques."[49] The elements of the sadness are in place, Walcott concedes, in the light, the climate, the vegetation that exceeds even the wasteful fecundity of Faulkner's south. The melancholy is in some sense endemic, and yet "there is something alien and ultimately wrong in the way such a sadness, even a morbidity, is described by English, French, or some of our exiled writers."

Despite the manifest intensity of grief, "The Bounty" still appears to be working against the myth of tropical *tristesse*. Grief is shunted off, finding odd conduits to other landscapes. John Clare, shipwrecked by madness, carries the elegy off to his shire in England. But the cast-away energies always return. Clare too clearly represents an aspect of Walcott's mother to be held at a distance. A remark in Irish poet and critic Tom Paulin's *Minotaur: Poetry and the Nation State* puts Clare in the middle of the dialect issue as well:

> John Clare wrote before the long ice age of standard British
> English clamped down on the living language and began to break
> its local and vernacular energies.[50]

The standard against which Clare's romanticism—as opposed to his language—was judged is visible nearby in a line that remembers Wordsworth surprised by his joy: "yet the bounty returns each daybreak, to my surprise, / / to my surprise and betrayal, yes, both at once" (4). If Clare comes into the poem even partly as an emblem of pre-standard, and therefore non-standard dialect, there is something close to betrayal in the way Walcott emends Clare's characteristic *prog* to prod.[51]

Because it can never reach its address, the language of elegy is almost unavoidably the language of betrayal, making elegy a concentration of the usually more dissolute problems of naming, which becomes a problem of reading, of hearing, of connecting. With elegy made somehow realer by the death of his mother, Walcott is now faced with the widest gulf of his career. W. S. Merwin's "Elegy" consists of only one line: "Who would I show it to," no question mark, just the fragment of truth. Walcott finally asks outright the question to which elegies are always themselves the negative answer.

> But can she or can she not read this? Can you read this,
> Mamma, or hear it? If I took the pulpit, lay-preacher
> like tender Clare, like poor Tom, so that look, Miss!
>
> the ants come to you like children...

Here the ants, tropical substitutes for worms, deliver the answer. Expectations of the elegy call for a motion toward conciliation with that answer. But this poem is to elegy as *Omeros* was to epic. *Omeros* learned to perform its inability to fit the individual, end-stopped, narratives—lives— into the epic story that the sea keeps telling and erasing. In this way "The Bounty" looks back, too, to Walcott's reading of James and to the link he wanted to make between James's project and the project of *Omeros*. *Omeros* was driven by the tension between the epic landscape and the truth of island isolation, the ironically small dimensions forced on lives lived out in the middle of nowhere. "The Bounty" translates that geographic paradox into the language of time. Death is ultimately a mirror of the design of Caribbean life; it takes away the seasons. In the poem's final section it is difficult to decide at times whether Walcott is describing the nature of Alix's life or the state of nature resulting from her death.

> But here there is one season, our viridian Eden

> There is no change now, no cycles of spring, autumn, winter,
> nor an island's perpetual summer; she took time with her;
> no climate, no calendar except for this bountiful day.

What can it mean that she took time with her? She took the past, perhaps, but memory is always strongest under the pressure of loss. Walcott is engaging in a kind of mythmaking. His mother's death can at least be made to explain the conditions under which time is lived in the Caribbean. Her death justifies the lack of seasonal change that has always been part of Walcott's experience of distance from the English tradition. By the time of his Nobel lecture in 1992, Walcott could read the climate as one component of outsiders' contempt for a life disconnected from the natural rhythms that condition European experience.

> They know nothing about seasons in which leaves let go of the
> year, in which spires fade in blizzards and streets whiten, of the
> erasures of whole cities by fog, of reflection in fireplaces; instead,
> they inhabit a geography whose rhythm, like their music is
> limited to two stresses: hot and wet, sun and rain, light and
> shadow, day and night, the limitations of an incomplete metre,
> and are therefore a people incapable of the subtleties of
> contradiction, of imaginative complexity. So be it. We cannot
> change contempt.[52]

But "The Bounty" can try to change climates. The last section reaches toward a literary spring. A chorus of crocuses open, glaciers shelve, but the squirrels that spring up are questions, interrogating the season. Spring is for Walcott a pastoral word, detached from the truths of life and labor, like much of the vocabulary of the temperate English tradition.

So the seasons don't move, neither by its end has the poem moved; only the ants make progress. Like a swimmer treading water, the poem has maintained its equilibrium on the surface of grief—a sort of fiction of the pop-psychology stages of grief, the poem gives the appearance of movement through apposition. Walcott gradually substitutes one thing for another until the poem, without moving, and with no real moments of crisis other than those at which it bids itself to stop, reaches its destination. So where, in the end, does it wind up? Where it started, maybe, with the recognition that those little adjustments to perception that the poet makes in each infinitesimally unsettling novelty of usage amount at last to the work of giants. The idea was already there at the end of the first section, where Walcott discovers a kind of peace—a resting, remember, one of the lies— "in the Egyptian labors / of ants moving boulders of sugar, words in this sentence." But that sugar, Walcott has already said, is artificial.

What follows the elegy in the volume *The Bounty* is a return to the form of *Midsummer* with its sonnet-like poems swollen, in the tropical heat, to twenty or twenty-five lines. It is as if the heat and light, outside the shadow of grief, have also faded the stress from the poems. Lines that give a deep pentameter resonance trail their syllables increasingly close to the right margin. A tight, regular pentameter line has ten, even nine, syllables, but Walcott can create a sense of the pentameter tradition in lines that bubble over with syllables:

> Bound volumes echoed city-blocks of paragraphs
> with ornate parenthetical doorways, crowds on one margin
> waiting to cross to the other page; as pigeons gurgle epigraphs

The thematic stress of the reference to Dante's *Paradiso* in "The Bounty" is still audible in those "bound volumes." Many of these later poems echo the elegy, not least in their exploration of various fictions of place, in "Spain" or "Italian Eclogues" or the overtly fictive "Six Fictions."

The place that most deeply resounds with the elsewhere of elegy in "The Bounty" is Ireland. The poem "28," placed near the end of the volume, rises out of Walcott's memory of Yeats's Nobel speech, published under the title "The Bounty of Sweden," and his sense of what his own Nobel Prize has bought him. The poem reaches a kind of resolution that "The Bounty" could not find. It comes as a revival of the poet's sense of the bounty of his native place, its benevolence now making a line to the wider and temporally longer world:

> Awakening to gratitude in this generous Eden,
> far from frenzy and violence in the discretion of distance,
> my debt, in Yeats's phrase, to "the bounty of Sweden"
> that has built this house facing the white combers that stands
> for hot, rutted lanes far from the disease of power,
> spreads like that copper-beech tree whose roots are Ireland's,
> with a foam-haired man pacing around a square tower
> muttering to a grey lake stirred by settling swans,
> in the glare of reputation; whose declining hour
> is exultation and fury both at once.[53]

That rhyme of Eden with Sweden reverses Stevens and makes available in Walcott's viridian south the whole vocabulary of the north, giving him license on the words that name a landscape in which Yeats can be present. In "The Bounty" this same effect, evoking Clare in place of Yeats, demands an image of sacrifice, that "dead hare / white and forgotten as winter with spring on its way."[54] Here the sacrifice has to do with the status of language. The phrase "stands for" evokes the sense of *signifies*, but also of *tolerates*. It is as if the poem, in imagining the house as a construction which refers to its landscape, is acknowledging and accepting its own complicated referential nature. The image becomes a way of pointing to the strained relationship between an English literary heritage—already displaced onto its Anglo-Irish scion—and the Caribbean world to which it was never meant to refer, and for Walcott always does.

Later in the poem that schizophrenic referral subsides into the Caribbean crisis of time. In a landscape painted in the hues of heraldry—inappropriate to the place and time—the absence of history merges with the absence of seasonal change. "The Bounty" began to read the static nature of the islands as continuous with the end of change suffered by Alix. The notion of cyclical change, rendered in those deep heraldic colors, looks even stranger here. It may be that the watercolorist's palette with which Walcott has habitually recorded his landscape cannot even register the absence of those dense, opaque tints without recourse to language drawn from outside his experience; at any rate what is missing finally does not seem missed. Somewhere in that turn on the usual image of the island longing for the history of the continent Walcott discovers what he needs to separate that general sadness, the *tristesse* of *triste tropiques*, from the new absences of individual grief, of grief at the conclusion of individual histories:

> There is no wood whose branches bear gules of amber
> that scream when they are broken, no balsam cure,
> nothing beyond those waves I care to remember,
> but a few friends gone, and that is a different care
> in this headland without distinction, where December
> is as green as May and the waves soothe in their unrest.

Walcott's world is not, in other words, Coole. Home is neither Yeats' landscape, with its "trees in their autumn beauty," nor his poem which has recourse to those and to the woodland paths that lead Yeats to his own epiphany on change and permanence in "The Wild Swans at Coole," its insight put to use in the elegy "In Memory of Major Robert Gregory," which followed "Wild Swans" in the volume of 1919. But Walcott can manufacture those things by simile out of precise attention to the bounty of his own place:

> I heard the brass leaves of the roaring copper-beech,
> saw the swans white as winter, names carved on the breast
> of the tree trunk in the light and lilt of great speech,
> and the prayer of a clock's hands at noon that come to rest
> over Ireland's torment. No bounty is greater
> than walking to the edge of the rocks where the headland's
> detonations exult in their natural metre,
> like white wings at Coole, the beat of his clapping swans.[55]

Walcott is still playful in all of this, as he borrows something of Yeats's foam-hair to turn that copper beech to beach. There is a darkness present, though. The headland's detonations exult in their natural meter in contrast, presumably, to the un-natural rhythm of detonations that signal Ireland's torment. The mixture creates another version of the between-ness of "The Bounty." Walking to the edge of the rocks could almost be walking to the edge of an epoch, a cusp at which one post-colonial talent lets go of his agon with another already assimilated into the main stream of tradition. Yeats would want to talk here of gyres and one age giving way to next.

Despite the similarities in the emergent, post- or late-colonial conditions of nineteenth-century America, early twentieth-century Ireland and the late-twentieth century Caribbean, the job of making, or of understanding a corporate literature is more difficult in the Caribbean. "Corporate" because the word national, which might be used with America or Ireland, won't work for the West Indies. "It is harder for one to understand the beginnings of West Indian literature than it would be to understand the emergence of American literature," Walcott said in an interview in 1975. Melville and Hawthorne, he went on, "had one common racial experience. They were on solid ground with no broken islands."[56] Walcott's effort has been to give a sense of solidity to the islands. His poems register in language the weight of their rocks *and* epochs. The landscape pervades the poetry as the one common bedrock of experience that allows a sense of West Indian history to emerge.

One of the ghosts enlisted ironically in *Midsummer* as a "fellow traveler," James Anthony Froude, wrote in *The English in the West Indies: or, The Bow of Ulysses* a passage that shows the habit of reading only rocks in the Caribbean already established in 1888:

> To the man of science the West Indies may be delightful and instructive. Rocks and trees and flowers remain there as they always were, and Nature is constant to herself; but the traveler whose heart is with his kind, and cares only to see his brother mortals making their corner of this planet into an orderly and rational home, had better choose some other object for his pilgrimage.[57]

Leaving aside his cultural bias, I can hear in Froude's description a longing for what Walcott described as the concomitants of poetry—explanation, justification, order. Walcott used this passage from the same book as an epigraph to "Air" in *The Gulf*:

> There has been romance, but it has been the romance of pirates and outlaws. The natural graces of life do not show themselves under such conditions. There are no people there in the true sense of the word, with a character and purpose of their own.

The poem it introduces looks back to the disappearance of the native cultures of Carib and Arawak as an image for the region still struggling with its own identity in the shadow of colonial rule, still unconverted by poetry into a space habitable, either in the mind of Europe or in the minds of West Indians themselves, by truer stories than those romances of pirates and outlaws. The unconverted forest, the poem remembers,

...devoured
the god-refusing Carib, petal
by golden petal, then forgot,
and the Arawak
who leaves not the lightest fern-trace
of his fossils to be cultured
by black rock.

but only the rusting cries
of a rainbird, like a hoarse
warrior summoning his race
from vaporous air
between this mountain ridge
and the vague sea
where the lost exodus
of corials sunk without a trace—

there is too much nothing here.

The nothing that's there is the nothing that now happens in the poem. Walcott's success here and across his body of work is to bring those physical conditions of his region—its rocks and trees and flowers—into the text of a humanistic tradition, so that people, in the true sense, may inhabit history's image of the West Indies.

NOTES

1. "A Tribute to C.L.R. James," *Critical Perspectives on Derek Walcott*, Robert D. Hamner ed. (Washington D.C.: Three Continents Press, 1993), p. 45.

2. Seamus Heaney, *The Government of the Tongue* (London: Faber and Faber, 1988), pp. 26-27.

3. "A Tribute to C.L.R. James," p. 45.

4. *The New York Times Book Review*, June 29, 1997, p.11.

5. Although the book was first published commercially in 1966, Williams took out copyright on the text in 1964. It may be that no revisions were made between the time of James' arrest and the publication.

6. Eric Williams, *British Historians and the West Indies* (London: Andrea Deutsch Limited, 1966), pp. 209-210.

7. Derek Walcott, "A Tribute to C.L.R. James," *C.L.R. James: His Intellectual Legacies*, Ed. Selwyn Cudjoe and William E. Cain (Amherst, Mass: University of Massachusetts Press, 1995), p. 34.

8. Sharon Ciccarelli, "Reflections Before and After Carnival: An Interview with Derek Walcott," *Conversations with Derek Walcott*, ed. William Baer (Jackson, Mississippi: University Press of Mississippi, 1996), p. 40.

9. "The Figure of Crusoe," *Critical Perspectives on Derek Walcott*, Robert D. Hamner ed. (Washington D.C.: Three Continents Press, 1993), p. 33.

10. Sharon Ciccarelli, p. 40.

11. Ibid.

12. *Crediting Poetry: The Nobel Lecture* (New York: Farrar Straus Giroux, 1995), p. 20.

13. "The Irish Dramatic Movement: Lecture delivered to the Royal Academy of Sweden by W. B. Yeats," *The Bounty of Sweden: A Meditation, and a Lecture Delivered Before the Royal Swedish Academy and Certain Notes by William Butler Yeats* (Dublin: Cuala Press, 1924, reprinted 1971), p. 33.

14. *The Antilles: Fragments of Epic Memory* (New York : Farrar, Straus and Giroux, 1993), [unpaged].

15. Ibid.

16. Ibid.

17. See Shaw's "Preface for Politicians," reprinted in *Modern Irish Drama* (New York: Norton, 1991), p. 475.

18. "What the Twilight Says: An Overture," *Critical Perspectives on Derek Walcott*, Robert D. Hamner ed. (Washington D.C.: Three Continents Press, 1993), p. 31.

19. *Midsummer* (New York : Farrar, Straus, Giroux, 1984).

20. *Omeros* (New York: Farrar, Straus and Giroux, 1990), p. 296.

21. "The *Paris Review* Interview," *Conversations with Derek Walcott*, p. 281.

22. "The Figure of Crusoe," p. 35

23. Ibid

24. *The Antilles: Fragments of Epic Memory*, [unpaged].

25. Cyril Hamshere, *The British in the Caribbean* (London: Weidenfeld and Nicolson, 972), p. 215.

26. Antonia Benítez-Rojo, *The Repeating Island* (Durham: Duke University Press, 1992), p. 4.

27. Ibid.

28. *The Gulf, Poems* (London: Weidenfeld and Nicolson, 1972), p. 40.

29. *The Castaway and other Poems* (London: Cape, 1965).

30. "You taught me language, and my profit on't / Is, I know how to

curse" (*Tempest* I.ii.365-6).

31. Edward Kamau Brathwaite's dedication of *History of the Voice*, though, gives evidence of an exception: "For Michael Smith, poet / Stoned to death on Stony Hill / Kingston, Jamaica / 17 August 1983."

32. Edward Hirsch, "The Art of Poetry XXXVII: Derek Walcott," *Conversations with Derek Walcott*, p. 116.

33. *History of the Voice: The Development of Nation Language in Anglophone Caribbean Poetry* (London: New Beacon Books, 1984), p. 20.

34. "Old England," *Songs of Jamaica* (Kingston, 1912), p. 63.

35. "The Schooner *Flight*," *The Star-apple Kingdom* (New York : Farrar, Straus, and Giroux, c1979), p. 3.

36. Brathwaite, p. 9.

37. "The Murmur of Malvern," *The Government of the Tongue* (London: Faber and Faber, 1984).

38. *History of the Voice* (London: New Beacon Books, 1984), p. 49.

39. Ibid., p. 75.

40. "What the Twilight Says," p. 10.

41. "The *Paris Review* Interview," *Conversations with Derek Walcott*, p. 273.

42. *The Bounty* (New York : Farrar, Straus, and Giroux, 1997).

43. "Summer Elegies," *Arkansas Testament* (New York: Farrar, Straus and Giroux, 1987), p. 95.

44. "An Elegie upon the death of the Deane of Pauls, Dr. Iohn Donne," *The Poems of Thomas Carew with his Masque Coelum Britannicum*, ed. Rhodes Dunlap (Oxford: Clarendon Press, 1949), pp. 71-77. It's an interesting coincidence, in this context, that the other of Carew's most famous elegies, for Maria Wentworth, uses a tetrameter version of the tercet stanza.

45. "What the Twilight Say: An Overture," p. 5.

46. Ibid.

47. Derek Walcott, "The Figure of Crusoe," presented at the University of the West Indies, St. Augustine, Trinidad on October 27, 1965, reprinted in *Critical Perspectives on Derek Walcott*, ed. Robert D. Hamner (Washington, D. C. : Three Continents Press, 1993), p. 35.

48. "The Figure of Crusoe," pp. 34-35.

49. *The Antilles: Fragments of Epic Memory*, [unpaged].

50. Tom Paulin, *Minotaur: Poetry and the Nation State* (Cambridge, Massachusetts: Harvard University Press), p. 47.

51. A contemporary reviewer included *progged* in a catalog of words by which Clare's *The Sheperds Calendar* was distinguished, and for the use of which the poet was to be faulted: "There was nothing, perhaps, which more

provoked our spleen than the want of a glossary; for, without such an assistance, how could we perceive the fitness and beauty of such words as — crizzling — hings — progged — spindling — siling — struttles — &c. &c." in Paulin, p. 53.

52. *The Antilles: Fragments of Epic Memory*, [unpaged].

53. *The Bounty*, p. 61.

54. *The Bounty*, p. 15.

55. W.B. Yeats, *The Collected Poems of W.B. Yeats*, edited by Richard J. Finneran (New York : Scribner Paperback Poetry, 1996).

56. Robert D. Hamner, "Conversation with Derek Walcott," *Conversations with Derek Walcott*, p. 28.

57. Anthony Froude, The English in the West Indies: or, The Bow of Ulysses, p. 349.

Chronology

1930	Born Derek Alton Walcott on June 23 in Castries, St. Lucia, British West Indies to Warwick Walcott, a civil servant, and Alix Walcott, a teacher. Siblings include twin brother Roderick Alton and older sister Pamela.
1931	Death of his father, Warwick Walcott.
1941	Begins at St. Mary's College in St. Lucia and stays through 1950.
1948	*Twenty-five Poems* privately printed.
1949	*Epitaph for the Young* privately printed.
1950	Founds St. Lucia Arts Guild. First play, *Henri Christophe*, is performed. Attends University College of the West Indies in Mona, Jamaica.
1951	*Poems* published.
1953	Graduates college with a Bachelor of Arts Degree.
1954	Marries Faye A. Moyston. Teaches at St. Mary's College.
1955	Teaches at Jamaica College, Kingston, Jamaica.
1957	Wins Drama Festival Prize for *Drums and Colors*. Visits the United States for the first time.
1958	Receives Rockefeller Foundation Fellowship to study theater in the United States.
1959	Founds Little Carib Theatre Workshop, known later as the Trinidad Theatre Workshop.

1960	Becomes Feature Writer for the Trinidad Guardian in Port-of-Spain.
1961	Receives Guinness Award for Poetry for "A Sea-Chantey."
1962	Marries Margaret Maillard. Publishes *In a Green Night: Poems 1948-1960*. Receives Ingram Merrill Foundation Grant.
1964	Publishes *Selected Poems*.
1965	Publishes *The Castaway and Other Poems*.
1966	Founds the Basement Theatre in Port-of-Spain. Becomes Fellow of the Royal Society of Literature.
1967	*Dream on Monkey Mountain* premiers in Toronto.
1970	Publishes *The Gulf and Other Poems*, as well as *Dream on Monkey Mountain and Other Plays*.
1971	Wins Obie Award for *Dream on Monkey Mountain*.
1973	Publishes *Another Life*. Receives honorary doctoral degree from the University of the West Indies.
1976	Publishes *Sea Grapes*. Resigns directorship of Trinidad Theatre Workshop.
1977	*Remembrance* is performed. Receives Guggenheim Fellowship.
1978	Publishes *The Joker of Seville and O Babylon!: Two Plays*.
1979	Publishes *The Star-Apple Kingdom*. Elected to the American Academy and Institute of Fine Arts.
1981	Teaches at Columbia University and then at Boston University as a Visiting Professor. Wins John D. and Catherine MacArthur Foundation Grant.
1982	Publishes *The Fortunate Traveller*. Marries Norline Metivier. Teaches at Harvard University as Visiting Professor.
1984	Publishes *Midsummer*.
1983	*A Branch of the Blue Nile* is performed.
1985	Returns to Boston University as a Visiting Professor.
1986	Publishes *Collected Poems 1948-1984*. Receives the *Los Angeles Times* Book Review Prize.
1988	Publishes *The Arkansas Testament*. Receives the Queen's Gold Medal for Poetry.
1989	Publishes *Omeros*.

1992	Receives the Nobel Prize for Literature.
1993	Publishes *Antilles: Fragments of Epic Memory*.
1997	Publishes *The Bounty*.
1998	Publishes *What the Twilight Says: Essays*.
2000	Publishes *Tiepolo's Hound*.

Contributors

HAROLD BLOOM is Sterling Professor of the Humanities at Yale University and Henry W. and Albert A. Berg Professor of English at the New York University Graduate School. He is the author of over 20 books, including *Shelley's Mythmaking* (1959), *The Visionary Company* (1961), *Blake's Apocalypse* (1963), *Yeats* (1970), *A Map of Misreading* (1975), *Kabbalah and Criticism* (1975), *Agon: Toward a Theory of Revisionism* (1982), *The American Religion* (1992), *The Western Canon* (1994), and *Omens of Millennium: The Gnosis of Angels, Dreams, and Resurrection* (1996). *The Anxiety of Influence* (1973) sets forth Professor Bloom's provocative theory of the literary relationships between the great writers and their predecessors. His most recent books include *Shakespeare: The Invention of the Human* (1998), a 1998 National Book Award finalist, *How to Read and Why* (2000), and *Genius: A Mosaic of One Hundred Exemplary Creative Minds* (2002). In 1999, Professor Bloom received the prestigious American Academy of Arts and Letters Gold Medal for Criticism, and in 2002 he received the Catalonia International Prize.

SEAMUS HEANEY, one of the most distinguished living poets and winner of the Nobel Prize, is the author of *Opened Ground: Selected Poems 1966-1996*, which draws from nine of his collections of poetry. His most recent collection is entitled *Electric Light*. He teaches regularly at Harvard University.

CALVIN BEDIENT teaches English at the University of California, Los Angeles. His works span poetry and criticism and include *Candy Necklace*, *Violence of the Morning*, and *In the Heart's Last Kingdom: Robert Penn Warren's Major Poetry*.

HELEN VENDLER teaches at Harvard University. Her books include studies of Yeats, Stevens, George Herbert, Keats, Seamus Heaney, and Shakespeare's sonnets.

JOSEPH BRODSKY (1940-1996) was awarded the Nobel Prize in Literature and has served as Poet Laureate of the United States. His essays are collected in *Less Than One* and *On Grief and Reason*. His books of poetry include *A Part of Speech* and *So Forth*.

PETER BALAKIAN is Donald M. and Constance H. Rebar Professor of the Humanities in the English department at Colgate University. His books included *June-tree: New and Selected 1974-2000*, a memoir entitled *Black Dog of Fate*, and a study of Theodore Roethke's poetry.

RITA DOVE has taught at Arizona State University and currently is Commonwealth Professor of English at the University of Virginia. She has served as Poet Laureate of the United States. Her books include *The Yellow House on the Corner*, *Darker Face of the Earth*, and most recently, *On the Bus with Rosa Parks*.

STEWART BROWN teaches at the University of Birmingham and has edited the *Oxford Book of Caribbean Short Stories*, *All Are Involved: The Art of Martin Cartier*, and *Caribbean Poetry Now*.

DAVID MIKICS is Associate Professor of English at the University of Houston. He is the author of *The Limits of Moralizing: Pathos and Subjectivity in Spenser and Milton*.

GREGSON DAVIS is Andrew W. Mellon Distinguished Professor in the Humanities at Duke University. He has translated the work of Aimé Cesaire and is the author of *Polyhymnia: The Rhetoric of Horatian Lyric Discourse*.

PAULA BURNETT teaches at Brunel University and has edited the *Penguin Book of Caribbean Verse in English*.

JAHAN RAMAZANI teaches English at the University of Virginia and is the author of a study of Yeats as well as *Poetry of Mourning: The Modern Elegy from Hardy to Heaney*.

PAUL BRESLIN teaches English at Northwestern University. He is the author of a collection of poems entitled *You Are Here* and *The Psycho-Political Muse: American Poetry Since the Fifties*.

WES DAVIS is Assistant Professor of English at Yale University. He specializes in 20th century American and British literature and has published essays on James Joyce, Seamus Heaney, and Robert Hass. Most recently he edited and introduced *The Milberg Collection of Jewish American Writing*.

Bibliography

Asein, Samuel Omo. "Derek Walcott and the Great Tradition." *The Literary Criterion* 16, no. 2 (1981): 18-30.

Ashalolu, Albert Olu. "Allegory *Ti Jean and His Brothers*." *World Literature Written in English* 16, no. 1 (April 1977): 203-11.

Atlas, James. "Derek Walcott: Poet of Two Worlds." *New York Times Magazine* 23 (May 1982): 32-38.

Balakian, Peter. "The Poetry of Derek Walcott." *Poetry* 148, no. 3 (June 1986): 169-77.

Baugh, Edward. *Derek Walcott: Memory as Vision*. London: Longman, 1978.

Bedient, Calvin. "Derek Walcott, Contemporary." *Parnassus* 9, no. 2 (1981): 31-44.

Breslin, Paul. *Nobody's Nation: Reading Derek Walcott*. Chicago: University of Chicago Press, 2001.

Brodsky, Joseph. "The Sound of the Tide." *Less Than One: Selected Essays*. Farrar, Straus and Giroux, 1986.

Brown, Stewart, ed. *The Art of Derek Walcott*. Chester Springs, PA: Dufour Editions, 1991.

Burnett, Paula. *Derek Walcott: Politics and Poetics*. Gainesville, FL: University Press of Florida, 2000.

Carruth, Hayden. "Poets on the Fringe." *Harpers* 260 (Jan. 1980): 80-81.

Cordua, Carla. "Walcott, El Afrosajon." *Caribbean Studies* 22, nos. 3-4 (1989): 87-89.

Daizal, R. Samad. "Cultural Imperatives in Derek Walcott's *Dream on Monkey Mountain.*" *Commonwealth Essays and Studies* 13 (Spring 1991): 8-21.

Davis, Gregson. "'With No Homeric Shadow': The Disavowal of Epic in Derek Walcott's *Omeros.*" *The South Atlantic Quarterly* 96, no. 2 (Spr. 1997): 321-333.

Dove, Rita. "Either I'm Nobody or I'm a Nation." *Parnassus* 14, no. 1 (1987): 49-76.

Fido, Elaine. "Images of Dream: Walcott, Soyinka, and Genet." *African Theatre Review* 1, no. 1 (Apr. 1985): 99-114.

Goldstraw, Irma E. *Derek Walcott: An Annotated Bibliography of His Works.* New York: Garland, 1984.

Hamner, Robert D. "Caliban Agonistes: Stages of Cultural Development in the Plays of Derek Walcott." *The Literary Half-Yearly* 26, no. 1 (Jan. 1985): 120-31.

———, ed. *Critical Perspectives on Derek Walcott.* Washington, DC: Three Continents Press, 1993.

———. "Exorcising the Planter Devil in the Plays of Derek Walcott." *Commonwealth* 7, no. 2 (Spring 1985): 95-102.

Heaney, Seamus. "The Language of Exile." *Parnassus* 8, no. 1 (Fall-Winter 1979): 5-11.

Hirsch, Edward. "The Art of Poetry." *Paris Review* 28 (Winter 1986): 197-230.

Ismond, Patricia. "Walcott's Later Drama: From 'Joker' to 'Remembrance.'" *Ariel* 16, no. 3 (July 1985): 89-101.

King, Bruce, ed. *West Indian Literature.* London: Macmillan, 1979.

Leithauser, Brad. "Ancestral Rhyme." *New Yorker* 66, no. 52 (11 Feb. 1991): 91-95.

Mariani, Paul. "Summoning the Dead: Politics and the Sublime in Contemporary English Poetry." *New England Review and Breadloaf Quarterly* 7, no. 3 (Spring 1985): 299-314.

McClatchy, J. D. "Divided Child." *The New Republic* 194, no. 12 (24 Mar. 1986): 36-38.

McCorkle, James. "Re-Mapping the New World." *Ariel* 17 (Apr. 1986): 3-14.

Mikics, David. "Derek Walcott and Alejo Carpentier: Nature, History, and the Caribbean Writer." In *Magical Realism: Theory, History, Community*, ed. Lois Parkinson Zamora and Wendy B. Faris. Durham, NC: Duke University Press, 1995.

Questal, Victor D. "The Trinidad Theatre Workshop 1966-67." *The Literary Half-Yearly* 26, no. 1 (Jan. 1985): 163-179.

Ramazani, Jahan. *The Hybrid Muse: Postcolonial Poetry in English*. Chicago: University of Chicago Press, 2001.

Stewart, Marion. "Walcott and Painting." *Jamaica Journal* 45 (May 1981): 56-68.

Thieme, John. *Derek Walcott*. Manchester: Manchester University Press, 1999.

Willis, Susan. "Caliban as Poet: Reversing the Maps of Domination." *Massachusetts Review* 23, no. 4 (Winter 1982): 615-30.

Vendler, Helen. "Poet of Two Worlds." *New York Review of Books* (4 Mar. 1982): 23, 25-27.

Acknowledgments

"The Murmur of Malvern" by Seamus Heaney from *The Government of the Tongue* by Seamus Heaney, copyright © 1989 by Seamus Heaney. Reprinted by permission.

"Derek Walcott, Contemporary" by Calvin Bedient from *Parnassus: Poetry in Review* 9, no. 2 (Fall/Winter 1981), copyright © 1981 by Calvin Bedient. Reprinted by permission of the author.

"Poet of Two Worlds" by Helen Vendler from *The New York Review of Books* 29, no. 3 (4 Mar. 1982). Reprinted by permission of *The New York Review of Books*. Copyright © 1982 by NYREV, Inc.

"The Sound of the Tide" by Joseph Brodsky from *Less Than One* by Joseph Brodsky, copyright © 1986 by Joseph Brodsky. Reprinted by permission of Farrar, Straus and Giroux, LLC.

"The Poetry of Derek Walcott" by Peter Balakian from *Poetry* 148, no. 3 (June 1986), copyright © 1986 by The Modern Poetry Association. Reprinted by permission of the Editor of *Poetry*.

"Either I'm Nobody, or I'm a Nation" from *Parnassus* 14 no. 1, © 1987 by Rita Dove. Reprinted by permission of the author.

"The Apprentice: *25 Poems, Epitaph for the Young, Poems,* and *In a Green Night*" by Stewart Brown from *The Art of Derek Walcott,* edited by Stewart Brown, copyright © 1991 by Stewart Brown. Reprinted by permission.

"Derek Walcott and Alejo Carpentier: Nature, History, and the Caribbean Writer" by David Mikics from *Magical Realism: Theory, History, Community,* edited by Lois Parkinson Zamora and Wendy B. Faris, copyright © 1995 by Duke University Press. Reprinted by permission.

"'With No Homeric Shadow': The Disavowal of Epic in Derek Walcott's *Omeros*" by Gregson Davis from *The South Atlantic Quarterly* 96, no. 2 (Spring 1997), copyright © 1997 by Duke University Press. Reprinted by permission.

"'The Theatre of Our Lives': Founding an Epic Drama" by Paula Burnett from *Derek Walcott: Politics and Poetics* by Paula Burnett, copyright © 2000 by the Board of Regents of the State of Florida. Reprinted with permission of the University Press of Florida.

"The Wound of Postcolonial History" by Jahan Ramazani from *The Hybrid Muse: Postcolonial Poetry in English* by Jahan Ramazani, copyright © 2001 by the University of Chicago. Reprinted by permission.

"*Another Life*: West Indian Life and the Problems of Narration" by Paul Breslin from *Nobody's Nation: Reading Derek Walcott* by Paul Breslin, copyright © 2001 by the University of Chicago. Reprinted by permission.

"Derek Walcott: The Sigh of History" by Wes Davis, printed for the first time in this volume, copyright © 2002 by Wes Davis. Printed by permission.

Index